Praise for previous editions of

Louisiana
Off the Beaten Path®

"To learn more about our own state, buy a copy of Gay Martin's guidebook....
[I]t qualifies as a bible for those who want to roam the roads of Louisiana."
—*Times-Picayune*, New Orleans

"A conversational, in-depth, parish-by-parish guide to towns and attractions."
—*Louisiana Life* Magazine

"Nowhere in the United States are there more unique places than in
Louisiana.... I've been back there twice, and this guide makes me want more."
—*Endless Vacation* magazine

"Designed to bring the traveler into contact with Louisiana culture and
traditions ... this is an important adjunct to any standard guide to the state."
—*Midwest Book Review*

Help Us Keep This Guide Up to Date

Every effort has been made by the author and editors to make this guide as accurate and useful as possible. However, many things can change after a guide is published—establishments close, phone numbers change, and facilities come under new management.

We would love to hear from you concerning your experiences with this guide and how you feel it could be improved and kept up to date. Although we may not be able to respond to all comments and suggestions, we'll take them to heart and we'll also make certain to share them with the author. Please send your comments and suggestions to the following address:

The Globe Pequot Press
Reader Response/Editorial Department
P.O. Box 480
Guilford, CT 06437

Or you may e-mail us at:
editorial@globe-pequot.com

Thanks for your input, and happy travels!

OFF THE BEATEN PATH® SERIES

Louisiana

SIXTH EDITION

by **Gay Martin**

Revised and Updated
by **Carolyn G. Kolb**

The Globe Pequot Press

Guilford, Connecticut

Text design by Laura Augustine
Illustrations by Carole Drong
Maps created by Equator Graphics © The Globe Pequot Press

ISSN 1539-3763
ISBN 0-7627-2439-0

Manufactured in the United States of America
Sixth Edition/First Printing

To my husband, Carlton,
who remains wonderful—"Here is for Papou."

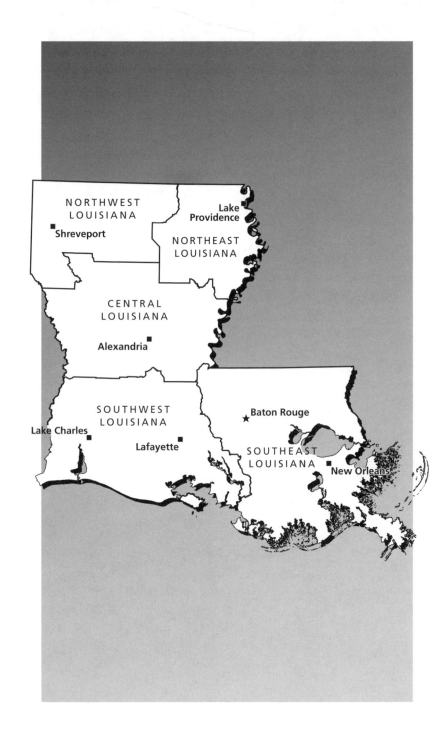

Contents

Acknowledgments viii

Introduction ix

Northwest Louisiana................................... 1

Northeast Louisiana.................................... 27

Central Louisiana 43

Southwest Louisiana................................... 67

Southeast Louisiana 111

Indexes... 167

General Index 167

Special Indexes 173

Bed-and-Breakfasts 173

Plantation Homes 173

Restaurants 173

Recipes 174

About the Author..................................... 175

Acknowledgments

A great big collective thank you goes to all the wonderful people who helped me during the past decade with previous editions of this book. Because that list grew so long, I'm clearing the decks to start all over with a millennium file, and at the top goes Carolyn G. Kolb for her splendid work on this edition of this book.

For the chefs, restaurateurs, and cooks who contributed recipes for this edition, I convey my appreciation. Thanks to all who shared some of their Louisiana with me, particularly Bruce Morgan, Charles N. Fisher, Jeff Richard, Preston Friedley, Stacy Brown, Jennifer Adams, Linda Hilt, Marguerite Plummer, Debra Ortego, Iris Harper, Ann and Jack Brittain, Cathy Judd, Georgiana Hary, Betty McLemore, Dennis LaBatt, Kathy Tarver, Robin Gaspard, Melinda F. Anderson, Ann Johnson, Kelly Strenge, Kay Broussard, Janice LeBlanc, Sue DeVille, Chris Pease, Sybil McCann, Anne Butler, Jan Worthy, Judy Pennington, Christine DeCuir, Beverly Gianna, Jordan Gillis, and Tom Fitzmorris. I also want to acknowledge the Louisiana Office of Tourism, the New Orleans Metropolitan Convention and Visitors Bureau, and the many chambers, bureaus, and parish tourism offices throughout the state for their help with this project.

And always, a special thanks to family and friends, who offer encouraging words and understand about the bane of writers—deadlines.

Introduction

Research is the heart of writing, especially travel writing, and lucky is the writer whose research leads her through Louisiana. Something about describing this extraordinary state always seems to send me to my kitchen. (Fortunately, a flight of stairs separates my keyboard from my cutting board.)

Louisiana's 4.3 million residents represent a rich ethnic mix. This includes not only the famous French heritage, but the Scotch-Irish-English background common to many white southerners. African-American, Hispanic, and Native American with dashes of Vietnamese, German, Lebanese, and even Hungarian all spice the cultural gumbo of the state.

During a recent trip to New Orleans, I visited Foodies Kitchen in Metairie. While browsing through this gourmet food emporium owned by Ti Adelaide Martin, a member of the renowned Brennan family of restaurateurs, I noticed a prominently placed quote by Ella Brennan: "In some places, they eat to live—in our town, we live to eat."

And it's true. In Louisiana, you can end your gastronomic wanderings. For food enthusiasts who enjoy preparing as well as eating, this edition contains recipes reflecting the state's varied cuisine, from peachy Ruston to Natchitoches with its famous meat pies to St. Francisville, where the real "Spinach Madeline" stood up and shared her classic creation. Specialties from Cajun country, Baton Rouge, and New Orleans may inspire you when you're having trouble coming up with ideas for dinner.

Traveling through the state I conducted a personal poll. "What's the best thing about Louisiana?" I asked almost everyone I met. Responses ranged from fishing, hunting, and history to climate and "flowers that bloom all year long," but the majority came up with two emphatic answers: "the people" and "the food." And I have to agree—both are wonderful.

"The people here are wonderful, gentle, and kind," said a man from West Monroe (who also maintains a home in New Hampshire). "They say good morning to everyone they meet, even strangers. That's what I like most about Louisiana." Both locals and transplanted citizens claimed, "You won't find better seafood anywhere else in the world." Menus feature everything from broiled, baked, boiled, blackened, steamed, and fried fish to delectable concoctions of gumbo, shrimp Creole, crabmeat crepes, crawfish bisque, étouffée, jambalaya, oysters Rockefeller, and pompano *en papillote*. With cuisines ranging from Acadian and Creole to Southern—well, what more can be said?

INTRODUCTION

In selecting trip souvenirs consider cookbooks. In each region you'll come across excellent cookbooks featuring local specialties, not surprising in a state that takes food seriously and regards cooking as an art.

Louisiana offers diversity with a capital D. The state's shape looks like a boot or perhaps a Santa Claus stocking, raveling at the toe. Both its culture and geography can be described as unique. Nowhere else in this country do you find parishes instead of counties—a carryover from the original divisions drawn by the Roman Catholic Church.

Natives tend to divide their state simply—North Louisiana and South Louisiana with New Orleans as a third entity. North and south merge at Alexandria, in the middle of the state. Actually the internal "Mason-Dixon" line can be drawn just south of Alexandria at Bayou Boeuf (called *BYE-yoo BUFF* by natives of French origin and *BYE-yoo BEFF* by other local folks).

Weather-wise

Given the humid, subtropical (meaning not-quite-tropical) climate of the state, summers can be hot in Louisiana. Winters, blissfully, are mild. Hurricanes are an occasional coastal area hazard. Whatever the season, prepare for rain.

For the purpose of clustering regional attractions, this book breaks the "boot" into five sections. Starting with the northwestern region, the text moves from west to east in zigzag fashion, culminating in the southeastern area on the doorstep of New Orleans. "The city that care forgot" would serve as a fitting finale for a Louisiana holiday, and several enticements, such as the Garden District and Vieux Carré (French Quarter), are suggested as part of a New Orleans itinerary. As the state's principal tourist magnet, New Orleans (that's pronounced *Noo or-LYUNS*) hardly qualifies as being off the beaten path; however, it would be a shame to miss some of this grand city's unique attractions.

From blues, jazz, and Cajun to country, swamp rock and pop, and progressive zydeco, music starts with a capital M in Louisiana. Fans flock from afar to Plaisance for the annual Zydeco Festival, where the music's hot and so's the temperature (but the heat doesn't daunt the dancing, clapping throngs).

Because Louisianians love festivals, practically any topic is good enough for a celebration—possums, peaches, pecans, poke salad, pirates, sweet potatoes, frogs, catfish, rice, oil, crawfish, and the list goes on. (Incidentally, despite what your biology teacher may have told you, the proper term here is crawfish—not crayfish.)

The merrymaking, which always includes good music and great food,

INTRODUCTION

can also feature such festivities as frog derbies, crawfish-eating contests, and pirogue races. At Morgan City's Shrimp & Petroleum Festival, now nearing its seventh decade, two big boats meet in a bow-to-bow "kiss" as the king and queen lean forward from their respective decks for a traditional champagne toast. Of course all the world knows about the state's biggest festival, Mardi Gras (French for "fat Tuesday"), with its magic, music, and mystique. To enhance your visit to a particular area, find out about any nearby festivals—they fill the calendar.

Renowned for its richness of outdoor activities, Louisiana refers to itself as a "Sportsman's Paradise"— as in the longtime state license plate motto. Fishing and hunting are much favored leisure activities. Among spectator sports, loyalties are divided between professional football's New Orleans Saints and the popular college teams, such as the LSU Tigers and Tulane University Green Wave.

The state boasts a number of the South's grand plantation manors, and many are mentioned in this guide. If you're a history buff, be sure to check the area through which you're traveling for other showplaces that may be in the same vicinity. Some historic homes, not open on a regular basis, can be visited by appointment. A great number, especially along River Road, offer year-round tours. Best of all, many of these mansions now open their doors to travelers, inviting them to sleep in canopied beds, wake up to coffee delivered on a silver platter, and enjoy a full plantation breakfast of grits, ham, eggs, and biscuits or perhaps sugared stacks of French toast with sausages. For a different slant on life along River Road, visit Laura, a Creole plantation and the American home of the legendary "Br'er Rabbit" tales.

You can also take a look at the lifestyles of early citizens who endured hardship and privation. Their customs and contributions are commemorated in museums across the state—from the Acadian Village and Homer's Ford Museum to Shreveport's Pioneer Heritage Center and Baton Rouge's Rural Life Museum.

Some general observations: North Louisiana's culture and topography resemble those of surrounding states—Mississippi, Arkansas, and Texas. This area is primarily Protestant. In contrast, most of South Louisiana's landscape features marshes, swamps, bayous, and bottomlands. Predominantly Catholic, many of its inhabitants descended from the French Acadians, who were forced by England to leave Canada in 1755. *Evangeline,* Longfellow's epic poem, tells their story. In time the pronunciation of "Acadian" was reduced to "Cajun." Known for their *joie de vivre,* or joy of life, Cajuns treasure their ancestry, and many still speak the Cajun-French language.

INTRODUCTION

The state's economy took a dip during the '80s when gas and oil prices plummeted, and the economic sector broadened to focus on other resources, such as tourism. Casinos and riverboat gambling represent "the biggest change on the landscape," notes one state official.

"There is a growing recognition of the importance of tourism throughout the entire state of Louisiana," says Preston Friedley of the Shreveport-Bossier Convention and Tourist Bureau. "Our area of northwest Louisiana has seen significant growth due to the expansion of riverboat gaming in Shreveport and Bossier City. The ripple effect of the millions of visitors has expanded job opportunities and growth in our riverfront and many areas such as hotel, restaurant, and retail related jobs."

Wherever you enter the state, stop at the first welcome station you see and collect information on local attractions. Although these centers no longer distribute tourism literature bags touting LOUISIANA—AS AMERICAN AS CRAWFISH PIE, the state's cultural differences remain apparent each time you encounter a word that appears unpronounceable at first (example: Zwolle, a small town near Toledo Bend on the state's western border, rhymes with *tamale*).

One native recommends "calling any place before you visit, as this is the country, and folks are liable to just leave and go fishin'." When traveling off the beaten path or before driving long distances, take this advice because dates, rates, times, attractions, and facilities *do* change.

For a free tour guide or road map of the state, write to the Louisiana Travel Promotion Association, P.O. Box 3988, Baton Rouge, LA 70821-3988, or call (800) 33-GUMBO. You can also request a directory of state festivals and fairs, a bed-and-breakfast guide, a booklet on the state's African-American attractions, and a vacation packet tailored to your interests. For more information, check out www.louisianatravel.com.

Unless otherwise noted, all museums and attractions with admission prices less than $5.00 per adult will be designated as modest. A restaurant meal (the price of a single entree without beverages) listed as economical costs less than $8.00, moderate prices range between $8.00 and $20.00, and entrees more than $20 are classified as expensive. As for accommodations, those that cost less than $80 per night will be listed as standard, an overnight stay falling in the $80 to $150 range is labeled moderate, and lodging more than $150 is designated deluxe.

Louisiana possesses many wonderful, tucked-away towns and special spots—more than can be included in this volume. If this sampler whets your appetite for a statewide exploration of your own, you'll discover a smorgasbord of tempting offerings. Take along your curiosity and your appetite when you head for Louisiana and let the good times roll! Or, as they put it in Cajun country, *"Laissez les bons temps rouler!"*

FYI

There's plenty to love and learn about the state of Louisiana. Here are some fun-filled facts, practical health notes, and a selected Web site that will better prepare you for your off-the-beaten-path adventure.

Symbolically Speaking

Louisiana has a wealth of state symbols. The two state songs are the not-too-well-known "Give Me Louisiana" and the perennial favorite "You Are My Sunshine," composed by former Louisiana governor Jimmie Davis. The state amphibian is the green tree frog; the state insect, the honeybee; the state fossil, petrified palmwood; the state wildflower, the iris; and the state dog, the Catahoula hog dog (a usually blue-eyed hound with distinctive whorls in its coarse black-and-white or grayish coat, said to be descended from early Spanish dogs).

The official Louisiana State seal shows a pelican feeding three young birds, with the motto "Union, Justice, Confidence" below. Perhaps significantly, the early Louisiana explorer Iberville captained a ship named *Pelikan* in a seventeenth-century victory over the English in Canada.

Health Notes

Exercise common sense: That's the best health information you need before any vacation. There are, however, a few things to keep in mind.

Because of the weather in Louisiana, pay special attention to temperature changes. Drink lots of water when it's hot. Stay dry and wear warm clothing in the winter—Louisiana duck hunters can be in danger of hypothermia when sudden cold fronts arrive in the marshes. Follow water safety rules and wear your life jacket in any watercraft. Obey all weather warnings from the media—if they say get out, go immediately.

Tuck in your shirt and pull your socks over your pant cuffs when you walk in the woods—Lyme disease ticks are found in the state, mainly in the Florida Parishes. Out in the wild, look where you walk: Snakes and poison ivy are both avoidable hazards. Nature is bountiful in Louisiana, but don't nibble on fruits, berries, or mushrooms in the wilderness unless you are absolutely sure of their identity.

In larger cities practice good sense. Don't walk alone on dark streets. Stay with the lights and the crowds. Obey the laws. And use alcohol in moderation. Even on vacation you still need a designated driver.

After all, you're going to want to come back here.

Internet Lagniappe

Louisiana may be a laid-back, steeped-in-history state, but when it comes to the Internet, it's got a one-stop super site that will knock your cyber socks off.

Set the browser to www.artscl.lsu.edu/poli/newla.html. This gets you to a site operated through the Louisiana State University library. Here you will find "Selected Louisiana Resources on the Internet" with connections to more than 300 sites (government, commercial, educational, and nonprofit) and a tool bar with separate buttons for Education, Politics, Cajun/Creole, New Orleans, Internet, Churches, Media, Lagniappe, and Baton Rouge. You can check out local newspapers to read the police reports, find out if the Louisiana Department of Finance is holding unclaimed funds in your name, try out your French, collect recipes, get details on tourist attractions and coming events, and even look at Louisiana photographs.

You can also reach state Web sites through any state university library connection. For example: go to the Web page for the University of New Orleans (www.uno.edu). Go to the library (click on the Earl K. Long Library button). Go to "about the library" then to "subject guide" then to "Internet resources on Louisiana." There you are.

As they might say around Lafayette: Poo Yi! That one is sure worth a bookmark, cher!

The prices and rates listed in this guidebook were confirmed at press time. We recommend, however, that you call establishments to obtain current information before traveling.

Northwest Louisiana

Northwest Louisiana (on a map, the top of the back of the boot) has the greatest range of temperatures in the state. The all-time high was 114 degrees in Plain Dealing and the low was minus 16 degrees recorded in 1886 in Minden.

Geologically speaking, this is the oldest part of the state. Louisiana's "hill region" includes the Sabine Uplift, around which curve outcrops of rock strata called "wolds." The Nacogdoches Wold (named for a town in nearby Texas) includes Driskill Mountain, which rises to 535 feet above sea level in Bienville Parish. The Red River and various tributaries and old channels drain the area.

The close proximity of Texas is readily seen not just in the hot weather but also in the local culture, a nice blend of Southwestern and Louisiana Southern that finds chicken-fried steak on the menu as well as shrimp and crawfish, and Wrangler jeans as proper attire for most local events.

Shreveport is the second largest city in Louisiana and, along with its across-the-Red-River sister city of Bossier, is the commercial center of this section of the state.

Ark-La-Tex

Entering Louisiana at its northwest corner, a person can stand in three states at the same time. North of Rodessa, the Three States Marker shows where the borders of Louisiana, Texas, and Arkansas all converge. Shreveport and Bossier City, farther south, serve as the hub for a 200-mile radius known as the *Ark-La-Tex.* The Shreveport-Bossier area makes a convenient starting point for exploring other portions of Louisiana. From here you can either proceed eastward or you can angle south into the central section. Both regions provide plenty of off-the-beaten-path attractions.

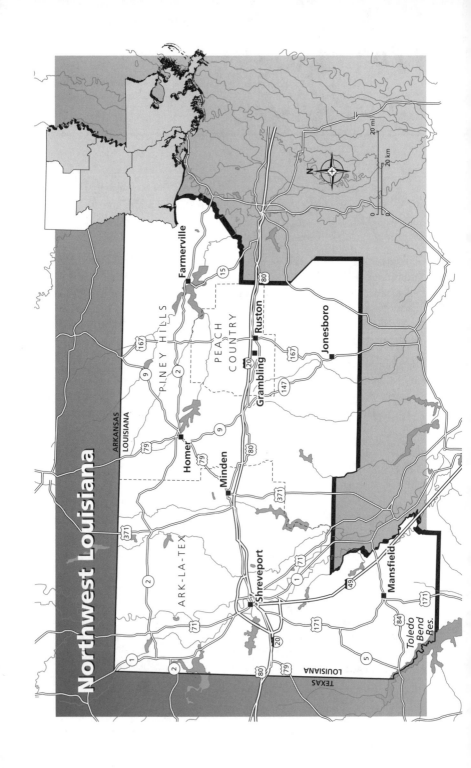

Northwest Louisiana

GAY'S FAVORITES IN
NORTHWEST LOUISIANA

American Rose Center,
Shreveport

*Ark-La-Tex Antique and
Classic Vehicle Museum,*
Shreveport

*Germantown Colony
Museum,* Minden

Kisatchie National Forest,
Homer

Louisiana Downs racetrack,
Bossier City

*Louisiana State Oil and
Gas Museum,* Oil City

Meadows Museum of Art,
Shreveport

R. W. Norton Art Gallery,
Shreveport

Sci-Port Discovery Center,
Shreveport

Town of Keatchie

Ford Museum, Homer

Named for the Native Americans who once lived here, Caddo Parish was created in 1838. The Caddo (or Kadohadacho) Native Americans who occupied the surrounding forests sold one million acres to the United States government on July 1, 1835.

Afterward, with the discovery of oil, the area turned from happy hunting grounds to hootin' and hollerin' hysteria almost overnight. In one year land values jumped from 50 cents an acre to $500 an acre. Oil City sprang up to become the first wildcat town in the Ark-La-Tex. The resulting large red-light district and influx of rough characters gave the town an unsavory reputation.

When you enter today's Oil City via Route 1 from the state's northwestern corner, you'll find a small, quiet hamlet with few reminders of its brawling boomtown days. One clue is Discovery Well, an exact replica of the area's first oil well, drilled here in 1906. Located about 2 blocks off Route 1, this derrick stands near the **Louisiana State Oil and Gas Museum** (318–995–6845) at 200 South Land Avenue (Oil City's main street). Currently the complex consists of three buildings dating from the early 1900s plus a new museum now under construction.

Start your tour at the museum, housed in the town's old railroad depot, which was donated by Kansas City Southern Railroad. You'll see an adjacent caboose and displays of early oil field equipment, railroad artifacts, old photographs, Native American relics, a collection of pearls found in mussels from Caddo Lake, and other items relating to the area's history.

A fifteen-minute video presentation acquaints you with North Caddo Parish's history, and your guide will share some of the region's colorful legends, such as the story of an Indian chief who divided his extensive land holdings between his twin sons. Each brave was told to walk for two and a half days—one toward the rising sun and the other toward the setting sun. The eastward-bound son received Louisiana's Natchitoches area as his legacy, and the other's inheritance was the region around Nacogdoches, Texas.

The museum is open Monday through Friday from 9:00 A.M. until 4:00 P.M. Admission is modest.

Back to Nature

*One pleasant way to
dawdle away a Shreveport
afternoon is on the paths
and by the fountains of the
**R. S. Barnwell Memorial
Garden and Art Center,**
(318–673–7703), 601
Clyde Fant Parkway. This
art gallery and plant-and-
flower exhibit facility is free
and open daily. There's a
sculpture garden and a spe-
cially scented garden, but
the best program is just let-
ting nature take its course
and following the walkways
through the quiet greenery.
Before some recent land-
scaping you could find
bonus vegetation: Pokeweed
growing on the slopes of
the nearby Red River
levee attracted lots of busy
gatherers each spring for
poke salad.*

After touring the museum, step across the street to see the century-old bank and post office (which was moved from nearby Trees City); both are enclosed by a chain-link fence. A security system now protects the small bank, although none was there when the bank did a booming cash business.

Perhaps the closest Oil City comes to its lively past occurs each spring when citizens celebrate the oil industry with their *Gusher Days Festival.* On tap are such events as arts-and-crafts exhibits, street dancing, parades, and a beard contest. Previous festivals featured a spirited competition in which local businessmen vied for the dubious distinc-tion of being named Miss Slush Pit.

Not only was the first oil well in Northwest Louisiana drilled in this area, but the world's first marine well was drilled in nearby Caddo Lake. Until May 1911, when this original offshore well was completed, underwater drilling remained in the realm of theory.

Water sports enthusiasts will appreciate Caddo Lake for other reasons. The large cypress-studded lake, which can be reached via Route 1, offers opportunities for boating, skiing, fishing, hunting, and camping. Consulting your map you'll see that the lake also spills over into Texas.

Continue south to Mooringsport and pick up Route 169. At the junction of Route 169 north and Blanchard-Furrh Road, you'll see the *Stumpwa-ter Inn Restaurant* (318–929–3725). This family restaurant, decorated in a country theme with shelves of old farm tools and mounted heads of deer, features good country cooking with a Cajun flavor.

You may want to try the Neptune casserole, a tasty combination of crab and shrimp over baked fettuccine. Catfish and steaks are perennial favorites. For dessert, try the French kiss if you're a chocolate lover or the restaurant's popular lemon icebox pie. The Stumpwater features an all-you-can-eat seafood buffet on Friday and Saturday. Hours are 4:00 to 9:00 P.M. Tuesday through Thursday, 4:00 to 10:00 P.M. Friday and Satur-day, and 11:00 A.M. to 9:00 P.M. Sunday. The Stumpwater is closed on Monday. Prices are economical to moderate.

Continue to 8012 Blanchard-Furrh Road, where you'll find the *Walter B. Jacobs Memorial Nature Park* (318–929–2806)—2.9 miles east of Longwood (Route 169) and 2.8 miles west of Blanchard (Route 173). Dedicated to nature's preservation, the park invites those who want to use it for walking, hiking, photography, painting, writing, bird-watching, or simply the pure enjoyment of being outdoors.

At the interpretive building you'll see an exhibit on predators and prey, coiled live snakes in glass cages, and a colony of bees in action. Other displays feature mounted specimens of native wildlife such as a Louisiana black bear, coyotes, and river otters. One of the building's classrooms contains "feel" boxes, helpful for using a hands-on approach with students. Youngsters can reach inside a box, guess what object they're touching, and then describe it for their classmates. This leads to follow-up discussions on different aspects of nature. (I was relieved that my box contained an antler instead of something squirmy.)

Trail and terrain maps are given to visitors who want to hike through the 160-acre park of pine, oak, and hickory forest. Markers identify natural features and animal habitats along the trails. Local woods are populated by deer, snakes, lizards, turtles, rabbits, squirrels, opossums, raccoons, armadillos, and other animals. Plant lovers will want to check out the medicinal and herb garden and the wildflower trail.

The park provides a picnic area with pavilion for people who want to pack a lunch and spend the day. Also two full-time and three part-time naturalists are available to arrange guided tours, present programs, teach sessions, and, in general, share expertise.

You can visit from 8:00 A.M. to 5:00 P.M. Wednesday through Saturday and from 1:00 to 5:00 P.M. on Sunday. The park is closed New Year's Day, Easter, Thanksgiving, and Christmas Day. Admission is free.

Top Annual Events in Northwest Louisiana

Louisiana Redbud Festival, Vivian, third weekend in March. (318) 375–5300

Holiday in Dixie, Shreveport, April. (318) 865–5555

Mudbug Madness, Shreveport, May. (318) 222–7403

Mayhaw Festival, Marion, mid-May. (318) 292–4716

Louisiana Peach Festival, Ruston, second week in June. (318) 255–2031

Red River Revel Arts Festival, Shreveport, first week in October. (318) 424–4000

Louisiana State Fair, Shreveport at Louisiana State Fairgrounds, last week in October. (318) 635–1361

Christmas in Roseland, Shreveport, fourth Friday in November through December. (318) 938–5402.

December on the Red, Shreveport-Bossier, December. (800) 551–8682

Rosa Monstrosa

A personal favorite: By far the oddest flower at the American Rose Center is the "Rosa Monstrosa," an all-green flower with petals the same color as its leaves. It has a certain creepy charm and must look rather like roses do to the color-blind.

Don't miss the **American Rose Center** (318–938–5402) at 8877 Jefferson-Paige Road, Shreveport 71130. Located just off Interstate 20, the American Rose Center is 5 miles east of the Texas state line and about 10 miles west of downtown Shreveport. Take exit 5 and follow the signs.

Now America's national flower (Congress made it official in 1986), the rose reigns supreme here at America's largest rose garden. The American Rose Society, established in 1892, also makes its headquarters at the center. You can stroll along pathways edged by split-rail fences to see more than sixty individual gardens at this facility that spreads over 118 acres. You don't have to be a rose expert to appreciate the beauty of this place. A label next to each planting provides such pertinent information as the rose's name, type, and heritage. Like the flowers themselves, the names are intriguing: White Masterpiece, New Year, Show Biz, French Lace, Angel Face, Touch of Class, Double Delight, and Sweet Surrender are among the rose varieties you can see here. While sampling this buffet of blossoms, be careful when you sniff—bees like the roses too.

The Windsounds Carillon Tower rises impressively from plantings of award-winning roses in reds, pinks, yellows, mauves, and a medley of other colors. You'll also find a picturesque log cabin chapel, a gift shop, sundials, gazebos, inviting benches, and picnicking facilities. The gardens and chapel serve as a beautiful backdrop for more than one hundred weddings a year.

Christmas in Roseland makes the place more magical than ever with such entertainment as choral groups, soloists, dancers, and storytellers. Displays include illuminated wire sculptures depicting the Nativity scene, Eiffel Tower, Statue of Liberty, a spotlighted group of seventy large wooden Christmas card panels designed and painted by area students, a model train exhibit, and other festive displays.

You can visit the Rose Center from April through October between 9:00 A.M. and 5:00 P.M. weekdays and till dusk on Saturday and Sunday. Holiday hours, from Thanksgiving through New Year's Eve (except for Christmas Day), change to 5:30 till 10:00 P.M. on weekends. Though the Center and gift shop are open during this holiday season from 9:00 A.M. to 5:00 P.M., this is not the best time to tour the grounds because they are covered with holiday decorations and the flowers (yes, roses do bloom in December) are taking a midwinter break. Admission is modest.

Lake Bistineau State Park.
Doyline; (318) 745–3503 or (888)
677–2478. This park has facilities for camping and cabin rental. State parks make a welcome break in a driving vacation, even if you don't stay overnight. For information on camping and rentals, write to Lake Bistineau State Park, 103 State Park Road, Doyline 71023, or call (877) 226–7652, the reservations number for all Louisiana state parks.

Louisiana State Fairgrounds.
Highways 79 and 80 (Greenwood Road), Shreveport; (318) 635–1361. Even when it's not fair week (last week in October) the Louisiana State Fairgrounds is worth visiting for the Louisiana State Exhibit Museum. Inside the marble rotunda, a long, circular corridor leads past dioramas of Louisiana industry and life. You'll find an oil refinery, a sulfur mine, a salt dome, an Indian village . . . in short, a wealth of small tableaux that explain Louisiana, along with murals, other exhibits, and an art gallery.

Sci-Port Discovery Center.
820 Clyde Fant Parkway; (318) 424–3466 or (877) SCI–PORT. This hands-on science museum on Shreveport's riverfront offers some 200 programs and interactive exhibits. Here you might lie on a bed of nails and learn why and how you can do this without flinching or screaming. Besides participating in Sci-Port's interactive discovery areas, you can take in an engrossing IMAX production on a 60-foot dome screen. Open daily, Monday through Friday from 10:00 A.M. to 5:00 P.M., Saturday from 10:00 A.M. to 6:00 P.M., and Sunday from 1:00 to 6:00 P.M.

Shreveport Sports Arena.
3207 Pershing Boulevard, Shreveport; (318) 752–BUGS (2847).
Although snow is something of a rarity in the area, there's ice galore at Hirsch Coliseum, and it's exciting to watch the Shreveport Mudbugs battle it out with other professional hockey teams from November through March.

Shreveport Swamp Dragons Baseball.
Fairgrounds Field, Shreveport; (800) 467–3230. This "AA" team is affiliated with the San Francisco Giants. A minor-league game can be a lot of fun for visiting sports fans—who knows, you might see one of tomorrow's World Series stars.

Continue into Shreveport, now big and bustling. The city truly qualified as an off-the-beaten-path kind of place before Captain Henry Miller Shreve appeared on the scene in 1833 to unclog the Red River. Using snag boats, Shreve and his crews divested the river of a logjam known as the "Great Raft," which extended some 180 miles—a project that took five years and cost $300,000. Later the town that sprang up on the banks of the Red River was named in honor of Captain Shreve. It's a safe bet to say that today the captain would not recognize his riverfront, which has taken on a Las Vegas look with dockside riverboat gaming, specialty shops, lounges, live music, and crowds courting Lady Luck via video poker, blackjack, craps, roulette, slots, and similar pursuits.

The Louisiana legislature officially recognized Shreveport as a town in 1839. During the Civil War Shreveport served as the state's capital for a short time. The last place in Louisiana to concede defeat, its official Confederate flag was not lowered until Federal troops arrived to occupy the city.

Start your visit to Shreveport with a drive through the historical Highland-Fairfield area, a setting for many of the city's elegant mansions. Fairfield Avenue, one of Shreveport's most attractive streets, features grand houses in a diversity of architectural styles. One of these lovely homes, *Fairfield Place* (318–222–0048), in the city's Highland Historic District, can be your base while here. When Janie Lipscomb first saw this classic Victorian house located at 2221 Fairfield Avenue, she fell in love with it and immediately signed a sales contract on the hood of her car.

With two crews of carpenters and artisans, she worked day and night seven days a week for the next five months to restore the home and convert it into an elegant guest house. The bed-and-breakfast facility was opened in 1983. Dating from the 1870s, the home still contains many of its original brass light fixtures and much of its copper hardware.

A former dental hygienist, Janie has effervescence and energy that serve her well in her current career as innkeeper. "I've tried to give each room and suite everything I ever wanted in a hotel room," she says, "and eliminate everything I hate about hotel rooms." Janie's an avid gardener, and you will admire her well-kept grounds and flower gardens. She serves full gourmet breakfasts with rich Cajun coffee and usually offers an afternoon tea cart with light refreshments. Rates range from moderate to deluxe, and credit cards are accepted.

While tooling around downtown Shreveport, stop by *Ark-La-Tex Antique and Classic Vehicle Museum* (318–222–0227) at 601 Spring Street. Here, on the premises of a 1920s automobile assembly area and showroom, you'll view a choice selection of vintage vehicles. At one time, you could purchase a Graham truck or Dodge car here. Now you'll see an assortment of antique automobiles, all polished to a high sheen and "peopled" with mannequins in period costumes. There are also motorcycle exhibits and a room focusing on the fire-fighting profession with antique fire trucks and related equipment. More than forty classic cars from private collections throughout the country and abroad may be admired at any given time, and exhibits rotate every six months. Tools, toys, historic photos, and related items complement the nostalgic settings. The facility houses a gift shop and an automotive library; some exhibit vehicles are for sale. The museum is open Monday through Saturday from 9:00 A.M. to 5:00 P.M. and Sunday from 1:00 to 5:00 P.M. Admission.

NORTHWEST LOUISIANA

> **Courthouse Copycat**
>
> *President Harry S. Truman liked Shreveport's Caddo Parish Courthouse (500 Texas Street) so much that he used part of its design for his presidential library in Independence, Missouri.*

Afterward, continue your sentimental journey by taking in **Spring Street Historical Museum** (318–424–0964), only a few steps away. Here at 525 Spring Street, you'll get a real feel for the city's history. Built as a bank in 1865 and recently restored, this fine structure with its cast-iron balcony is one of the town's oldest existing buildings. An eight-minute video presentation acquaints you with the city's early history. Rotating exhibits allow the museum to showcase its historical collections of furniture, clothing, jewelry, firearms, books, and newspapers.

Don't miss seeing the upstairs with its permanent collection of Victorian furnishings. Beautiful period pieces include American Chippendale chairs that date from 1760 to 1775, paintings from the 1800s, various pieces of carved rosewood furniture, an 1878 cherry and walnut organ that has been restored to playing condition, a child's harp, a melodeon, and a Persian carpet. You'll also see a chair that belonged to Shreveport's famous madam (who received a three-month bank loan for her business and repaid it within two weeks). Hours are from 10:00 A.M. to 4:00 P.M. Tuesday through Saturday. Modest admission.

While in the area you can stop for a meal at the **Blind Tiger** (318–226–8747) on the corner of Spring and Texas Streets in historic Shreve Square. Harking back to the time of Prohibition and speakeasies, when saloons operated behind facades or "blinds" such as museums with wild animal displays to mask back rooms where alcoholic beverages were sold, the restaurant's name serves as a reminder of the town's past.

Erected in 1848, the building burned in 1854 and was rebuilt later to house several businesses, including the Buckelew Hardware Company. The interior echoes the nostalgic theme with stained glass, dark wood paneling, brass rails, and Tiffany chandeliers.

"Our menu offers plenty of variety, although the emphasis is on seafood," says Rick Sloan, who with Glenn Brannan owns the Blind Tiger. Consider an appetizer of tiger wings or pigskins for starters, then try one of the snapper specialties. The restaurant also serves a Cajun sampler of five different entrees as well as great steaks and hamburgers. Prices are moderate. Hours are from 11:00 A.M. to 10:00 P.M. Monday through Thursday, 11:00 A.M. to 11:00 P.M. Friday and Saturday, and noon to 9:00 P.M. Sunday. The bar is open all night—until 6:00 A.M. daily.

Located at 619 Louisiana Avenue in Shreveport, the **Strand Theatre** (318–226–1481) is a must-see, although parking can present a problem.

Be sure to notice the dome and the exterior's decorative details as you approach. Now restored to its previous grandeur, the neobaroque theater originally opened in 1925 with the operetta *The Chocolate Soldier*. Listed on the National Register of Historic Places, the 1,636-seat theater boasts an organ of 939 pipes, ornate box seats, and gilt-edged mirrors. The interior features a color scheme of rich burgundy with gold accents. Don't forget to look up at the magnificent ceiling and dazzling chandeliers.

Reopened in 1984, this downtown landmark again attracts crowds for performances that range from ballet and musical extravaganzas on ice to touring Broadway hits. The Strand is open for performances or by appointment.

Continue to the ***Meadows Museum of Art*** (318–869–5169), located at 2911 Centenary Boulevard in Shreveport 71104, on the Centenary College campus. The museum features a fascinating one-man collection of Indochinese art. On request, visitors can view the museum's award-winning film, *Indochina Revisited: A Portrait of Jean Despujols.* This twenty-eight-minute documentary will provide some glimpses into the life and work of an extraordinary artist. A seven-minute slide presentation also offers an overview of the Despujols collection.

From December 1936 to August 1938, French artist Jean Despujols made his way through French Indochina's interior, capturing its people and landscapes with pencil, ink, oil, charcoal, and watercolor. This rare collection of 360 works is personalized by excerpts from a diary he kept while traveling through the remote areas of Vietnam, Laos, and Cambodia. Despujols moved to Shreveport in 1941 and became an American citizen in 1945. His collection (hidden at his parents' home in France) survived World War II only to disappear in transit later when the artist requested that it be shipped to him in America. Lost for seven months during the trip from France, the valuable collection surfaced in Guadeloupe, where it had mistakenly been unloaded. The treasure finally arrived in Shreveport in December 1948.

The Smithsonian Institution exhibited Despujols's works in 1950, and *National Geographic* borrowed twenty-one of his paintings to illustrate a 1951 article on Indochina. Despujols died in 1965, and his works were kept in a Shreveport bank vault. In 1969 Centenary alumnus Algur H. Meadows purchased the collection, presented it to the college, and also provided funds for a museum to house the rare body of work.

The Meadows Museum also displays major traveling exhibits throughout the year. The museum is open to the public from noon to 4:00 P.M.

Tuesday, Wednesday, and Friday; from noon to 5:00 P.M. on Thursday; and from 1:00 to 4:00 P.M. Saturday and Sunday. Admission is free.

For a delectable meal of award-winning fare, make reservations at **Monsieur Patou,** "Your French Restaurant" (318–868–9822), housed in Suite 135 at 855 Pierremont Road, Shreveport 71106. Don't let the officelike facade fool you. Inside awaits a comfortable ambience with some mirrored and gilt opulence punctuated by dashes of whimsy. (Visit the ladies' room for a touch of the boudoir.)

"We are a very small restaurant," said Horia-Muriel, Chef Patou's charming wife, "and we concentrate on quality."

A graduate of the French Culinary Institute, Patrick Francis Henri Hébert (a.k.a. Monsieur Patou) worked with several fine European restaurants, including London's Savoy Hotel, where he personally prepared meals for the Queen of England and other members of the royal family. After coming to the United States, he spent four years at an acclaimed New Orleans eatery before choosing Shreveport as the location for his own restaurant, which he dedicated to Horia-Muriel, who assists him, and to their children.

A meal at Monsieur Patou is best savored slowly and thoroughly. Tantalizing starters include a slice of foie gras with green olive dressing and another French classic, burgundy escargots in parsley garlic butter, or perhaps puff pastry filled with lump crab and topped with champagne sauce. Entrees might range from a fresh seafood dish or rack of lamb with artichokes to medallions of veal or crispy roasted duck with orange and cranberry sauce. Lemon Bavarian cream and crème brûlée make grand finishes.

Let Monsieur Patou treat you to the authentic tastes of France. Hours are 6:00 to 11:00 P.M. Monday through Saturday. Open for lunch for parties of eight or more, with advance reservations. Expensive.

More treasures await at the **R. W. Norton Art Gallery** (318–865–4201), surrounded by forty landscaped acres that showcase masses of azaleas each spring. Designed in a contemporary style, the gallery at 4747 Creswell Avenue, Shreveport 71106, houses twenty exhibition rooms. Here is one of the three largest collections in the country of American Western paintings and sculptures by Frederic Remington and Charles M. Russell, as well as Flemish tapestries (circa 1540) and works by Corot, Auguste Rodin, Sir Joshua Reynolds, and other masters. In addition to its collections of decorative arts, sculptures, and paintings representing four centuries, the Norton Gallery offers a reference/research library. Except for national holidays, the museum is open from 10:00 A.M. to 5:00 P.M. Tuesday through Friday and 1:00 to 5:00 P.M. Saturday and Sunday. Admission is free.

After a visit to the art gallery, take Route 1 to the campus of Louisiana State University in Shreveport. Near the northeast corner of the campus you'll find the *Pioneer Heritage Center.* The complex is composed of six authentic plantation structures that give you a picture—outside the pages of a history book—of how the area's early settlers lived.

The Webb and Webb Commissary serves as a visitor center where you'll get an overview of the operation and an interesting history lesson about the pioneers who settled the northwest corner of Louisiana. The building itself is typical of a company store in an agricultural community, where purchases could be made on credit before a crop was harvested and paid off later when the crop was sold.

You'll come away with a new appreciation for modern dentistry after seeing the dental drill displayed in the doctor's office at the Pioneer Heritage Center. There's also a collection of medical and surgical instruments from the "olden days." One room contains displays of various herbal home remedies.

Docents dressed in period clothing demonstrate pioneer skills, which range from churning butter to making bricks, as they interpret life from the 1830s period and provide eye-opening experiences for youngsters

Horsing Around

*O*ne of the best reasons to go to Bossier City is the racetrack, **Louisiana Downs,** *with its grandstand towering over the flat landscape. The horse industry is the fifth biggest agribusiness in Louisiana, and one of the nation's top owners, John Franks, has his spread north of here. (Franks was named "best horseman in the country" as recipient of the New York Jockey Club's Eclipse Award.)*

Every race card will have a special

"Louisiana Bred" race for local talent during the eighty-six days a year that Thoroughbred racing is held. (The Fair Grounds in New Orleans race meeting goes from Thanksgiving to Easter; the Louisiana Downs meet begins in late June and ends at Thanksgiving.)

The regulars on the backstretch (the work area where owners, trainers, and other horse people are found) spend time here and at the track in Hot Springs, Arkansas.

Webb and Webb Commissary at Pioneer Heritage Center

and adults. Students can try making a clay and straw "cat" for a chimney, braid a rug, or learn to shoot marbles.

You'll see the restored 1856 "Big House," a frame antebellum cottage from Caspiana Plantation, and an outside kitchen. A nearby structure, the Thrasher log house, illustrates the dogtrot style. The dogtrot (an open passage supposedly favored by the family dogs) provided a cool covered area for performing household chores during hot weather. The complex also features an equipped blacksmith's shop.

The Pioneer Heritage Center serves as a "history laboratory" for area schools and visitors. Visiting hours are 9:00 A.M. to noon Tuesday through Friday, or by appointment. For information on special events or to schedule a tour, call (318) 797–5339. To reach the director, call (318) 797–5332. The complex closes for major holidays and from mid-December through February. Admission is modest, and children get in free.

At *Savoie's,* "The Cajun Restaurant" (318–797–3010), located at 2400 East Seventieth Street, you can sample special Cajun dishes in a North Louisiana locale. Savoie's offers such delights as court bouillon (*koo boo-YON*), crawfish stew, shrimp, oyster or catfish po'boys (submarine sandwiches for "poor boys"), stuffed crab, and jambalaya. You also can opt for steaks—a rib-eye or a filet mignon that comes with french fries and coleslaw.

If it's lunchtime and you're in a hurry, order from the items with stars—they require less time to prepare. Try the shrimp fettuccine or the Louisiana fried oysters with jambalaya.

Open daily, the restaurant operates from 9:30 A.M. until 10:00 P.M. Monday through Thursday, 9:30 A.M. to 10:30 P.M. on Friday and Saturday, and 11:00 A.M. to 9:00 P.M. Sunday. Prices are moderate.

Before continuing east, you may want to sweep south a short distance for a look at a charming little town called *Keatchie* (*KEY-chi*—the second syllable sounds like the *chi* in "child").

To reach Keatchie, about 25 miles southwest of Shreveport, take U.S. Highway 171 south (the Mansfield Road), then turn west on State Route 5. Incorporated in 1858 as Keachi, the town takes its name from a Native American tribe of Caddo ancestry. You will see a sign that says WELCOME TO HISTORIC KEACHI because Travis Whitfield and other members of the local heritage foundation worked hard to get the original spelling restored.

Predominantly Greek Revival, which Travis describes as "kind of a Parthenon temple style," much of the town's architecture dates from the 1840s and 1850s and is on the National Register of Historic Places. A short drive takes visitors by three Greek Revival–style churches, the large Keatchie Plantation Store, the Masonic Hall, and a Confederate cemetery. On Highway 172 west of downtown stands the 1852 Keatchie Baptist Church, originally the chapel for a women's college (no longer in existence). Future plans call for a cultural center on what was once the campus.

Afterward, you can head southeast to historic Natchitoches (described in the section on Central Louisiana) via Interstate 49 or return to Shreveport for an eastward thrust.

Traveling east, Bossier City begins where Shreveport ends. Bossier boasts a well-beaten path, Louisiana Downs, one of the country's top racetracks for Thoroughbreds.

The *Touchstone Wildlife and Art Museum* (318–949–2323) is located 2.2 miles east of the Louisiana Downs racetrack on U.S. Highway 80 near Bossier City. Founded by professional taxidermists Lura and Sam Touchstone, this natural history museum features hand-painted dioramas as backdrops for mounted mammals, birds, and reptiles from all over the world. The collection contains more than 1,000 specimens of wildlife displayed in habitats simulating their natural environments. Sam practices "taxidermy in action," and all his animals are engaged in lifelike pursuits. Be sure to notice the giraffe and the family of red foxes as well as the 310-pound gorilla that died at age twenty-seven in a zoo.

NORTHWEST LOUISIANA

Take the nature trail behind the museum and see some mesquite growing, a rarity for Louisiana. Also on display are collections of insects, Native American artifacts, war relics, and antique tools. The museum is open Tuesday through Saturday from 9:00 A.M. until 5:00 P.M. Parking is free, and admission is modest.

Tree Facts
Forestry is an important factor in Louisiana's economy because paper mills demand vast quantities of wood pulp pine trees. New varieties of the loblolly pine can be brought to market in only nine years.

Continue east from Bossier City, by way of either Interstate 20 or U.S. Highways 79–80, and you'll arrive in Minden. Take time to drive along Minden's brick streets to see the downtown area with antiques shops and several homes on the National Register of Historic Places.

Located 7 miles northeast of Minden (and some 30 miles east of Shreveport), you'll find the **Germantown Colony Museum** (318–377–6061) on Route 114. Several German families established a village here in 1835, and their furniture, documents, letters, tools, and other artifacts are exhibited both in replica buildings and in original cabins made of hand-hewn logs.

On display is a copy of an 1826 document signed by an archduke ordering Count von Leon (who became the group's leader) to leave Germany. In Pennsylvania the count and his wife met other German families who shared similar religious beliefs. They joined forces and began a journey south to the Minden area, the site they selected to establish a community. During the trip the count died of yellow fever at Grand Encore, Louisiana. Undaunted, the countess carried on and saw the group's goal of establishing a self-sufficient religious colony fulfilled. Germantown functioned as a communal system for more than three and a half decades. The countess earned money by giving music lessons. (Her pupils came from Minden.) Other colonists performed work according to their talents and interests. The group grew grape and mulberry trees for making jellies and wine.

You'll see the cabin where the countess lived and the kitchen–dining hall where the colonists gathered for meals, as well as reproductions of a smokehouse (on the site of the original), a doctor's cottage, and a blacksmith shop with authentic equipment. All the buildings contain items that the Germantown settlers used, and a map shows where other structures, such as barns and workhouses, once stood.

On the walls of the countess's cabin, you can see remnants of the original wallpaper that she ordered from New Orleans. Among the interesting items on display are the countess's piano, Count von Leon's coronet, the colony's book of laws, German Bibles, ledgers, and slave passes.

15

The museum is open Wednesday through Saturday from noon until 5:00 P.M. and also by appointment. Admission is modest.

Piney Hills

Travel south on Route 154 for about 3 miles to Gibsland. Each year on the weekend closest to May 23, the town stages its *Authentic Bonnie and Clyde Festival* with robbery reenactments and more civilized events such as an antique car parade and a street dance. Gibsland's *Authentic Bonnie and Clyde Museum* contains newspaper accounts and photos relating to the criminal careers of the gunslinging couple. Check with the Town Hall for more information.

Afterward, continue south on Route 154 to Mount Lebanon. Located on a downtown corner, the *Stagecoach Museum* is open Friday through Sunday from 2:00 to 5:00 P.M.

From Mount Lebanon continue south for 5 miles. Here under Ambrose Mountain's shady pines stands a simple marker denoting the *Bonnie and Clyde Ambush Site.* The notorious couple had vowed never to be taken alive. At this spot a surprise attack by Texas Rangers brought the fugitives' spree of bank robberies to a screeching halt. The stone marker, erected by the Bienville Parish Police Jury, reads AT THIS SITE MAY 23, 1934, CLYDE BARROW AND BONNIE PARKER WERE KILLED BY LAW ENFORCEMENT OFFICIALS.

One local legend has it that during an attempted robbery of a Ruston

Tall Tales

Swapping Stories: Folktales from Louisiana *is a compilation of stories mostly told at festivals around the state in 1990 and edited by Carl Lindahl, Maida Owens, and C. Renee Harvison. Some are folktales, some are ghost stories, some are legends, and some are just anecdotes of Louisiana communities.*

You get a true sense of Louisiana's many cultures, including everything *from Harold Talbert of Arcadia reminiscing about going to the picture show, to former governor Jimmie Davis telling jokes, to a story by Ruston restaurant owner Sarah Albritton.*

Published in 1997 by the University Press of Mississippi for the Louisiana Division of the Arts, Swapping Stories *will set you back a double sawbuck (that's $20 for the paperback), but it's well worth the price.*

bank, the couple took an undertaker as hostage. Clyde's bargain: the man's life for his future services. He was released in Arkansas when Clyde extracted a promise from the mortician to make him "look good" after the inevitable occurred. Later, upon learning the couple had been killed, the undertaker traveled to the Arcadia funeral home (where the bodies had been taken), determined to keep his end of the bargain. Although he found the two corpses beyond salvaging, he was allowed to restore one of Clyde's hands.

After your visit return to Mt. Lebanon and continue north to the intersection of U.S. Highway 80. Travel east on this road until you reach Arcadia. This small town, along with nearby Homer, Athens, and Sparta, all took their names from ancient Greece.

In Arcadia you can stop by the **Bienville Depot Museum** to see a permanent exhibit of memorabilia related to Bonnie and Clyde as well as other items of local history. Located downtown, the circa 1884 depot stands adjacent to the **Bienville Parish Courthouse.** Arcadia also hosts **Bonnie & Clyde Trade Days** on Route 9 about 2.5 miles south of town. This monthly event takes place the weekend prior to the third Monday.

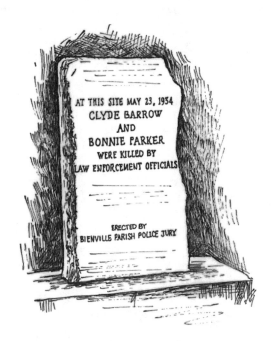

Bonnie and Clyde Ambush Site

For more information on local attractions in northern Bienville Parish, such as **Driskill Mountain,** Louisiana's highest point, call Bill Atteridge at the **Civil War Naval Museum** (318–263–8247), 153 Museum Road in Arcadia. The museum is open Wednesday through Saturday from 10:00 A.M. to 4:00 P.M. and from 1:00 to 4:00 P.M. on Sunday. Mr. Atteridge is currently gathering information for a Bonnie and Clyde Tourism Trail.

Homer, located 23 miles north of Arcadia, can be reached by taking Route 9 north, which runs into U.S. Highway 79 just outside town.

Proceed to Homer's town square. On the square's south side, you'll see the **Ford Museum** (318–927–9190), located at 519 South Main Street. This museum owes its existence to a German infantry officer's helmet, which inspired the museum's collection. When Herbert S. Ford's sons retrieved the helmet from the town dump, he embarked on a personal campaign to preserve for posterity other items of historical significance.

In 1918 Ford started his collection, and as he accumulated additional artifacts, storage became a problem. At various times the collection occupied a room at the local high school, a railroad car, and the town hall. This remarkable assemblage now has a permanent home in the handsome Hotel Claiborne, a building that dates from 1890.

Downstairs you will see interpretive exhibits for each of the area's major development stages, starting with a dugout canoe and other Native American artifacts. Illustrating Claiborne Parish's pioneer period is an authentic log cabin moved from nearby Haynesville. The structure had to be dismantled and then reassembled inside the museum. Other items of interest at the Ford Museum include a moonshiner's still for making corn whiskey, a scale for weighing cotton bales, an 1830 loom, a collection of handwoven overshot coverlets, and an 1868 Grover and Baker sewing machine. You'll also see a circa 1832 piano brought by barge and oxcart from New Orleans to nearby Minden. The museum also features a collection of thirty plantation bells, which came from schools and farms throughout the parish.

Don't miss the upstairs area, where individual rooms focus on various themes. You'll see a series of historical settings featuring a doctor's office, chapel, school, general store, hotel room, military room, and the like. Also on display are antique firearms (including Confederate weapons) and a doctor's buggy that was used in a John Wayne movie, *The Horse Soldiers,* filmed in nearby Natchitoches.

Even though the Ford Museum could be considered off the beaten path, about 2,000 persons find their way to this fascinating facility each year.

Community volunteers serve as guides and play a major role in the museum's operation. Monday, Wednesday, and Friday hours are from 9:30 A.M. to noon and from 1:30 to 4:00 P.M.; Sunday's hours run from 2:00 to 4:00 P.M. To see the museum on other days, call for an appointment.

From the Ford Museum you can walk across the street to the **Claiborne Parish Courthouse,** in the middle of Homer's town square. A classic example of Greek Revival architecture, the structure was completed in 1861 and is still in use. The courthouse served as the departure point for area soldiers mustering for the Confederate cause and remains one of only four pre–Civil War courthouses in Louisiana. Some artifacts from the courthouse are displayed at the Ford Museum.

From Homer, take State Route 2 east to Bernice, a distance of about 25 miles.

You will enjoy a stop at the **Bernice Depot Museum** (318– 285–2433) and adjacent park. Located at Louisiana and Main Streets, the restored 1899 railroad depot features exhibits on railroading, such as its Rock Island memorabilia and a 1938 wooden caboose called *The Captain Henderson.* You'll also see material on local "Big Woods" history. Open Monday through Friday, the museum's hours are 10:00 A.M. to noon and 1:00 to 3:00 P.M., or by appointment.

Afterward, take U.S. Highway 167 to Ruston, about 20 miles south.

Peach Country

*Y*ou are now in Lincoln Parish, in the heart of peach country. From mid-March through early April, this region becomes a landscape of blooming peach trees. **Mitcham's Peach Orchard** (318– 255–9292), located just outside Ruston on Routes 181 and 182, offers fresh peaches for sale during June, July, and August.

Ruston hosts the annual **Louisiana Peach Festival,** which has been chosen one of the Southeast Tourism Society's top twenty events for June. Besides eating lots of peach ice cream, festival-goers can enjoy a parade, treasure hunt, cooking contests, craft exhibits, and musical entertainment.

Founded in 1884 as Russ Town, the city of Ruston was named for Robert E. Russ, who gave the Vicksburg, Shreveport, and Pacific Railroad some acreage to build a railroad and town site on his property. An early center of culture, Ruston was the site of the Louisiana Chautauqua, a summer program providing opportunities for citizens to immerse themselves in

Peaches, Peaches Everywhere

*K*aylon Thompson French created the following dish featuring Ruston peaches to complement a Cornish hen/wild rice combination. Her recipe took top honors in Ruston's 1997 Peach Cookery Contest and proved so delectable the judges could not stop with a sample taste or two. Rumor has it they tossed restraint to the winds and all but licked the platter clean.

Peach-A-Doodle-Do

4 Cornish hens

1 tablespoon Cajun seasoning

1 cup peach jelly or preserves

1 teaspoon ground cinnamon

Preheat oven to 350° F. Clean hens and cavities. If desired, the hens may be cut in half lengthwise. Place hens in a shallow 9"x 13" roasting pan, skin side up. Season with Cajun seasoning to taste and roast 25 minutes. Meanwhile, place peach jelly or preserves in a microwave-safe container and melt in a microwave oven for approximately 1 minute. Consistency should be loose, not runny or boiling. Stir cinnamon into melted jelly. Remove hens from oven and brush with melted jelly until fully coated. Return to oven and roast for another 20 minutes. Baste once more 5 minutes before serving. Discard remaining glaze. Remove from oven and serve with the following:

Wild About Peaches Rice

2 boxes wild rice (fast cooking)

4 tablespoons peach preserves

1 small package of walnut pieces

1 small bunch of green onions, chopped

In a nonstick boiler, prepare rice according to directions on box (including spice packet and butter). Approximately 2 minutes before the cooking time has finished, stir in peach preserves and walnut pieces. Cover boiler and finish cooking. Remove from heat. Garnish with chopped green onions.

music, drama, art, and the like. The parish is now home to two universities, Grambling and Louisiana Tech.

The **Lincoln Parish Museum** (318–251–0018), 609 North Vienna Street, Ruston 71270, serves as a good starting point to begin your exploration of this inviting city. Housed in the lovely Kidd-Davis home, built in 1886, the regional museum features a collection of period furniture, paintings, and other items of historical interest. In the entry hall be sure to notice the hand-painted wall murals that illustrate the Chautauqua and scenes from local history.

You'll see a dollhouse, exquisitely furnished with tiny period pieces, on display downstairs and another on the second floor. The museum's upstairs exhibits feature various collections such as vintage wedding dresses and original textiles designed during the 1930s as part of the government's Works Progress Administration program. Other displays include household items ranging from cornshuck brooms and kitchen utensils to antique radios and tools.

The museum is open Tuesday through Friday from 10:00 A.M. to 4:00 P.M. and on Saturday and Sunday by appointment.

Jimmie Davis, twice governor of Louisiana (1944–48 and 1960–64) and professional country-music artist and composer, started his singing career in 1928. One of his original songs, "You Are My Sunshine," became a hit in 1939 and was later recorded in thirty-four languages. Until his death, Davis paid an annual visit to a Homecoming held at the *Jimmie Davis Tabernacle,* south of Ruston in Jackson Parish. The revival-style Homecoming, which is held the first Sunday in October, attracts lots of folks. Everyone is invited to bring a dish and enjoy an old-fashioned dinner and a fish fry on the grounds. (At many places in the South, dinner is served at midday, with a lighter supper in the evening.)

Professional gospel groups from across the country join the function held on the site of Davis's parents' home close to the Peckerwood Hill Store. The Tabernacle, built in 1965 by a group of Davis's friends, is located near the junction of Highways 542 and 811 midway between Quitman and Jonesboro.

In Ruston be sure to stop by the *Piney Hills Gallery* (318–255–1450), located at the Dixie Center for the Arts. Original works, ranging from traditional and contemporary crafts to fine arts by some forty North Central Louisiana artists, are displayed in this consignment sales gallery.

You'll see paintings, pottery, furniture, quilts, crocheted items, cornshuck hats, dolls, stuffed toys, puppets, stained glass, jewelry, lamps, sculpture, calligraphy, and photography. Also on display are textile arts, wood carvings, and handmade musical instruments. Articles at the gallery can range in price from $2.00 to $2,000.00. The gallery is open from 10:00 A.M. until 4:00 P.M. Monday through Friday and closes on holidays.

Unique pieces from the *Kent Follette Pottery Studio* are among the gallery's distinctive offerings. Kent Follette, a nationally acclaimed potter, maintains a studio on Route 455, 4 miles north of Ruston, which is open from 10:00 A.M. to 5:00 P.M. Monday through Saturday.

After leaving the studio, take time to stop by *Trenton Street Bistro* (318–251–2103), housed in a century-old building in Ruston's Historic

Hot off the Gridiron

Grambling State University *at Grambling, near Ruston, is one of Louisiana's historic African-American colleges. What it is best known for, though, is the large number of its alumni who go on to play pro-football—more than most schools could ever hope for. Drive around the stadium grounds and note the signage directing the media. What the sports reporters know is that if you want to see what the National Football League will look like in the future, go to a Grambling game and read the team roster. And don't miss the halftime show!*

District. Located at 201 North Trenton, the building served as a local drugstore for more than six decades. Owners Debra Stall and Pete Schumacher offer interesting cuisine downstairs with "pub grub" available at Pete's Pub upstairs. The cafe is open from 11:00 A.M. until 9:00 P.M. Friday and Saturday. Sunday hours are 11:30 A.M. to 1:30 P.M.

At some point during your Ruston visit, plan to stop by the *Log Cabin Smokehouse* (318–255–8023), located a quarter mile north of Interstate 20 at 1906 Farmerville Highway. Housed in an 1886 dogtrot home of hand-hewn logs, the eatery serves barbecue sandwiches or hickory-smoked beef, turkey breast, ham, pork ribs, chicken, and sausage. Texas toast, hickory-smoked beans, and coleslaw or potato salad complete your meal. Prices are economical. From Monday through Friday, serving hours run from 11:00 A.M. to 2:00 P.M. and from 4:30 to 9:00 P.M. Hours are from 11:00 A.M. to 9:00 P.M. on Saturday. Closed Sunday.

Youngsters will enjoy seeing *Idea Place* in Woodard Hall on the campus of *Louisiana Tech University,* located on the town's west side. This children's museum features hands-on exhibits designed to encourage both you and the kids to investigate scientific and mathematical concepts and have fun at the same time. For an appointment call (318) 257–2794.

Tech is also *the* place in Ruston to get ice cream—both cones and large containers—filled with such flavors as blueberry cheesecake and the old standbys vanilla, strawberry, and chocolate. During summer months you can enjoy peach ice cream, and at Christmastime, peppermint and rum raisin flavors are available. Thanks to the college's cows, you can also purchase other premium dairy products: fresh milk (including chocolate), cheeses, and butter along with rolls and bread—all at extremely reasonable prices. These products are sold daily at the *Louisiana Tech Farm Salesroom,* located behind Reese Hall (about 1.5 miles south of the main campus) just off U.S. Highway 80 west. You can line up with local students and professors Monday through Friday from 8:30 A.M. to 5:30 P.M. (With advance notice visitors can tour the nearby dairy plant, which processes these products.)

Nearby you'll also see the *Louisiana Tech Equine Center,* where Thoroughbreds and quarter horses are boarded, bred, and trained. You can tour the paddocks, barns, and stables and watch the horses being exercised. The center is open Monday through Friday except during holidays, and there's no admission fee. Call (318) 257–4502 for an appointment.

Before leaving Ruston, you may want to indulge in some soul food at *Bee's Cafe* (318–255–5610), located at 805 Larson Street. Bee's hotwater cornbread is scrumptious any time of the day—even at breakfast. Speaking of breakfast, this is a good place to fortify yourself for the rigors of the road. You can enjoy a pork chop (or bacon or sausage if you're a traditionalist) along with grits, eggs, and toast. A plate lunch might consist of smothered steak and vegetables (perhaps sweet potatoes or black-eyed peas), rice, and peach cobbler. All selections are written on a blackboard. Prices are economical. Hours are 6:00 A.M. to 2:30 P.M. Monday through Friday.

PLACES TO STAY IN NORTHWEST LOUISIANA

ARK-LA-TEX
Best Western of Minden,
I–20 at exit 47,
Highway 7 near Minden,
(318) 377–1001 or
(800) 528–1234.

Days Inn,
4935 West Monkhouse Drive, Shreveport,
(318) 636–0080 or
(800) DAYS–INN.

Fairfield Place,
2221 Fairfield Avenue,
Shreveport,
(318) 222–0048.

Hampton Inn,
1005 Gould Drive, Bossier,
(318) 752–1112 or
(800) HAMPTON.

Holiday Inn Express–
Airport,
5101 Westwood Park Drive,
Shreveport,
(318) 631–2000.

Holiday Inn Financial Plaza,
5555 Financial Plaza,
Shreveport,
(318) 688–3000.

LeBossier Hotel,
4000 Industrial Drive,
Bossier,
(318) 747–0711.

Sheraton Shreveport,
1419 East Seventieth Street,
Shreveport,
(318) 797–9900 or
(800) 325–3535.

PEACH COUNTRY
Days Inn,
I–20, exit 86,
1801 North Service Road,
Ruston,
(318) 251–2360 or
(800) DAYS–INN.

PLACES TO EAT IN NORTHWEST LOUISIANA

ARK-LA-TEX
Blind Tiger,
Spring and Texas Streets,
Shreveport,
(318) 226–8747.

Bon Appetit,
4832 Line Avenue,
Shreveport,
(318) 868–1438.

Chianti,
6535 Line Avenue,
Shreveport,
(318) 868–8866.

Country Tavern,
823 Brookhollow Drive,
Shreveport,
(318) 797–4477.

For More Information

Arcadia Chamber of Commerce
P.O. Box 587, Arcadia 71001
(318) 263–9897

Homer Chamber of Commerce
519 South Main Street, Homer 71040
(318) 927–3271

Kisatchie National Forest
324 Beardsley, Homer, 71040
(318) 927–2061
(for information on recreation and accommodations in this national forest)

Ruston-Lincoln Parish Tourist Commission
P.O. Box 150, Ruston 71273
(318) 255–2031

Shreveport-Bossier Convention and Visitors' Bureau
629 Spring Street, Shreveport, 71101-3645
(800) 551–8682
www.shreveport-bossier.org

There are visitor centers at 100 John Wesley Boulevard in Bossier City and in the Pierre Bossier, South Park, and St. Vincent Malls.

Webster Parish Convention and Visitors Bureau
P.O. Box 819, Minden 71055
(318) 377–4240

Area newspapers include *The Minden Press-Herald* in Minden; *The Bienville Democrat-Ringgold Record* in Arcadia; the *Bossier Press-Tribune* in Bossier City; *The Guardian-Journal* in Homer; the *Daily Leader* in Ruston; and *The Shreveport Times* in Shreveport. The *Times* will have the most comprehensive entertainment listings for the area. When near a university, always pick up a copy of the school paper; the local entertainment listings might be useful (and sometimes there are good coupons to clip).

Ernest's Orleans Restaurant and Lounge,
1601 Spring Street,
South Shreveport,
(318) 226–1325.

Grandy's,
6811 Pines Road,
Shreveport,
(318) 687–0718.

Karen's Cafe and Kitchen,
505 Milam Street,
Shreveport,
(318) 424–7067.

Monsieur Patou,
855 Pierremont Road,
Suite 135,
Shreveport,
(318) 868–9822.

Murrell's,
539 East Kings Highway,
Shreveport,
(318) 868–2620.

Ralph and Kacoo's,
1700 Old Minden Road,
Bossier,
(318) 747–6660.

Savoie's "The Cajun
Restaurant,"
2400 East Seventieth Street,
Shreveport,
(318) 797–3010.

Semolina,
4801 Line Avenue,
Pierremont Mall,
Shreveport,
(318) 868–6884.

PEACH COUNTRY
Bee's Cafe,
805 Larson Street,
Ruston,
(318) 255–5610.

Log Cabin Smokehouse,
1906 Farmerville Highway,
Ruston,
(318) 255–8023.

Trenton Street Bistro,
201 North Trenton,
Ruston,
(318) 251–2103.

Northeast Louisiana

The top northeast corner of Louisiana has some of its richest land along the river bottoms. This is mostly farming country; soybeans predominate, cotton was once king. Settlements grew up along river shipping points.

The area near Monroe has natural gas reserves for mineral wealth. Economically this is a region of sharp contrasts, with a unique cultural blend that affords visitors a pleasant experience among friendly folk.

The upper part of Louisiana is much more akin to nearby Southern states than to the French-Catholic culture near the coast. Notice that older homes look a little different here—the typical saltbox style Cajun cottage and the New Orleans Victorian shotgun give way to simple farmhouses and the occasional dogtrot (center breezeway) house that derives from log cabin construction.

Cotton Country

After leaving Ruston, travel east on Interstate 20 to West Monroe, the first of several stops in Ouachita (*WASH-a-taw*) Parish. You won't find a more inviting place to take a driving break than **Kiroli Park** (318–396–4016). Located at 820 Kiroli (*ka-ROLL-ee*) Road, the park's entrance is framed by tiers of flower beds. Nature trails for hiking and paved paths for jogging provide a pleasant interlude. With a park permit and state license, you can try your luck in the fishing pond. The 150-acre park also features picnic facilities, tennis courts, a lodge, playgrounds, an amphitheater, a conservatory, and rest rooms.

Car-Window Forestry

Driving along I–20 you get a good view of Louisiana forests. Note that the vegetation near the highway is different (and denser) than that back in the woods. More sun, different roadside soils, and mowing by the highway department create a different ecosystem here. Country roadsides are where you find blackberries (late May) and pokeweed (for edible poke salad, late March and early April).

In the woods the predominant upper story (tallest) trees are pine (shortleaf and loblolly, some grown from planted seedlings and some natural), plus oak and hickory trees. On the highlands you will see more pines. In the lowlands you will see more hardwoods, which shed leaves in winter.

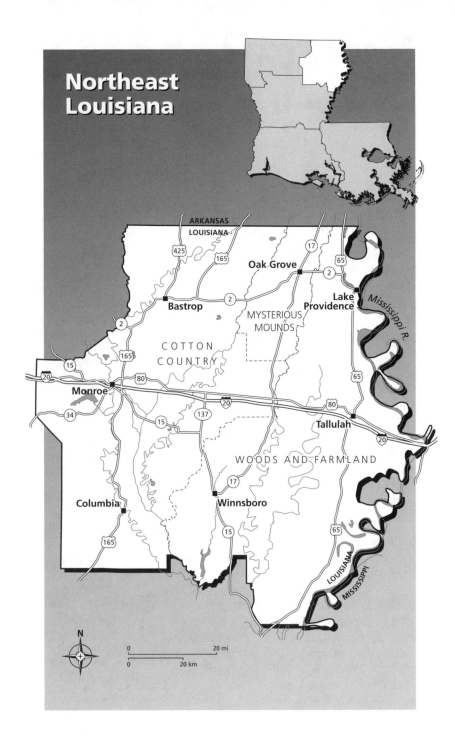

Northeast
Louisiana

ARKANSAS
LOUISIANA

425
165
17
65
Oak Grove
2
Bastrop
2
Lake
Providence
Mississippi R.
MYSTERIOUS
MOUNDS
COTTON
COUNTRY
165
65
15
20
80
Monroe
20
80
Tallulah
34
15
137
20
WOODS AND FARMLAND
17
Columbia
Winnsboro
65
15
LOUISIANA
165
MISSISSIPPI

N

0   20 mi
0   20 km

GAY'S FAVORITES IN NORTHEAST LOUISIANA

Emy-Lou Biedenharn Foundation,
Monroe

Louisiana Purchase Gardens and Zoo,
Monroe

Masur Museum of Art,
Monroe

Poverty Point State Historic Site,
Epps

Tensas River National Wildlife Refuge,
Delhi

Formerly used as a Boy Scout camp, the park is now owned and operated by the City of West Monroe. There's a modest admission fee.

For a look at original works by area artists, visit the **Ouachita River Art Guild Gallery** (318–322–2380). Located at 211 Trenton Street, West Monroe 71291, the fine art sales gallery features watercolor, oil, and acrylic paintings, stained glass items, pottery, sculpture, jewelry, calligraphy, and other art forms. The gallery is open from 10:00 A.M. to 5:00 P.M. Tuesday through Saturday.

Antique buffs will want to save time for exploring **Antique Alley** in West Monroe. Between Trenton Street's 100 and 300 blocks, you'll find a concentration of antiques and gift shops with more than twenty dealers, along with several art galleries and eateries. These renovated shops are housed in downtown buildings dating from the 1880s. Inventories feature American and European antiques, Oriental vases and rugs, silver, crystal, linens, primitives, baskets, railroad and nautical artifacts, quilts, Coca-Cola memorabilia, jewelry, coins, original paintings, and other decorative objects. Most shops are open Tuesday through Saturday from 10:00 A.M. until 5:00 P.M.

Continue east until West Monroe merges with Monroe. For a fine dinner, try **Warehouse No. 1 Restaurant** (318–322–1340) at One Olive Street. The eatery, which retains its original roof and flooring, occupies a restored warehouse on the Ouachita River. Featured menu items include Louisiana catfish, blackened jumbo shrimp, red snapper, and rib-eye. Prices are moderate to expensive. Restaurant hours are 5:00 to 9:00 P.M. Monday through Thursday and 5:00 to 9:30 P.M. Friday and Saturday; closed Sunday.

In Monroe head north to 2006 Riverside Drive, the location of the **Emy-Lou Biedenharn Foundation** (318–387–5281 or 800–362–0983), which consists of the Biedenharn family mansion, the Bible Museum (housing a remarkable collection of rare Bibles, books, illuminated manuscripts, musical instruments, and antique furnishings), and ELsong Garden and Conservatory, with piped music, splashing fountains, and a profusion of blooming plants.

A world-renowned concert contralto who once performed in Europe, Emy-Lou Biedenharn was forced to return to America when World War II brought her successful operatic career to an abrupt halt. Upon arriving at her Monroe home in 1939, her father, Joseph A. Biedenharn

Emy-Lou Biedenharn Foundation

(Coca-Cola's first bottler), presented her with an original John Wycliffe Bible. This gift inspired her to start collecting rare Bibles. She later bought the next-door mansion to contain her vast collection and named it ELsong (for "Emy-Lou's Song").

From the time you walk past the 700-pound solid bronze door (with its unique handle from an English castle), you realize you've entered a treasure trove. Changing exhibits from the permanent collection and outside exhibitions are also displayed from time to time.

The theme gardens are gorgeous. You'll see the Garden of Four Seasons with its marble cherubs, an Oriental garden featuring a gazebo and potted bonsai specimens, the Plants of the Bible Garden adjacent to the museum, the Ballet Lawn (where a bride was being photographed when I visited), and other delightful settings.

Except on national holidays, the facility is open Monday through Saturday from 10:00 A.M. to 5:00 P.M. and Sunday from 2:00 to 5:00 P.M. Admission is free.

Take time to drive through Monroe's square-mile *Historic District,* which overlooks the Ouachita River. Founded by Don Juan Filhiol, the original settlement was known as Fort Miro. Later the town's name was changed to Monroe in honor of the first steamboat to pass that way. Be sure to notice the Ouachita Parish Courthouse. At 520 South Grand Street, near the site of old Fort Miro, stands the frontier-style *Isaiah Garrett House,* a redbrick structure that dates from 1840.

Continue to **Masur Museum of Art** (318–329–2237), a modified English Tudor–style building at 1400 South Grand Street. In addition to the museum's permanent collection of paintings, graphics, sculpture, photographs, and other artworks, traveling exhibits are featured throughout the year.

A remodeled carriage house serves as an on-premises workshop for art classes. Trained volunteers conduct tours through the museum, which is open Tuesday through Thursday from 9:00 A.M. until 5:00 P.M. and Friday through Sunday from 2:00 until 5:00 P.M. Admission is free.

At the **Louisiana Purchase Gardens and Zoo** (318–329–2400), 1405 Bernstein Park Drive, Monroe 71202, you can enjoy a delightful outing. Stroll along tree-lined paths, take a leisurely cruise on a canopied pontoon boat along Bayou Safari, or chug around the eighty-acre park's Lewis and Clark Railroad via miniature train. The Louisiana Territory's historic events and points of interest serve as the park's theme and a backdrop for an animal population that ranges between 450 and 550. Especially noted for its primate collection, the zoo's large group of lemurs (whose forebears came from Madagascar) were all bred on the premises.

As you cruise through varied settings that simulate the animals' natural habitats, you'll see the zoo's resident ham—Solomon, the llama.

Several of the zoo's animals were transported to nearby Winnfield when the movie *Blaze* was being filmed. In one scene, a spider monkey named Juanita wanted to commend Paul Newman (who portrayed former Louisiana governor Earl K. Long) for his fine performance. Immediately after the Long character delivered some lines to his stripper-girlfriend Blaze Starr, the monkey reached out of her cage and emphatically patted Newman on the shoulder.

Early Mon-ro(e)ver

In his far-ranging expedition of present-day Monroe in the 1540s, Hernando de Soto wrote about crossing the "Washita," as he spelled it, River.

Among lush gardens with live oaks and a host of flowering plants, the zoo offers a gift shop and concessions. Except for Christmas Day, the facility is open 10:00 A.M. to 5:00 P.M. daily. Admission is modest; children two and under are admitted free.

Continue south on U.S. Highway 165 to Columbia in Caldwell Parish. Don't miss the **Martin Homeplace** (318–649–6722) about a mile north of Columbia on Martin Lane off U.S. Highway 165. Watch for the turnoff sign beside O'Neal Butane Company for the two-story circa 1878 farmhouse.

TOP ANNUAL EVENTS IN NORTHEAST LOUISIANA

Franklin Parish Catfish Festival, Winnsboro, April. (318) 435–7607.

Deep South Rodeo, Winnsboro, August. (318) 435–7607.

Louisiana Folklife Festival, Monroe, second weekend in September. (800) 843–1872.

Southern Pickin' and Ginnin' Festival, 815 Louisa Street, Rayville, third weekend in September. (318) 728–4127.

North Louisiana Folklife, Inc., Columbia, second weekend in October. (318) 495–5468.

The Martin Homeplace offers a glimpse of rural life during the early 1900s. Canned jellies from wild fruits make splashes of purple, green, red, and gold on scallop-edged pantry shelves. Martin Homeplace is open Tuesday through Friday from 9:00 A.M. to 4:30 P.M. year-round with tours for a small fee. Call ahead for a place at the table if you want to enjoy a country-style meal, cooked and served on the premises each Thursday from 11:00 A.M. to 1:30 P.M. Economical prices.

As a result of Columbia's participation in Louisiana's Main Street program (a project of the National Trust for Historic Preservation), many once-forgotten structures have been rescued and restored, such as the unique *Schepis Museum* (318–649–9931 or 649–0726). Head for 107 Main Street at the levee, where you'll see this structure topped by life-size statues of George Washington and Christopher Columbus beneath a bald eagle's spread wings. Built by Italian architect John Schepis, the former mercantile store resembles a Renaissance-style palazzo of the mid-fifteenth century.

The museum offers travel information and hosts ongoing exhibits. One of the museum's past exhibits showcased the 1927 Flood and its devastating impact on eleven states. Other exhibits have featured black-and-white photography depicting rural life in Louisiana from 1939 to 1963, bayous and wetlands, and cowboys as heroes. Hours are Tuesday through Saturday from 10:00 A.M. to 4:00 P.M. Free admission.

After seeing the museum's current exhibit, step next door to the *Watermark Saloon* (318–649–0999), the last building before the levee. The oldest saloon on the Ouachita River, the Watermark dates back to the steamboat era during the reign of King Cotton. Hours are noon till midnight, Monday through Saturday.

After strolling along Main Street and browsing for antiques, plan a drive by the nearby *First United Methodist Church.* Ask someone to point you in the direction of this picturesque building, painted dark green with white trim. Constructed from plans brought from Europe by a church member and completed in 1911, the church is listed on the National Register of Historic Places. If time permits, plan a walking tour through the town's hillside cemetery. At this point, you can easily continue south on U.S. Highway 165 to Alexandria and launch an exploration of the state's central section or continue your sight-seeing through the state's northeastern corner.

If you're near Richland Parish the third Saturday in August, consider taking in the spirited **Southern Pickin' and Ginnin' Festival** held annually in nearby Rayville. For now, proceed to Bastrop—the seat of Morehouse Parish—north of Monroe.

Across from the Morehouse Parish Courthouse on the town square, you'll see the **Rose Theater,** restored and used for local productions throughout the year. Call (318) 283–0120 for a recording that provides information on current or upcoming events. Tours are available by reservation.

Before leaving Bastrop, follow U.S. Highway 165 east until it becomes Mer Rouge Road. You'll pass right by the **Snyder Memorial Museum and Creative Art Center** (318–281–8760) at 1620 East Madison Street, Bastrop 71220. Housed in a brick building with a roof of red tile, the museum contains furniture from the eighteenth and nineteenth centuries, an Oriental rug in an unusual design, clothing, maps, documents, china, and kitchen utensils. In the living and dining rooms, notice the antique oak furniture with legs carved in a barley-twist design. The museum also features a country store with old-fashioned merchandise, Native American artifacts, historic documents, and monthly art exhibits.

First United Methodist Church

Fishy Guests

Although catfish farming is more common in the delta area of neighboring Mississippi, there are some commercial catfish ponds in Louisiana. The strangest "tourists" to discover these attractions are the cormorants, fishing birds that come up from their usual haunts on the Gulf to fish in these productive waters. These large black birds with long necks usually perch on utility lines.

A separate carriage house holds old farm implements, sidesaddles, cotton scales, and a horse-drawn hearse. The grounds offer gardens and picnic facilities, and the museum is open Tuesday through Friday from 9:00 A.M. until 4:00 P.M. There is no admission charge.

From Bastrop take Route 133 south until you reach Route 134, which leads east to Epps. Located slightly northeast of Epps (and 15 miles north of Delhi) on Route 577 off Route 134, you'll discover Poverty Point State Historic Site, one of North America's most remarkable archaeological wonders.

Mysterious Mounds

I f you happen to fly over Louisiana's northeastern corner during winter months when the earth is not camouflaged by foliage, you can see the outline of a great bird with a wingspan of 640 feet. This bird mound was built some 3,000 years ago by the advanced people of Poverty Point.

The mind boggles to think about the millions of loads of dirt (carried in baskets of animal skin and woven materials and weighing perhaps fifty pounds a load) required to create the site's huge complex of concentric ridges and ceremonial mounds. This tremendous undertaking involved not only tedious labor but also a high degree of engineering expertise. Now known as **Poverty Point State Historic Site** (318–926–5492 or 888–926–5492), the area is as archaeologically significant as England's Stonehenge.

"A whopping total of 1 percent of Poverty Point has been excavated so far," says manager Dennis LaBatt. But that 1 percent tells a remarkable story. When these ridges and mounds were built along Bayou Macon between 1700 and 700 B.C., they were the largest earthworks in the Western Hemisphere. Poverty Point's inhabitants, evidently a bird-revering people, possessed an uncanny degree of astronomical awareness; two of the aisles line up with the summer- and winter-solstice sunsets.

Excavations have uncovered numerous articles of personal adornment, many with bird motifs. Pendants, bangles, and beads of copper, lead, and red jasper appear among the finds. Designs feature various geometric shapes, bird heads, animal claws, locusts, turtles, clam shell replicas, and tiny carved owls. Artifacts also include stone tools, spears, and numerous round earthern balls used for cooking.

When LaBatt stages a cooking demonstration to show visitors how the cooking balls may have been used, he heats fifty balls and puts them in a pit; he then places venison or fish (wrapped in green leaves) on the heated balls. The food is covered with fifty more balls and allowed to cook slowly.

You can explore the park on foot—it takes between one and two hours to complete the 2.6-mile walking trail—or you can opt for a ride in an open-air tram, which seats thirty adults. The forty-five-minute tram tour operates from Easter through Labor Day and features stops at Mound A, Mound B, and the terrace ridges.

The Atl-Atl (at-ul at-ul) is a bit of early technology known at Poverty Point in its heyday. It is a spear-throwing aid—a wooden hand-grip supports the spear and enables the thrower to increase range and accuracy. Covering the distance of a football field would be no problem.

The guides at Poverty Point State Historic Site will demonstrate how one works and let you try your hand, too. And, you can make your own.

At the visitor center, an audiovisual presentation provides some background on Poverty Point, and you'll see displays of artifacts found on the site. There are also picnic facilities here as well as a wooden observation tower that affords an overview of the mounds. If you visit Poverty Point during summer, you may see an archaeological dig in progress. Several state universities schedule digs during this time, and visitors are welcome to watch the excavations.

Poverty Point's hours are from 9:00 A.M. to 5:00 P.M. seven days a week year-round, excluding Thanksgiving, Christmas, and New Year's Day. Admission is modest; senior citizens and children under twelve are admitted free.

The area surrounding Poverty Point is agricultural country, and the terrain is flat. Along the road you'll see pastureland, crops, cotton gins, and sawmills.

Woods and Farmland

After leaving Poverty Point, head south to Delhi and take U.S. Highway 80 east, watching for a sign to turn right onto a gravel road to reach **Tensas River National Wildlife Refuge** (318–574–2664). To reach the visitor center, continue south to the end of the road. (When I entered the refuge via a nearby dirt road, five white-tailed deer leaped across the trail in front of me.)

The Tensas (*TEN-saw*) Refuge's visitor center is a large, rustic building with a rough cedar exterior. Here you can pick up a refuge map and see dioramas and exhibits of birds, mammals, and reptiles indicative of regional wildlife. The building also houses an auditorium where films and slide shows on the refuge's activities may be viewed. The Hollow Cypress Wildlife Trail, extending about a quarter of a mile, takes you to an observation platform. Along the way you may see birds, squirrels, and, yes, snakes.

As part of the National Refuge System, Tensas serves as a protected habitat for native wildlife such as the Louisiana black bear. According to the Fish and Wildlife Service, some sixty to one hundred of these bears currently roam the Tensas woods (including the refuge and surrounding forests in Madison Parish).

The Louisiana black bear inspired America's beloved teddy bear. Although the story varies as to locale, it seems that President Theodore Roosevelt, while on a hunting trip to the deep South, wanted to shoot a bear. He once wrote, "I was especially anxious to kill a bear . . . after the fashion of the old Southern planters, who for a century past have followed the bear with horse and hound and horn. . . ." Members of Roosevelt's hunting party, knowing of his keen desire to bag a bear, captured a black bear and tied it to a tree—an easy target for the president. Roosevelt's refusal to shoot the helpless animal resulted in much publicity, triggering several editorial cartoons. Soon after the hunting incident, a New York shopkeeper named Morris Michtom came up with the idea of marketing some stuffed toy bears made by his wife, Rose. He called them "Teddy's Bears," and the president gave his approval. The Michtoms' cuddly bears became an instant success, and the rest is history.

When I visited the refuge, radios had been placed on fifteen black bears to monitor their activity in a program aimed at preserving and improving their habitat. The radio collars emit signals, which enable refuge personnel to keep track of the bears' whereabouts.

According to Talbert Williams, a range technician at the refuge, "These small black bears are barely holding their own." Talbert, who was born in a log cabin on the banks of the Tensas River, served for more than three decades as a state game warden before going to work for the federal government to "save these woods." He can tell you plenty of local stories, including anecdotes about Ben Lilly, a legendary hunter from these parts.

This habitat also provides food and shelter for many other animals, including the bobcat, otter, raccoon, mink, squirrel, woodchuck, wild turkey,

OTHER ATTRACTIONS WORTH SEEING

barred owl, and pileated woodpecker, as well as thousands of waterfowl and other migratory birds.

In this bottomland forest you'll also see a great variety of trees—several kinds of oak, three or four species of elm, cypress, sweet gum, maple, black locust, honey locust, red haw, and others. Spiky palmetto, muscadine vines, shrubs, and other plants grow here as well.

Deep in the heart of the woods stand the ruins of an old plantation house—about ten handmade-brick pillars (from 10 to 12 feet tall) are all that remain of the former three-story structure. Also hidden in the forest are an old cemetery with eight or nine tombstones and the towering chimney of a pre–Civil War cotton gin.

Primitive canoe launches allow visitors to explore parts of the refuge by boat. Some public hunting is allowed here, but hunters need to familiarize themselves with refuge regulations. Deer hunting permits, which must be requested in advance by writing or phoning, are issued on the basis of drawings. The refuge is open year-round for fishing, but no camping is allowed. As Talbert says, "If you like the natural things, this is the place to come."

Downtown Columbia. *Stop and walk about in this pleasant old steamboat stop. Main Street has been revived and focuses on the Ouachita River. Columbia was the hometown of former Louisiana governor John McKeithen.*

Lake D'Arbonne State Park. *P.O. Box 236, Farmerville 71241; (318) 368–2086 or (888) 677–5200. Excellent fishing (buy a license!) and water sports on a man-made lake. Lots of places to picnic.*

Northeast Louisiana University. *Off Bonair Drive, Monroe. There is always something interesting to see on a university campus. The library will have exhibits, there will be art displays, and you can pick up the campus newspaper for events.*

The public is welcome to visit the refuge, which offers an active environmental education program, any time of the year. Except for holidays the visitor center is open Monday through Friday from 8:00 A.M. until 4:00 P.M., on Saturday from 10:00 A.M. to 4:00 P.M., and on Sunday from 1:00 to 4:00 P.M. For further information contact the Refuge Manager, Tensas River National Wildlife Refuge, Route 2, Box 295, Tallulah 71282.

After exploring the refuge, head northeast to **Tallulah.** In this area of flat farmland, you'll drive past pecan groves, pastures of grazing cattle, and fields of soybeans, cotton, rice, and wheat.

Tallulah was founded in 1857 and is said to have been named by a traveling railroad engineer in honor of his former sweetheart back home (after he was jilted by a local lady). A bayou winds its way through town and is especially lovely during the holiday season, when

Battle of Get-This-Bug

Tallulah was the site of the U.S. Department of Agriculture station that studied the boll weevil and how to exterminate it beginning in 1909.

lights from a series of Christmas trees placed in the water reflect across its surface.

During the early 1900s Tallulah was the site of a government laboratory where experiments were conducted to find a weapon in the war against the boll weevil. By the 1920s aerial crop-dusting techniques were being developed here. In 1924 Delta Airlines (then called Huff Daland Dusters) entered the picture and established the first commercial crop-dusting company.

Traveling north on U.S. Highway 65 takes you to East Carroll Parish and the town of Transylvania, a tiny community with a spooky name. ***Transylvania General Store*** (318–559–1338) stands adjacent to a small post office; beyond looms a white water tower emblazoned with a black bat.

The store, owned by Nancy and Phillip Koehn, has attracted sightseers from England, Italy, Iceland, Japan, and even Romania's Transylvania—including a visitor who identified himself as a descendant of Count Dracula.

Besides food, dry goods, and hardware, the owners sell life-size rubber bats, skull replicas, and about 250 dozen T-shirts a year—some with a Dracula likeness and others with a bat logo. (Be sure to take a peek at the "baby vampire bats" in a lighted box.)

You can get cold soft drinks here and order sandwiches of your choice as well as hamburgers, fried chicken, and plate lunches. The store, open Monday through Saturday from 6:00 A.M. until 8:00 P.M. (7:00 P.M. in winter), is closed on Sunday.

After leaving Transylvania, continue north on U.S. Highway 65 (a direct route through the state's northeastern corner to Arkansas) for 10 miles to ***Lake Providence,*** located on a 6-mile-long oxbow lake that appeared on the local landscape when the Mississippi River couldn't decide which way to go.

According to parish lore, the town's name sprang from early years when Captain Bunch and his band of pirates attacked and robbed travelers on the Mississippi. If settlers got past Bunch's Bend, they thanked Providence for their safe passage. Fortunately, today's visitors don't have to worry about pirates and can stop to enjoy the lake's recreation opportunities.

Located downtown at 208 Lake Street, the ***Ole Dutch Bakery*** (318–559–1574) offers French, honey whole wheat, and cinnamon breads and other specialties. A perennial favorite, the poppy seed bread is made with almond, butter, and vanilla flavorings and topped with a glaze. Owners Kathy and Marlin Wedel also operate an adjoining cafe where you can enjoy lunch; the single daily special might range from a traditional Mennonite recipe to upside-down pizza or cheese enchiladas. The cafe's wooden tables and chairs were made by Marlin's brother, Errol. The business actually started in Kathy's kitchen. Her home-baked goods made from traditional Dutch and German recipes proved popular, and the Ole Dutch Bakery opened its doors in 1983. Hours are Tuesday through Friday from 6:30 A.M. until 5:00 P.M. and on Saturday from 6:30 A.M. to 4:00 P.M.

Afterward, continue to **Byerley House** (318– 559–5125) at 600 Lake Street (also U.S. Highway 65) in Lake Providence. This restored Victorian structure serves as a visitor and community center as well as home to the chamber of commerce. Here you can collect information and maps on local and state attractions, enjoy free coffee (or lemonade during summer months), unpack a picnic lunch on the grounds, or stroll on the pier over the lake. Byerley House is open from 9:00 A.M. to 5:00 P.M. Monday through Saturday and 1:00 to 5:00 P.M. Sunday.

A 500-foot overwater nature walk adjacent to Byerley Park offers a view of **Grant's Canal** through 300-year-old cypress trees. Part of the Civil War Discovery Trail, the channel proved to be a military failure for General Grant in his attempts to find an alternate way to slip Union gunboats past Vicksburg's heavy fortifications during his Southern attack.

Continue to the **Louisiana Cotton Museum** (318–559–2041), located a couple of miles or so north of town on U.S. Highway 65, for an overview of the history of cotton and its impact on westward expansion, society, culture, and the economy. Exhibits focusing on the period from 1820 through the 1930s interpret cotton's leading role in the state's heritage and its influence on life in Louisiana and the South as a whole. You'll see a large cotton gin (supposedly the state's first electric version) plus other museum exhibits and pavilions on the grounds. In early fall, you may get a chance to pick cotton on the premises. Hours are from 9:00 A.M. to 4:00 P.M. Monday through Friday. Open Saturday also in summer. Admission is free.

Saved from the Pirates

One explanation for the naming of Lake Providence is that river travelers escaping from upstream pirates gratefully called this safe site "Providence."

To see another agricultural product in its various phases, continue north about 8 miles on U.S. Highway 65 to **Panola Pepper Company**

The James Boys

The town of Oak Grove, near Lake Providence, was said to be frequently visited by outlaws Jesse and Frank James, who were such pleasant house guests that they were known to help local kids with their homework.

(318–559–1774) until you see the sign directing you east to Panola, about a quarter of a mile off the highway. If you call ahead, owner Grady Brown will line up a guide to give you a tour (except during the hottest summer months). From planting to pickling peppers, there's something seasonal and interesting to see at this family cotton plantation, which has diversified into food processing.

The company's country store stocks hot sauces, packaged mixes, gourmet mustards, pepper-stuffed olives, and seasonings. Panola Gourmet Pepper Sauce makes a great souvenir, although hard-core pepper lovers may prefer the Bat's Brew or Vampfire Hot Sauce (inspired by nearby Transylvania). For the undecided, Panola offers a variety pack. The store also carries home accessories, aprons, T-shirts, golf balls, and other gift items. Store hours are 8:00 A.M. to 4:30 P.M. Monday through Friday.

Before leaving the northeast section, consider taking U.S. Highway 65 south toward Newellton in Tensas Parish. ***Winter Quarters State Historic Site*** (318–467–9750 or 888–677–9468), the only plantation home along the banks of Lake St. Joseph that was not torched by Yankee troops during the Vicksburg Campaign, is located on Route 608, 6 miles southeast of Newellton (and north of St. Joseph). The original structure, a three-room hunting lodge, was built in 1805 by Job Routh. The plantation grew to more than 2,000 acres. Later, Routh's heirs added several rooms and a gallery to the lodge. In 1850, Dr. Haller Nutt and his wife, "Miss Julia" (Routh's granddaughter), bought the property and enlarged the house again.

Grant's Vicksburg Campaign brought many changes to Winter Quarters Plantation. The Union army marched south through Tensas during the spring of 1863, carrying out General William Tecumseh Sherman's orders to destroy everything not needed by Union troops. Fifteen plantation homes lined the banks of Lake St. Joseph before the Union troops passed through. When they left, only Winter Quarters remained standing.

According to a letter written by Dr. Nutt and dated October 1863, he and his family were in Natchez, Mississippi, when Union troops tramped through Tensas Parish. His overseer, Hamilton Smith "obtained letters of protection in my [Dr. Nutt's] name from advance officers of this army," Generals McPherson and Smith. Thus, Winter Quarters Plantation was saved. Regrettably, Union army stragglers destroyed all outbuildings, livestock, and crops.

The mansion, which overlooks Lake St. Joseph, features front, back, and side verandas. Furnished with period pieces, the house also contains documents, personal records, copies of diaries, and memorabilia from the Civil War period. Be sure to notice the rare billiard table, circa 1845. Except for Thanksgiving, Christmas, and New Year's Day, the site is open daily from 9:00 A.M. until 5:00 P.M. Modest admission.

PLACES TO STAY IN NORTHEAST LOUISIANA

COTTON COUNTRY
Days Inn,
5650 Frontage Road,
Monroe,
(318) 345–2220 or
(800) 325–2525.

Fairfield Inn,
I–20 at Thomas Road,
West Monroe,
(318) 388–3810 or
(800) 228–2800.

Hampton Inn,
1407 Martin Luther
King Drive,
Monroe,
(318) 361–9944 or
(800) 426–7866.

Holiday Inn Holidome,
I–20 and U.S. 165 Bypass,
Monroe,
(318) 387–5100 or
(800) 465–4329.

La Quinta Inn,
1035 U.S. 165 Bypass South,
Monroe,
(318) 322–3900 or
(800) 531–5900.

Ramada Limited Motel,
Highway 165 South,
Monroe,
(318) 323–1600 or
(800) 2–RAMADA.

MYSTERIOUS MOUNDS
D'Arbonne Lake Motel,
101 Dori Drive,
Farmerville,
(318) 368–2236.

Preferred Inn,
1053 East Madison Street,
Bastrop,
(318) 281–3621 or
(800) 227–8767.

WOODS AND FARMLANDS
Best Western Winnsboro,
4198 Front Street,
Winnsboro,
(318) 435–2000.

Super 8 Motel,
1604 Highway 65,
Tallulah,
(318) 574–2000.

For More Information

Doorway to Louisiana
600 Lake Street, Lake Providence 71254
(318) 559–5125

Monroe–West Monroe Convention and Visitors Bureau
P.O. Box 6054, Monroe 71211
(318) 387–5691 or (800) 843–1872

Winnsboro–Franklin Parish Tourist Center
3826 Front Street, Winnsboro 71295
(318) 435–7607
www.winnsboro.org

Area newspapers include the *News–Star* in Monroe (largest in the region, should have activities listings weekly), the *Banner–Democrat* in Lake Providence, the *Caldwell Watchman–Progress* in Columbia, the *Bastrop Daily Enterprise* in Bastrop, the *Franklin Sun* in Winnsboro, and the *Madison Journal* in Tallulah.

**PLACES TO EAT IN
NORTHEAST LOUISIANA**

COTTON COUNTRY
Barnhill's' Country Buffet,
3110 Louisville Avenue,
Monroe,
(318) 323–4883.

Chateau,
2007 Louisville Avenue,
Monroe,
(318) 325–0384.

Cracker Barrel
Old Country Store,
309 Constitution Drive,
West Monroe,
(318) 325–5505.

Danken Trail,
7702 DeSiard Street,
Monroe,
(318) 343–0773.

Genusa's Italian Restaurant,
815 Park Avenue,
Monroe,
(318) 325–5098.

Magnolia Bar & Grill,
1210 North Eighteenth
Street, Monroe,
(318) 387–3670.

Monroe's Restaurant,
1301 North Nineteenth
Street, Monroe,
(318) 387–0908.

Warehouse No. 1 Restaurant,
One Olive Street,
Monroe,
(318) 322–1340.

WOODS AND FARMLAND
Brown's Landing,
120 Brown's Landing Road,
Winnsboro,
(318) 435–5291.

Country Pride,
Highway 65, exit 171,
Tallulah,
(318) 574–5900.

Jesse's Steak and Seafood,
3942 Front Street
(Highway 15),
Winnsboro,
(318) 435–9948.

Ole Dutch Bakery,
208 Lake Street,
Lake Providence,
(318) 559–1574.

San Marcus,
4198 Front Street,
Winnsboro,
(318) 435–0002.

Central Louisiana

Central Louisiana is crossed by rivers and streams, with the old meanders of the Red River and even the Mississippi River still marked in the region's geology. The area around Marksville is on a raised terrace of land, but like most of Louisiana, the general characteristic of the terrain is flat. Rich soil and a long growing season made agriculture, especially of cotton, profitable along the rivers.

Around A.D. 100 the area was home to a Native American culture (named Marksville for its location) of mound building with distinctive pottery. This part of Louisiana was later the gateway to the Spanish colonies of the West, with an early frontier outpost just outside Natchitoches, a city that itself dates to the early eighteenth century.

Woodland and Water

About midway between Shreveport and Lake Charles on U.S. Highway 171, you'll find *Hodges Gardens* (800–354–3523), a site that lures visitors year-round. Created by conservation-minded A. J. Hodges, this forest retreat was once barren land, stripped by timber companies. During the 1940s Hodges replanted thousands of acres with pine trees to bring to pass this outdoor wonderland containing staggered gardens of formal plantings and hillsides strewn with wildflowers. Near the entrance of the main garden area, you'll see a petrified tree—supposedly thousands of years old.

A stone quarry serves as a striking backdrop for moss-covered rocks, waterfalls, and a profusion of wildflowers and other plants. Although featured flowers vary with the season, there's always a lavish display. Acres of daffodils, tulips, and other multicolored bulbs herald spring; camellias, dogwood, and azaleas blazing in reds, corals, and hot pinks confirm the season's arrival. With summer come assorted annuals and thousands of roses bursting into dazzling bloom. Fall furnishes vibrant displays of chrysanthemums—a fantasy in red, pink, purple, yellow, bronze, and white.

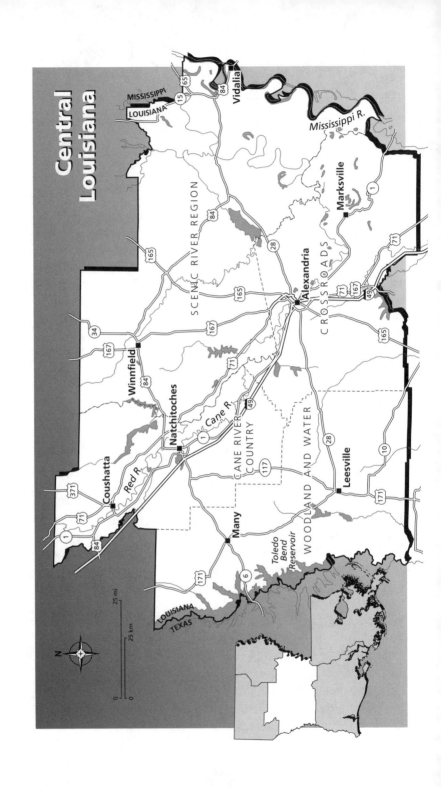

CENTRAL LOUISIANA

GAY'S FAVORITES IN CENTRAL LOUISIANA

Bayou Folk Museum,
Cloutierville

Kent House, Alexandria

Melrose Plantation,
Natchitoches

Toledo Bend Lake

*Los Adaes State
Commemorative Area,*
Many

Town of Natchitoches

Briarwood, Natchitoches

Wending your way along pebbled concrete walks that lead past streams and cascading waterfalls, you'll enjoy rainbows of blossoms with sweet aromas. Although the formal gardens are accessible only on foot, you may drive from point to point within the complex. Along the way various panoramic observation points provide breathtaking views. The 4,700 acres of pine forest also serve as home to various birds and animals. You'll see squirrels, wild turkeys, and deer (some 700 deer inhabit these woods). Barbados and mouflon sheep and buffalo roam pastures bordering a large lake on the property.

Rental boats for fishing are available. Two picnic areas—one nearby equipped with a vending area and rest rooms and the other (without these facilities) in a more remote setting—provide pleasant places for enjoying lunch or a snack. The grounds also offer a conservatory, greenhouses, and a gift shop.

Except Christmas Eve, Christmas Day, and New Year's Day, the gardens are open daily and admission is charged. For more information contact Hodges Gardens, P.O. Box 340, Florien 71429.

Across the road from the entrance to Hodges Gardens is **Emerald Hills Golf and Tennis Resort** (800–533–5031), where you may want to have dinner or stay overnight.

To reach **Fisher** (318–256–2001 or 256–6263), about a ten-minute drive from Hodges Gardens, follow U.S. Highway 171 north and watch for the turnoff sign. Surrounded by a pine forest and off the beaten path, this hamlet could challenge Garrison Keillor's own Lake Wobegon for the title "The Town That Time Forgot." But therein lies its charm—a quaint and quiet place in today's frenetic world.

When the Louisiana Long Leaf Lumber Company (also known as Four-L) located here in 1899 to harvest the nearby pine forest, it built Fisher as a base of operations. The town grew into a bustling place with red-dirt streets where mules hauled loads of logs. Fisher was built entirely of local lumber, including board sidewalks.

Although Fisher's sawmill days ended in 1966 when new owners bought the mill and sold the company houses, you can still see white picket fences, pine cottages, a post office, and an opera house where people stood in line to see movies that cost a dime. There's also an old commissary where folks once shopped, standing awhile on the store's long front porch to chat with neighbors. Antiques are now on sale here.

The Fisher Heritage Foundation has received grants to restore the commissary, depot, and opera house. Village residents are working to preserve the lumber town's past, and Fisher has been placed on the National Register of Historic Places. Other sites include a caboose painted a fire-engine red with canary yellow trim, an office building, and the Old Fisher Church.

Visitors can step back into the village's history at Christmas, when the entire village is lit with lights, and each May, when Fisher celebrates its heritage with *Sawmill Days,* a festival featuring music, food, entertainment, and a variety of logging and woodworking competitions.

Continuing north on U.S. Highway 171 about 6 miles takes you to Many (*MAN-ee*). Westward lies Toledo Bend country, an outdoor lover's paradise of some 185,000 acres. Famed for its fine bass fishing, this large recreation area offers marinas, public parks, restaurants, boating facilities, and camping. Should you decide to go fishing, *Toledo Bend Lake* promises prolific possibilities. The Sabine Parish Tourist and Recreation Commission (318–256–5880 or 800–358–7802) at 920 Fisher Road will answer your questions and point you in all the right directions on this big lake. Ask them about annual events such as the nearby *Zwolle Tamale Festival.*

Leaving Many, take Route 6 northeast to Natchitoches Parish.

Cane River Country

The lovely town of *Natchitoches* (pronounced *NAK-a-tush*), which sprang up on the Red River, is now located on the Cane River (actually a lake). The town didn't move—the river did. But perhaps that's why the place retains its historical charm. As Louisiana's oldest town, Natchitoches was a thriving steamboat port that showed promise of growing into a major metropolis, second in size only to New Orleans, until destiny, in the guise of a spring flood, deemed otherwise. When the Red River carved a new course, Natchitoches was separated from the main body of water and lost its strategic location as a trade center. The shrunken stream left flowing through the old channel was renamed the Cane River. A dam constructed in 1917 created Cane River Lake, which drifts through the city's heart.

Natchitoches also holds the distinction of being the oldest permanent

CENTRAL LOUISIANA

European settlement in the entire Louisiana Purchase Territory, a vast acreage from which all or parts of fifteen states were carved.

When French Canadian Louis Juchereau de St. Denis (*de-NEE*) docked here in 1714, he found the Native American Natchitoches (a Caddo tribe) living along the north bank of the Red River. The town takes its name from this tribe, and various translations of the word include "place of chinquapin eaters," "chestnut eaters," and "pawpaw eaters." St. Denis chose this spot to found Natchitoches, which evolved from a trading post with both the Native Americans (the French exchanged guns, knives, and trinkets for furs, bear oil, salt, and such) and the Spanish. To thwart Spanish advances **Fort St. Jean Baptiste** (318–357–3101) was established here in 1716. Located on Mill Street, the fort is open daily from 9:00 A.M. to 5:00 P.M. Modest admission.

You can see a replica of the old French fort with its walls of sharpened logs on the riverfront at Mill Street. The compound, which contains the commandant's house, a small warehouse, a chapel, barracks, and three huts, is not far from the American Cemetery (where some historians surmise St. Denis and his wife are buried).

If you happen to drive through Natchitoches during December, you'll see why it's called the City of Lights. Some 170,000 multicolored lights glow along the downtown riverbank during the Christmas Festival of Lights, an annual event that attracts thousands of sightseers. The movie *Steel Magnolias,* which was filmed in Natchitoches, features some night scenes showing this glittering spectacle. You may want to take a Steel Magnolias tour to see some of the locations used in the movie. For more information and a local map, stop by the Natchitoches Parish Tourist Commission (318–352– 8072 or 800– 259–1714) at 781 Front Street.

Top Annual Events in Central Louisiana

Choctaw-Apache Powwow, *Ebarb, April or May.*
(318) 645–2588.

Sawmill Days, *Fisher, third weekend in May.*
(318) 256–2001 or 256–6263.

Melrose Plantation Arts and Crafts Festival, *on the Cane River, Melrose, second weekend in June.*
(318) 379–0055.

Natchitoches-Northwestern Folk Festival, *Prather Coliseum, Northwestern State University, third weekend in July.*
(318) 352–8072.

Cenlabration, *315 Bolton Avenue, Alexandria, Labor Day weekend.*
(318) 473–1127 or (888) 77–CENLA.

Zwolle Tamale Festival, *Many, second weekend in October.*
(318) 256–5880.

Natchitoches Pilgrimage, *Natchitoches, second full weekend in October.*
(318) 352–8072.

Louisiana Pecan Festival, *Colfax, first full weekend in November.*
(318) 627–5196.

Christmas Festival of Lights, *Natchitoches, first Saturday in December and all December weekends.*
(800) 259–1714.

A Savory Specialty

Mrs. Charles E. Cloutier's recipe for these tasty meat pies first appeared in the *Cane River Cuisine* cookbook. Now you can enjoy this Natchitoches specialty in your own kitchen.

Natchitoches Meat Pie

Filling:

1 1/2 pounds ground beef

1 1/2 pounds ground pork

1 cup chopped green onions, tops and bottoms

1 tablespoon salt

1 teaspoon coarse ground black pepper

1 teaspoon coarse ground red pepper

1/2 teaspoon cayenne pepper

1/3 cup all-purpose flour

Crust:

2 cups self-rising flour

1/3 heaping cup solid shortening

1 egg, beaten

3/4 cup milk

Combine ground beef, pork, onions, and seasonings in large Dutch oven.

Cook over medium heat, stirring often until meat loses its red color. Do not overcook meat. Remove from heat and cool to room temperature. Drain off all excess grease. Sift 1/3 cup of flour over meat mixture, stirring until well combined.

Sift remaining 2 cups of flour and cut shortening into flour. Add beaten egg and milk. Form dough into ball. Roll about 1/3 of dough at a time on a lightly floured surface and cut into 5- to 5 1/2-inch circles. Separate circles with waxed paper.

To assemble: Place heaping tablespoon of filling on one side of circle. With fingertips, dampen edge of circle containing meat, then fold top over meat and crimp with fork dipped in water. With fork, prick twice on top.

To fry: Cook until golden brown at 350° F in deep-fat fryer.

These meat pies freeze beautifully if enclosed in plastic sandwich bags. When frying frozen meat pies, do not thaw before frying. Cocktail meat pies may be made the same way, using a biscuit cutter and 1 teaspoon of meat filling.

Makes 26–28 pies, 5- to 5 1/2-inch size.

Along the town's picturesque brick-paved Front Street, you'll pass many antebellum structures in the original downtown area. At the 1843 **Hughes Building,** be sure to notice the courtyard with its ornate spiral staircase of cast iron.

To continue your exploration you can park down by the riverside, just below Front Street, to see the **Roque House.** Located on the bank of Cane River Lake, the Roque (*rock*) House dates from the 1790s. Originally built as a residence at nearby Isle Brevelle, the French

Roque House

colonial structure of hand-hewn cypress was moved to its present site during the 1960s. The restored wood-shingled cottage is especially noted for its *bousillage (BOO-see-ahj)* construction. *Bousillage,* which was used in a number of the state's French colonial buildings, was made by boiling Spanish moss and combining it with mud and hair scraped from animal hides. When packed between wooden wall posts, the procedure was known as *bousillage entre poteaux.* Covered with plaster (sometimes made with lime and deer hair), this mixture provided good insulation.

Natchitoches offers a number of other attractions such as the **Old Courthouse** and the **Immaculate Conception Catholic Church,** both located on Second and Church Streets, and also the **Trinity Parish Church** at Second and Trudeau Streets.

Don't leave Natchitoches without stopping by **Lasyone's Meat Pie Kitchen and Restaurant** (318–352–3353), located at 622 Second Street. Meat pies, the featured specialty, resemble fried fruit pies except for the filling. To make his famous creations, James Lasyone (*lassie-OWN*) uses a combination of pork and ground beef with onions and spices. The slowly cooked meat is later thickened with a roux (flour sautéed in oil as a thickening agent) and chilled overnight. At serving time a dollop of the mixture is dropped on a circle of dough; after the crust is folded over and crimped on the edges, the pie is ready to fry.

A former grocer, Lasyone has been in the restaurant business more than thirty years and is assisted by his wife, Jo Ann, and other family members. The restaurateur remembers when men pushed charcoal-filled metal carts through the streets of Natchitoches, selling "hotta meat pies."

Los Adaes

Natchitoches was once an outpost on the frontier. **Los Adaes,** *near Robeline and Many on Louisiana Highway 6 at Highway 485, is where a mission was built by the Spanish in 1717 and a fort was established in 1721 to guard this section of the Camino Real (royal road).*

Until 1773 this was the capital of the Spanish Province of Texas. Los Adaes today is a state historic site where visitors will find reconstructions of buildings and evidence of archaeological explorations of the setting. Los Adaes is located at 6354 Highway 485, Robeline 71469; (318) 472–9449 or (888) 677–5378.

Order a meat pie with dirty rice (the name given to the dark-stained version cooked with chicken giblets) and a green salad. For dessert you'll want to try another house specialty, Cane River cream pie. The restaurant offers a complete menu and features daily luncheon specials, such as red beans and rice with sausage, veal cutlets, catfish, or chicken breast. Prices are economical. Hours are Monday through Saturday from 7:00 A.M. to 6:30 P.M.

Allow some time for driving through the fertile plantation country surrounding Natchitoches, where you'll see pecan groves and fields of soybeans and cotton. You'll also want to visit one or more of the many nearby plantation homes for which Cane River Country is famous, but be sure to call before you go because operating hours change. If possible, schedule an afternoon visit to **Beau Fort Plantation** (318–352–5340 or 352–8352), an antebellum home located 10 miles south of town via Routes 494 and 119, about halfway between Natchitoches and Melrose Plantation. An avenue of live oaks leads to the house, which occupies the grounds where historic Fort Charles stood during the 1760s. A wide cottage-style structure of Creole architecture dating from about 1790, the house features an 84-foot front gallery. Constructed of hand-hewn cypress timbers and *bousillage* walls, the home is listed on the National Register of Historic Places.

Over the dining room table, you'll see a punkah (also called a "shoo fly"), which was installed when the house was built. Be sure to notice the plantation scenes depicted on the library's wallpaper. Among the home's many interesting antiques are a rosewood plantation desk dating from 1790 and, in the Stranger's Room, a 1790 bed with hand-carved posts in a pineapple and acanthus leaf pattern. A brick and antique ironwork fence encloses a lovely rear garden.

Except for major holidays, Beau Fort is open from 1:00 to 4:00 P.M. daily for tours. Admission is charged.

Beau Fort also offers bed-and-breakfast accommodations. Moderate to deluxe rates.

Don't miss **Melrose Plantation** (318–379–0055), 2 miles east of Route 1 at the junction of Routes 493 and 119. Your guide will tell you the legend of the remarkable Marie Thérèse Coincoin, a freed slave who obtained a land grant from the Spanish colonial authorities and, with the help of her sons, established and operated what is now Melrose Plantation.

You'll see the Yucca House, Marie Thérèse's original two-room cypress-timbered home built in 1796, and the African House, supposedly the only original Congo-like architecture still standing in the United States. Other plantation buildings include the white clapboard Big House built in 1833 by Marie Thérèse's grandson, the Weaving House, the Bindery, Ghana House, and the Writer's Cabin. Also on the grounds is the cabin home of former Melrose cook Clementine Hunter, whose colorful and charming murals cover the upstairs walls of the African House.

At one time Melrose was one of the country's largest pecan orchards. John Henry and his wife, fondly known as Miss Cammie, restored Melrose and turned it into a renowned retreat for artists and writers. Among the many writers who accepted their hospitality were François Mignon, Erskine Caldwell, Lyle Saxon, and Caroline Dormon.

Melrose, which closes on all major holidays, is open daily from noon to 4:00 P.M. Admission.

Afterward, continue to **Magnolia Plantation Home** (318–379–2221) at 5487 Highway 119 in the town of Natchez near Derry. Surrounded by stately oaks and magnolias (which inspired the home's name), the large manor house replaces one built in the 1830s. During the Civil War, General Nathaniel Banks's Union forces burned the original home. The family restored it in 1896, using the same foundation and floor plan with fourteen fireplaces and twenty-seven rooms, including a Catholic chapel still used for Mass. Throughout the house, you'll see Louisiana-crafted and Southern Empire furnishings such as the parlor's square grand piano made of rosewood.

Scrapbook Heaven

Cammie Henry, longtime owner of Melrose, was renowned for her extensive collection of clippings and scrapbooks on Louisiana history. Everything is now in the Cammie Henry Collection at the Watson Library at Northwestern State University in Natchitoches. To learn more about "Miss Cammie" and her collections, tap into www.nsula.edu.

A working plantation of 2,192 acres, Magnolia has been in the same family since 1753, when Jean Baptiste LeComte II acquired it through an original French land grant. The property also features several dependencies and a massive mule-drawn cotton press. Once known for its racing stables, this

National Bicentennial Farm is open for tours daily except Sunday from 1:00 to 4:00 P.M., or by appointment. Admission is charged.

Approximately 25 miles south of Natchitoches, just off Route 1 on Route 495, you'll find the **Kate Chopin House** (318–379–2233), home of the **Bayou Folk Museum.** This building, which dates from the early 1800s, is located on Main Street in the charming village of Cloutierville (*KLOOCH-er-vil*). The only place to park is on the narrow street in front of the museum; local traffic, however, tends to be light.

Constructed of slave-made brick, cypress mortised with square wooden pegs, and *bousillage,* the raised cottage–style structure contains four fireplaces that share a single chimney. An exterior staircase leads to the second floor, which served as the living area.

Author Kate Chopin lived in this house with her husband and six children from 1879 until 1884. In the downstairs entrance room, you'll see a showcase featuring an original edition of *Bayou Folk,* a collection of Chopin's short stories about Creole life in which she uses Cane River Country as a setting. Portraits of the author and her family, along with a number of their possessions, are also on display at this National Historic Landmark.

Other rooms feature various collections of jewelry, china, glass, sewing machines, school desks, early phonographs, oak iceboxes, Civil War firearms, and antique furniture. On the upstairs rear porch, you'll see an unusual old sharpshooter coffin.

The museum complex also contains a blacksmith shop, a mule-operated sugarcane mill, and a country doctor's office, furnished with medical

Chopin on Screen

*K*ate Chopin, who wrote in the late 1800s, was an author out of favor for years, but she has been rediscovered and championed as an ahead-of-her-time feminist writer. One fan was actress Kelly McGillis, who managed to coproduce and star in a cinema version of Chopin's surprisingly modern novel about adultery, The Awakening, in 1992. The movie version had to be called Grand Isle because the film Awakenings, starring Robin Williams and based on the book by Dr. Oliver Sacks, had come out in 1990.

Grand Isle's costuming and set design are properly accurate, as are the well-photographed locations. As a bonus, lots of Louisiana actors found work in the project. The film, while not otherwise remarkable, is a nice compliment to a Louisiana author and is available on videotape.

equipment and instruments once used by plantation doctors. Except for major holidays, the Kate Chopin House is open from 10:00 A.M. to 5:00 P.M. daily. Admission is charged.

If time permits, drive south along Route 1, where you'll see acres of pecan groves. Several pecan processing plants dot the roadside in this area. In season you can stop and buy whole or shelled pecans, roasted pecans, candies made with pecans, and other nutty delights.

Afterward you can either drive on to Alexandria, the state's cross-roads, or head north of Natchitoches to take in some interesting sites in that direction.

Taking the northern option, you can retrace your route to Natchitoches or get on U.S. Highway 71 north for a visit to **Briarwood** (318–576–3379) in the northwest corner of Natchitoches Parish. This wonderful wooded area, some 19 miles north of Campti, is located just off Route 9, north of Readhimer and 2 miles south of Saline. (Saline is especially noted for its fine watermelons, so you may want to stop and buy one if you pass this way during summer months.) Briarwood, a wild garden definitely off the beaten path, will especially delight botanists and bird-watchers. A rustic sign suspended over a wooden gate marks the entrance to this 125-acre nature preserve, once the home of Caroline Dormon, America's first woman to be employed in forestry.

A pioneer conservationist, Dormon played a major role in establishing Louisiana's Kisatchie National Forest, which extends over seven parishes and covers 600,000 acres. Also known internationally for her work as a naturalist, Dormon described and painted rare native species of plants. Her books *Flowers Native to the Deep South* and *Wild Flowers of Louisiana* are both botany classics.

Briarwood boasts Louisiana's largest collection of plants native to the Southeast, where spring might bring spectacular shows of pink dog-woods, white pompons, crabapples, pale pink native azaleas, and mottled-green trilliums. The nature preserve is also home to a woodland iris garden and six different species of pitcher plants.

Briarwood's curators Jessie and Richard Johnson, who knew "Miss Car-rie" personally, will welcome you to this serene retreat, which can be explored on foot or aboard the "stealth cart." Richard, who calls Briar-wood a "place of renewal, a balm for the soul," will show you Miss Carrie's former log cabin home, deep in the woods. Now a museum, the house contains furniture, household items, and original illustrations from one of the naturalist's books. Be sure to spend a few minutes looking through

Corduroy Roads

At Briarwood the vegetation is not the only authentic Louisiana object underfoot. On the grounds is a segment of what was a "corduroy road." These old carriage roads were made of logs laid sideways along the roadbed, providing nineteenth-century riders with a jolting journey.

the scrapbooks, where you'll see some of Miss Carrie's correspondence. One note to a friend reads: "That everlastin' bird book is out at last! I'm bound to say I think it's a darlin'—even if I am its mama!"

Surrounding the cabin you'll see many giant trees, including a longleaf pine possibly three centuries old, known as Grandpappy. Nearby are tulip and sourwood trees, big-leafed magnolias, and native sasanquas—fall-blooming camellias with delicate blossoms and handsome dark foliage.

A trail winds past a pond and through tall pines, mountain laurel, and wild ginger to a one-room cabin on a gentle knoll even farther back in the forest. The simply furnished log house, called Three Pines Cabin, served as Miss Carrie's retreat for writing and painting when too many visitors found their way to Briarwood. "This was her hideaway," Jessie says, "when the world beat a path to her door."

Even though Briarwood does not advertise, some 2,000 visitors discover it each year. The nature preserve is open to the public every weekend in March, April, May, August, and November. Hours are from 9:00 A.M. to 5:00 P.M. on Saturday and from noon to 5:00 P.M. on Sunday. Tours at other times may be arranged by appointment. Admission is charged.

Scenic River Region

After exploring and savoring Briarwood, head for neighboring Winn Parish, the home of Winnfield and the birthplace of Huey P. Long, O. K. Allen, and Earl K. Long—all former governors of Louisiana. Both Routes 126 and 156 east will take you to Highway 167, where you'll turn south to reach Winnfield (less than an hour's drive from Briarwood).

Downtown, you'll see a statue of Huey Long on the courthouse lawn. Nearby, the *Louisiana Political Museum and Hall of Fame* (318–628–5928), housed in a circa 1908 train depot at 499 East Main Street, offers a look at the lives and times of Louisiana's prominent politicians. You'll see life-size wax figures of brothers Huey P. and Earl K. Long. Other exhibits include photos, campaign memorabilia, and audio and video excerpts from political speeches and public appearances. The museum is usually open Tuesday through Friday from 10:00 A.M. to 5:00 P.M., Saturday from 10:00 A.M. to 2:00 P.M. and other times by appointment. Free admission.

A pleasant place to stay overnight is **Southern Colonial Bed and Breakfast** (318–628–6087), located at 801 East Main Street, Winnfield 71483. The towering two-story house dates from about 1908, and owners Judy and John Posey will welcome you to their home, which features an inviting front porch and seven fireplaces. The Poseys occupy the downstairs portion. The second floor, reserved for overnight visitors, features a common parlor and large guest rooms with some interesting antiques. Amenities include cable television, phones, coffee, and wake-up alarms. Guests can enjoy refreshments on the balcony or on the large porch, shaded by an ancient oak tree. Mornings start with a traditional Southern breakfast. Standard rates.

A short stroll from the Poseys' home, you'll find the **Earl K. Long State Commemorative Area.** Established in honor of Louisiana's first three-term governor, the one-acre park features a symmetrical design and lovely landscaping. An 8-foot bronze statue, dedicated on July 4, 1963, stands as a memorial to Earl Kemp Long, younger brother of Huey Long. A hedged circular sidewalk leads to a pavilion, a pleasant spot for a picnic.

From Winnfield, take U.S. Highway 167 south via Pineville to Alexandria.

Crossroads

Arriving in Pineville, you'll cross the Red River via the O. K. Allen Bridge to reach Alexandria. Known as a crossroads city, Alexandria marks the state's geographic center. The parish seat of Rapides (*ra-PEEDS*), Alexandria lost most of its buildings and records in 1864 when the Yankees set fire to the city during the Civil War. Another disaster occurred with the flood of 1866. The Red River separates Alexandria from its sister city, Pineville.

Soon after your arrival, stop by **Kent House** (318–487–5998) at 3601 Bayou Rapides Road, Alexandria 71303. Believed to be Central Louisiana's oldest existing building (one of a few area structures to survive the Civil War), the home was completed in 1880. Kent House, which stands on brick pillars, exemplifies the classic Louisiana style of French and Spanish colonial architecture. An elevated construction protected buildings from floods and dampness.

Now restored, the house was moved to its present location from the original site, 2 blocks away. Kent House serves as a museum where visitors may see seven period rooms filled with Empire, Sheraton, and Federal furniture, authentic documents dealing with land transfers, and many interesting decorative items.

The four-acre complex also contains slave quarters, a notched-log carriage house, a barn, a blacksmith shop, a sugar mill, and gardens. You'll see a detached kitchen and milk house along with a collection of early nineteenth-century cooking utensils. From October through April open-hearth cooking demonstrations are given each Wednesday between 9:00 A.M. and noon. Prepared foods might include corn bread, chicken, corn soup, lima beans, and pie. Admission is modest. Kent House is open from 9:00 A.M. to 5:00 P.M. every day except Sunday, when the house is open by appointment only. Admission is charged. Check out the property at www.kenthouse.org.

Don't miss **Radisson Hotel Bentley** (318–448–9600), one of America's grand hotels, rich in history. Located at 200 DeSoto Street by the Red River, the hotel dates to 1908 and stands as a fine example of early-twentieth-century Renaissance Revival architecture.

It is said that some strategies for World War II battles were mapped out at Hotel Bentley, sometimes on napkins in the Mirror Room. Many troop commanders and other eminent military figures either lived at Hotel Bentley or visited during this period. The hotel's guest register records such names as Major General George Patton, General George C. Marshall, General Matthew B. Ridgway, Lieutenant Colonel Omar Bradley, Colonel Dwight Eisenhower, and Lieutenant Henry Kissinger. In the hotel's Venetian Room, couples danced to the music of Tommy Dorsey and many of the era's big bands.

Jerry Lee Has Left the Building . . .

In rock and roll's earliest days, Elvis's biggest rival for the top performer crown was Jerry Lee Lewis, the rambunctious piano player who composed "Great Balls of Fire" and shocked his fans when he married his thirteen-year-old second cousin.

Jerry Lee grew up in Ferriday, Louisiana (northeast of Alexandria via Louisiana Highway 28 and U.S. Highway 84). He came from an interesting family. Two other cousins were Mickey Gilley (no Texas music

fan can ignore him) and that tearful evangelist, Jimmy Swaggart.

Ferriday's musical legacy of black delta blues and juke joints coupled with white fundamentalist hymns is responsible for Jerry Lee's sound. If you want to hear more, Ferriday hosts the **Delta Music Festival** *each spring.*

For more information contact the Ferriday Chamber of Commerce, 1001 East Wallace Boulevard, Ferriday 71334; (318) 757–4297.

CENTRAL LOUISIANA

Along with its nostalgic past, the hotel promises charm and modern amenities for today's traveler.

From the Bentley it's a short walk to the ***Alexandria Museum of Art*** (318–443–3458) at 933 Main Street, Alexandria 71301. The museum occupies the original Rapides Bank building, which dates from 1898, the first major building to appear after twin disasters of fire and flood in the 1860s. The facility features a fine collection of modern and contemporary works as well as Louisiana folk arts, traveling exhibits, and a gift shop. The museum, which also sponsors educational and interpretive programs, is open Tuesday through Friday from 10:00 A.M. to 5:00 P.M. Saturday hours are from 1:00 to 4:00 P.M. Admission fee is nominal.

Continue to nearby ***River Oaks Square Arts Center*** (318–473–2670) at 1330 Main Street, Alexandria 71301. This lovely Queen Anne–style house, the original residence of the Bolton family, was given to the city by Peggy Bolton to be used for the arts. Adjacent to the home stands a new structure housing studios and galleries. About thirty local artists now work at the center, and you can watch creativity in action as painters, weavers, and sculptors practice their callings. In addition to showcasing artists at work, the center sometimes offers classes and workshops in drawing, watercolor, printmaking, sculpture, and collage for both children and adults. River Oaks Square is open from 10:00 A.M. to 4:00 P.M. Tuesday through Friday and 10:00 A.M. to 2:00 P.M. on Saturday. Besides browsing, you can also buy unique works of art.

A few steps behind River Oaks Square, you'll find the ***Arna Bontemps African-American Museum and Cultural Arts Center*** (318–473–4692) at 1327 Third Street, Alexandria 71301. Bontemps, a member of the Harlem Renaissance, wrote novels, poetry, plays, histories, folklore collections, biographies, and children's literature. Housed in the circa 1890 home where Bontemps was born in 1902, the museum contains the author's typewriter, books, letters, and memorabilia such as photographs of Louis Armstrong, Sidney Poitier, and other entertainers and arts figures. In addition to preserving a literary legacy, Bontemps's childhood home serves as a setting for traveling exhibits, area art displays, and writing classes for local youngsters. The center also

OTHER ATTRACTIONS WORTH SEEING

Alexandria Zoological Park, 3016 Masonic Drive, Alexandria; (318) 473–1143. This pleasant zoo has a miniature train to ride and more than 500 animals. Open daily, closed Thanksgiving, Christmas, and New Year's. Small admission fee.

Dewey Hills Wildlife Management Area, 20 miles east of Pineville, at 1995 Shreveport Highway; (318) 339–8751. More than 60,000 acres of preserve with bottomland forests, hiking trails, campsites, and boat launches.

Old LSU Interpretive Site, 2500 Shreveport Highway, Pineville; (318) 473–7160. All that remains of the first location of Louisiana State University are brick foundations in this site surrounded by the Kisatchie National Forest. On the National Register of Historic Places.

showcases the Hall of Fame collection originally kept at LSU's Alexandria branch. Except for major holidays, hours are Tuesday through Friday from 10:00 A.M. to 5:00 P.M. and Saturday from 10:00 A.M. to 2:00 P.M. A nominal donation is requested.

Afterward, head back toward the Hotel Bentley and cross the Jackson Street Bridge to Pineville's Main Street. You'll soon see a cemetery on the left and then *Mount Olivet Chapel.* Built in 1854, the church was dedicated by Bishop Leonidas Polk, who later "buckled sword over gown" to become a Confederate general. The picturesque chapel survived the Civil War, probably because it served as a headquarters for the Union Army.

The Gothic Revival structure, which features some Tiffany windows, was designed by Richard Upjohn, the architect of New York's Trinity Church. Except for its oak floor, the chapel is constructed entirely of native pinewood. Although the building is kept locked, the instructions for getting a key are posted on the side door. Take some time to explore the surrounding cemetery with tombstone dates as early as 1824 still discernible.

Military buffs may want to visit the *Alexandria National Cemetery* at 209 Shamrock Avenue, also in Pineville. This cemetery, an art gallery in stone, contains graves from the Civil War, Spanish-American War, and both World Wars.

After visiting Pineville take U.S. Highway 71 south to Lecompte, about 12 miles south of Alexandria. Here you'll find *Lea's Lunchroom* (318–776–5178), a country-style cafe that dishes up hearty Southern cooking. Lea Johnson established this popular eatery in 1928.

Cotton: Then and Now

*W*hile in this area, consider an eastward excursion to **Frogmore Plantation and Gins** *(318–757–2453), where owners Lynette and George Tanner offer a contrast between the old and the new. Located at 11054 Highway 84 in Frogmore near the Mississippi border, this 1,800-acre working cotton plantation features eighteen antebellum structures, including authentically furnished slave row cabins dating from 1810. Besides touring the buildings, you'll see a film on cotton's role in history, an 1884 antique steam gin, and today's computerized version. You may also get a chance to pick cotton here. Call ahead for hours, which vary by season. Admission.*

The staff believes in fast service and objects to written menus because "they take too much time." At Lea's the server recites the menu, which might feature red beans and sausage with rice and crackling corn bread or a choice of fried fish, beef tips, or ham along with turnip greens and sweet potatoes. Rates are economical. Milk is served in chilled glasses, and you can have a demitasse of coffee after your meal. The restaurant is famous

Grant Parish, north of Alexandria, comprises such a rural area that there are no traffic signals within its boundaries. Well, maybe a few blinking lights . . . but none of those red-yellow-green ones.

for its hams baked in dough and homemade pies made from secret family recipes. The staff makes about 71,000 pies a year, including apple, pecan, banana cream, cherry, blueberry, blackberry, lemon, chocolate, and coconut. In fact, the Louisiana Senate named LeCompte the Pie Capital of the state as a tribute to Lea's seven-plus decades of service.

The restaurant also offers a large selection of regional cookbooks and purchases much of its produce from local growers. Lea's is closed on Monday and opens at 7:00 A.M. on other days. Closing time is 6:00 P.M.

Lecompte (*le-COUNT*) was named after an 1850s record-breaking racehorse from a local plantation. Before a sign painter inadvertently inserted a *P*, the place was Lecomte. While in town stop by the **Old Lecompte School** (318–776–9520), which dates from 1924. Local citizens recently waged a campaign to resurrect their old school—where shouts of students and chiming class bells had not been heard for more than two decades—and won an award from the state for their success story. Now a community center, the large building houses a museum, dining room, public library, meeting rooms, gymnasium, and auditorium.

The remarkable thing about this project is that it was entirely a community effort. All money came from private donations, and local people volunteered their talents to renovate the structure. The building's distinctive historical features, including the auditorium's ornate plasterwork and balcony railing, have been preserved. The end result is a fine multipurpose facility that holds a treasury of memories for generations of former students. The most recent addition, a three-room museum, focuses on two centuries of Louisiana history. Visiting hours are Tuesday from 9:00 A.M. to 5:00 P.M., Wednesday through Friday from 1:00 to 5:00 P.M., and Saturday from 9:00 A.M. to 1:00 P.M.

Before leaving this area you may want to drive through the surrounding countryside. Some 300 nurseries are located in the nearby Lecompte– Forest Hill area. Along **Nursery Row** you'll find landscaping bargains in a variety of shrubs, trees, and plants, including ornamental and exotic plants. Although the nurseries supply commercial markets, most will accommodate drop-in retail customers.

Don't miss **Loyd Hall Plantation** (318–776–5641 or 800–240–8135) at 292 Loyd Bridge Road near Cheneyville. The plantation can be reached easily by taking exit 61 off Interstate 49, then traveling east on U.S. Highway 167 and following signs. Anne and Frank Fitzgerald and daughter Melinda will welcome you to their lovely three-story antebellum home, which dates from 1810. This classic white-columned plantation house features original pine-heart flooring, cypress woodwork, and medallioned ceilings.

You'll enjoy seeing the elegant furnishings and learning about the house's history. According to a New Orleans psychic, three resident ghosts prowl the huge rooms at Loyd Hall, and you'll hear some interesting stories about them. Supposedly a violinist appears at midnight on the second-floor gallery and plays sad songs. When visitors ask Anne if she's heard the ghostly tunes, she usually answers that after her exhausting day, she's sound asleep by midnight. (When I visited, I was asleep by that time too. I did go outside earlier, however, to snap a few night photos of the mansion. The resulting pictures contained some eerie white streaks, which I attributed to my photography—but who knows?) If you visit Loyd Hall, you won't have to worry about the ghosts

Loyd Hall Plantation

because they live in the big house, and overnight guests sleep in the plantation suites and cottages on the grounds. Moderate to deluxe rates.

Visitors to the plantation can see various agricultural operations in action. Cotton, corn, sugarcane, and soybeans are raised here. "We let our guests gather pecans and pick cotton," Anne notes. "People are intrigued with cotton." One visitor took a cottonseed back to her home in Paris, planted it in a pot on her balcony, and nourishes it like a houseplant.

The mansion is open for tours daily from 10:00 A.M. to 4:00 P.M. Admission.

At *Griffin's Antiques* (318–346–2806 or 318–346–9135), on the corner of Church and Main Streets in Bunkie, you'll see a large selection of stained-glass windows. Owner Toni Griffin, assisted by her daughter, Doris Maillet, will show you a selection of outstanding antiques, including many signed Louisiana pieces. The shop, which specializes in full- and half-tester four-poster beds and banquet tables, also carries mahogany marble-topped dressers and washstands, rosewood parlor tables, beds, consoles, cupboards, Meissen candelabra, fine china, silver, and cut crystal. Hours are Tuesday through Saturday from 10:00 A.M. to 5:00 P.M., or by appointment.

Before leaving Bunkie, be sure to stop by the *Courtney Gallery of Art* (318–346–9966) on Walnut Street near the Pershing Highway intersection, 1 block off Main Street. After a sojourn in Georgia, Juanita Courtney returned to her hometown and opened an art gallery. A professional painter for some thirty years, Juanita's subject matter ranges from landscapes, house portraits, zydeco musicians, and still lifes to barnyard animals, wild animals, and pet portraits. Her original oils and watercolors, along with a large selection of prints, wooden door-panel hangings of scenes from yesteryear, and antique wood engravings from vintage newspapers and magazines may be purchased here.

The gallery also carries Clementine Hunter paintings as well as an assortment of gifts such as pottery, sculpture, and decorative decoys. Unless Juanita is away exhibiting her work at an art show, you can visit during business hours of 9:00 A.M. to 5:00 P.M. Monday through Friday and 9:00 A.M. to 3:00 P.M. Saturday.

After exploring Bunkie, head northeast about 11 miles to Hessmer, where you'll be greeted by a host of barnyard sounds when you visit Howard Ducote's *Old Corner Antique Shop* (318–563–8247). Here in a former dairy barn, Howard houses an enormous collection of armoires, marble-topped tables, slipper chairs, cupboards, beds, mantels, mirrors, and china. Chickens, guinea fowl, ducks, geese, and turkeys strut about in a large pen behind the barn. You'll probably find Howard wearing a leather apron, busy at work refinishing an antique piece. Business hours are 7:00 A.M. to 5:00 P.M. daily.

While in the area, you may want to swing about 5 miles east to Mansura, where Howard's mother, Lena Ducote, lives at 440 Leglise Street. In her shop, housed in an old bank building adjacent to her home, Mrs. Ducote carries a selection of dolls and dishes along with some antique furnishings. She also offers caning and furniture refinishing services. Although Mrs. Ducote does not keep regular business hours, she often opens her shop by request.

Head northeast to Marksville. Located a half mile south of town, just off Route 1 south, you'll find the *Tunica-Biloxi Museum* (318–253–8174). On this 1,000-acre Indian reservation, a replica of a Tunica temple mound contains a collection of artifacts valued at $5 million—the famed Tunica Treasure. Tour guides will fill you in on the history of this extraordinary collection of Native American and European artifacts.

Taken from Tunica burial sites by pot hunters, these fruits of colonial entrepreneurship have finally been returned to the Tunica tribe (after a long legal battle). You'll see Native American and European artifacts dating from 1698 to 1800, which the Tunicas amassed in transactions with the French, Spanish, English, and other Native Americans during the state's colonial period. Among the many colorful exhibits are displays of Native American pottery, shell beads, basketry, almost 400 brass and copper kettles, 166 flintlock muskets, several hundred pieces of European ceramics, and 200,000 beads of European manufacture. There is also a display of paintings on Native American themes and a 40-foot-long diorama.

Pottery, baskets, beadwork, and other Native American crafts are sold here. The Tunica-Biloxi Museum is open Monday through Saturday from 8:00 A.M. to 4:30 P.M. Admission is modest.

Adjacent to the town of Marksville and about a mile or so from the reservation, you'll find the *Marksville State Historic Site* (318–253–8954 or 888–253–8954) at 837 Martin Luther King Drive, Marksville 71351. Marksville's Indian civilization flourished here some 2,000 years ago, and museum exhibits interpret that culture. Situated on a bluff overlooking Old River, the Marksville site encompasses six prehistoric Indian mounds as well as encircling earthworks ranging from 4 to 6 feet tall. Except for Thanksgiving, Christmas, and New Year's Day, the site is open daily from 9:00 A.M. to 5:00 P.M.

PLACES TO STAY IN
CENTRAL LOUISIANA

WOODLAND AND WATER
Landmark Hotel of
Leesville,
Highway 171 South,
Leesville,
(337) 239–7571 or
(800) 246–6926.

CANE RIVER COUNTRY
Beau Fort Plantation,
10 miles south of
Natchitoches,
(318) 352–5340 or
(318) 352–9580.

Best Western of
Natchitoches,
I–49 and Highway 6,
Natchitoches,
(318) 352–6655 or
(800) 528–1234.

Fleur de Lis Bed &
Breakfast Inn,
336 Second Street,
Natchitoches,
(318) 352–6621 or
(800) 489–6621.

Hampton Inn,
5300 Highway 6 West,
Natchitoches,
(318) 354–0010 or
(800) HAMPTON.

Holiday Inn Express,
5131 Highway 6 West,
Natchitoches,
(318) 354–9911 or
(800) HOLIDAY.

Judge Porter House,
321 Second Street,
Natchitoches,
(318) 352–9206 or
(800) 441–8343.

Ramada Inn,
7624 Highway 1 Bypass,
Natchitoches,
(318) 357–8281 or
(888) 252–8281.

Tante Huppé Historic Inn,
424 Jefferson Street,
Natchitoches,
(318) 352–5342 or
(800) 482–4276.

SCENIC RIVER REGION
Southern Colonial Bed
and Breakfast,
801 East Main Street,
Winnfield,
(318) 628–6087.

CROSSROADS
Best Western of Alexandria
Inn and Suites,
2720 West
MacArthur Drive,
Alexandria,
(318) 445–5530 or
(800) 528–1234.

Hampton Inn,
2301 North
MacArthur Drive,
Alexandria,
(318) 487–8500 or
(800) 426–7866.

Holiday Inn
Convention Center,
701 Fourth Street,
Alexandria,
(318) 442–9000.

Holiday Inn
MacArthur Drive,
2716 North
MacArthur Drive,
Alexandria,
(318) 487–4261 or
(800) 465–4329.

Loyd Hall Plantation,
292 Loyd Bridge Road,
Cheneyville,
(318) 776–5641 or
(800) 240–8135.

Paragon Casino Resort,
711 Grand Boulevard,
Marksville,
(318) 253–0777 or
(800) 642–7777. Next to
the casino venture of the
Tunica–Biloxi tribal
council.

Radisson Hotel Bentley,
200 DeSoto Street,
Alexandria,
(318) 448–9600 or
(800) 333–3333.

Ramada Limited
of Alexandria,
742 MacArthur Drive,
Alexandria,
(318) 448–1611 or
(800) 272–6232.

PLACES TO EAT IN
CENTRAL LOUISIANA

WOODLAND AND WATER
Country Boy Restaurant,
105 Highland Street,
Many,
(318) 256–3953.

For More Information

Alexandria/Pineville Area Convention and Visitors Bureau
*locations at 707 Main Street, Alexandria 71301 and
Alexandria Mall, 3437 Masonic Drive, Alexandria 71301*
(800) 742–7049
www.apacvb.org

Avoyelles Commission of Tourism
208 South Main Street, Marksville 71351
(318) 253–0585 or (800) 833–4195

Natchitoches Parish Tourist Commission
781 Front Street, Natchitoches 71457
(800) 259–1714

Sabine Parish Tourist and Recreation Commission
920 Fisher Road, Many 71449
(800) 358–7802

Vernon Parish Tourism and Recreation Commission
P.O. Box 349, Leesville 71496
(318) 238–0783 or (800) 349–6287

Winn Parish Tourist Commission
P.O. Box 565, Winfield 71483
(318) 628–4461

Area newspapers include *Alexandria Daily Town Talk* in Alexandria (largest paper in the area, should have weekly entertainment listings), the *Sabine Index* in Many, the *Natchitoches Times* in Natchitoches, the *Winn Parish Enterprise* in Winnfield, the *Record* in Bunkie, and the *Weekly News* in Marksville.

CANE RIVER COUNTRY
Just Friends,
750 Front Street,
Natchitoches,
(318) 352–3836.

Lasyone's Meat Pie Kitchen
and Restaurant,
622 Second Street,
Natchitoches,
(318) 352–3353.

Mariner's,
off Louisiana Highway 1
South Bypass at Sibley Lake,
Natchitoches,
(318) 357–1220.

Papa's Bar and Grill,
604 Front Street,
Natchitoches,
(318) 356–5850.

CROSSROADS
The Bentley Room
Restaurant
at the Radisson Hotel
Bentley,
200 DeSoto Street,
Alexandria,
(318) 448–9600.

Critic's Choice,
5208 Rue Verdon,
Alexandria,
(318) 445–1680.

El Reparo Mexican
Restaurant & Grill,
550 McArthur Drive,
Alexandria,
(318) 487–0207.

Julia's Place,
2204 Worley Drive,
Alexandria,
(318) 445–2405.

Lea's Lunchroom,
1810 Highway 71 South,
Lecompte,
(318) 776–5178.

Lee J's on the Levee,
208 Main Street,
Pineville,
(318) 487–4628.

Paradise Catfish Kitchen,
4820 Monroe Highway,
Pineville,
(318) 640–5032.

Stalnaker's Restaurant,
4230 Stalnaker Road,
Pineville,
(318) 640–1361.

Tunk's Cypress Inn,
9507 Highway 28 West,
Boyce,
(318) 487–4014.

Southwest Louisiana

The southwest portion of Louisiana includes coastal marshes with oak ridges along their edges. Inland are found prairie lands. The prairies are cut by several watercourses, including the Calcasieu and the Vermilion Rivers. The low meandering ridges of the prairies are also marked by intermittent, slow moving streams called coulees. Rice cultivation (which necessitates seasonal irrigation and is often rotated with crawfish farming) along with petroleum, cattle, and seafood industries make up a large portion of the regional economy.

Imperial Calcasieu

Forming the heel of the Louisiana boot, the parishes of Cameron, Calcasieu *(KAL-ka-shoe)*, Beauregard, Allen, and Jefferson Davis compose what was once called Imperial Calcasieu.

Made up mostly of marshlands and bayous, Cameron is Louisiana's largest parish. If you enter the state's southwestern corner via Interstate 10, consider making a side trip to the *Sabine National Wildlife Refuge* or the newer *Cameron Prairie National Wildlife Refuge,* both major stops on the 105-mile *Creole Nature Trail.*

Take the Sulphur exit off Interstate 10 and turn south on State Route 27 (which is also the Creole Nature Trail). To reach the Sabine Refuge headquarters, proceed about 25 miles.

At the visitor center you'll find an interpretive area, media room, wildlife exhibits, and information on the area's ecology. Displays demonstrate the importance of marshlands and the role the refuge plays in waterfowl and wildlife management.

An animated exhibit features the realistic figure of a Cajun fisherman sitting on a wharf, surrounded by marsh birds with attendant alligator. A close look reveals a snake under the wharf and a flounder in the water. At the press of a button, the fisherman launches into a tale, in Cajun dialect, about the area's history. He stands up, speaks of the value of the marshlands, and then reseats himself.

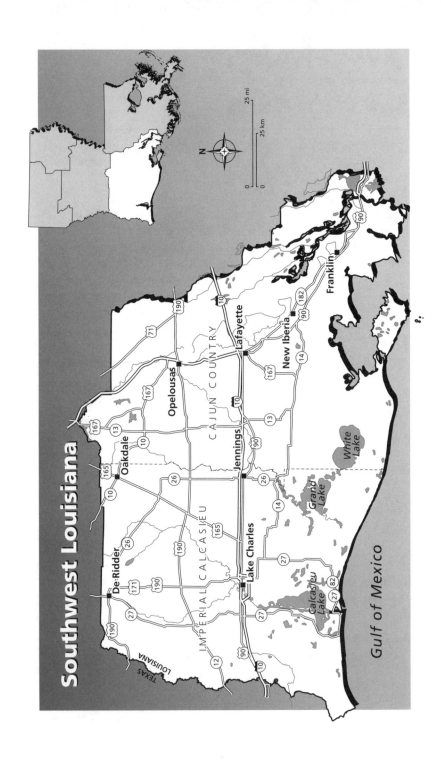

Southwest Louisiana

TEXAS
LOUISIANA

De-Ridder

Oakdale

Opelousas

CAJUN COUNTRY

Lafayette

New Iberia

Franklin

Jennings

IMPERIAL CALCASIEU

Lake Charles

Calcasieu Lake

Grand Lake

White Lake

Gulf of Mexico

N

25 mi
25 km
0
0

82

SOUTHWEST LOUISIANA

GAY'S FAVORITES IN SOUTHWEST LOUISIANA

Acadian Village,
Lafayette

Atchafalaya Basin,
near Henderson

Avery Island

Longfellow-Evangeline State Historic Site,
St. Martinville

Shadows-on-the-Teche,
New Iberia

Town of Abbeville

Town of Washington

Vermilionville, Lafayette

For a close-up view of the marshlands, you can take a self-guided tour along a nature trail, 4 miles south of the headquarters building. The 1.5-mile footpath changes from concrete to wooden walkway when it crosses the trail's water portions. For this hike bring along your binoculars and insect repellent. As you follow the footpath, you're likely to see alligators, especially on warm days when they surface to sun themselves. While these creatures may look lazy and sluggish, they can hurtle into fast-forward in a heartbeat, so maintain a respectful distance at all times. In cooler weather you'll spot small furry animals such as nutrias, rabbits, and raccoons. Red wolves, foxes, and deer live here, too.

Bird-watchers will be beside themselves with glee. This refuge has a national reputation as one of the country's best birding areas. Some 300 species of fowl consider the refuge either home or a nice place for a holiday. Established in 1937 mainly as a wintering area for migratory geese and ducks, the refuge also serves as home to the peregrine falcon.

About midway along the trail, you can climb a flight of wooden steps to an observation tower for a better view of this area of wetlands just above the Gulf of Mexico.

Popular times to visit are from mid-April to mid-May, when spring birds migrate, and September, when fall migration starts. The prime time for observing the refuge's waterfowl is from mid-November through January. Bird-watching, hiking, fishing, crabbing, and nature study are year-round activities. However, access to the refuge's interior is closed from October 15 to March 15. (Use along Route 27 is permitted year-round.)

You may use the marshlands trail from sunrise until sunset. The visitor center (337–762–3816) is open from 7:00 A.M. to 4:00 P.M. Monday through Friday and from noon until 4:00 P.M. on Saturday and Sunday. There's no admission charge.

Railroad buffs might like to start exploring the state's southwestern portion at DeQuincy, reached by taking Route 27 north. Once a rowdy frontier town with eight saloons to serve a transient population of some 200 persons, DeQuincy managed to live down its early reputation after the railroad's arrival, when it began attracting more serious settlers.

Both the **DeQuincy Railroad Museum** (337–786–2823) and the DeQuincy Chamber of Commerce occupy the Kansas City Southern Railroad's original depot on Lake Charles Avenue. Museum exhibits include a 1913 steam locomotive, a coal car, a vintage caboose, and several restored railcars. You'll also see telegraph and railroad equipment, local historical memorabilia such as tickets and timetables dating from the early 1900s, uniforms, and an old mail pouch. You may admire the ticket agent's ability to concentrate as he sits before an antique typewriter absorbed by his work and apparently oblivious to all activity around him . . . until you realize that he's a mannequin. Museum hours Monday through Friday are 9:00 A.M. to 4:00 P.M. Saturday and Sunday hours run from noon to 4:00 P.M. Admission is free, but donations are appreciated.

After leaving DeQuincy take Route 27 south to Sulphur and turn right on U.S. Highway 90 to reach Picard Road. The **Brimstone Historical Society Museum** (337–527–7142), located at 800 Picard Road, Sulphur 70663, is housed in the Southern Pacific Railway Depot at Frasch Park, and a one-ton block of sulfur marks the spot. You'll see a wildlife diorama, an antique medical instrument collection, photos of the town during its sulfur-mining heyday, and other exhibits related to the southwestern region.

The museum's focus concerns the history of the American sulfur industry, which started here, thanks to the ingenuity of Herman Frasch. Although it was no secret that sulfur deposits existed in the area, nobody knew how to tap this wealth. Extracting the yellow mineral from its underground home remained in the realm of the impossible until scientist-inventor Frasch solved the problem. He came up with a superheating water process that led to the commercial production of sulfur in the United States. (Prior to 1900 almost all sulfur came from Sicily.) The Brimstone Museum, established in 1976, commemorates Frasch's contribution. A display and short movie describe both the Frasch process and sulfur's importance to modern society. Among other things, sulfur is used in making medicines, rayon, fertilizers, insecticides, paper pulp, matches, and gunpowder.

The museum is open Monday through Thursday from 9:30 A.M. to 5:00 P.M., 9:30 A.M. to 2:00 P.M. on Friday, and Saturday from noon to 3:00 P.M. Admission is free.

From Sulphur you can either drive directly into the city of Lake Charles or take the long way around via the **Creole Nature Trail.** If you opt for the trail, be sure to pick up a self-guided tour brochure before leaving the Brimstone Museum. The Creole Nature Trail, which winds through the

---

TOP ANNUAL EVENTS IN SOUTHWEST LOUISIANA

Louisiana Railroad Days Festival,
300 Holly Street, DeQuincy, second
weekend in April. (337) 786–8241.

Festival International de Louisiane,
735 Jefferson Street, Lafayette, last
weekend in April. (337) 232–8086.

Breaux Bridge Crawfish Festival,
Breaux Bridge, first full weekend in May.
(888) 565–5939.

Contraband Days,
900 Lakeshore Drive, Lake Charles, first
two weeks in May. (337) 436–5508.

Shrimp Festival,
Main Street, Delcambre, mid-August.
(888) 9–IBERIA.

**The Original Southwest Louisiana
Zydeco Music Festival,**
off Highway 167,
Plaisance, last Saturday before Labor Day.
(337) 942–2392.

**Louisiana Shrimp and
Petroleum Festival,**
710 Third Street, Morgan City,
Labor Day weekend.
(800) 256–2931.

Frog Festival,
Rayne, Labor Day weekend.
(337) 334–2332.

Festivals Acadiens,
Lafayette, third weekend in September.
(800) 346–1958.

**Louisiana Sugar Cane Festival
and Fair,**
City Park, Parkview Drive,
New Iberia,
late September.
(888) 9–IBERIA.

International Rice Festival,
Crowley, third weekend in October.
(337) 783–3067.

Prairie Cajun Folklife Festival,
P.O. Box 1106, Eunice,
third weekend in October.
(337) 457–2565.

---

southern part of Calcasieu Parish and most of Cameron Parish, provides a good introduction to the area, but you need to allow at least half a day to complete the circuit—longer if you're prone to dally. The visitor center of the Cameron Prairie National Wildlife Refuge, accessible from Route 27, features robotics, dioramas, and a boardwalk overlooking the marsh.

Few parts of the country look the same as they did when early settlers arrived. This trail is one of the few. At places along the way, one must mentally subtract contemporary human clutter, but even so, the land looks much as it did in earlier days. To some people this area might appear desolate, but the more discerning will recognize a singular environment teeming with life.

Starting in Sulphur, the Creole Nature Trail follows Route 27 down to the Gulf of Mexico, heads east along the coast, and backtracks before going north to Lake Charles. Marked by signs with an alligator logo, the trail follows state highways, which change during the route.

Hurricane Audrey Memorial

On June 27, 1957, Hurricane Audrey hit Cameron Parish, leaving 525 dead. There is a monument in front of Our Lady Star of the Sea Church, 4 miles east of Cameron on Highway 82.

Along the way you'll pass through Hackberry, the crab capital of the world. Because hard-shell blue crabs are so plentiful here, you might be inclined to try your luck at **crabbing**. The basic equipment boils down to two pieces: a net to scoop up the crabs and a bucket to hold them. You can buy crabbing supplies at one of the area bait shops. With net in hand you can walk along a pier and capture any crabs you see on pilings, or you can wade in shallow water and scoop them up before they scurry away. Then there's the string-and-bait method. It entails attaching a one-ounce fishing weight plus a chunk of meat or fish to a string about 20 feet long. Toss the loaded line into the water, preferably near rocks or a dock. When you feel a slight tug, slowly pull the string toward you, keeping the net submerged and as still as possible so that it will look like part of the underwater scenery. As long as it's in the water, the crab will cling to the line. When it gets close enough, sweep it into your net. You have to be swift and synchronized, or the crab will win. After you collect enough crabs to constitute a meal, you can trade your bucket for a cookbook.

Just past Hackberry the driving tour intersects the Sabine Wildlife Refuge (described earlier in this chapter). Continue south on Route 27 toward Holly Beach (also called the Cajun Riviera) on the Gulf of Mexico. If you're a birder, you might want to get off the trail here and travel west on Route 82. This takes you to Johnson's Bayou and the Holleyman Bird Sanctuary, a popular bed-and-breakfast stop for many migrating songbirds crossing the Gulf each spring and fall.

From Holly Beach, the Creole Nature Trail stretches eastward along State Routes 27 and 82. Just before reaching Cameron, you'll drive aboard a fifty-car ferry that transports you across the Calcasieu Ship Channel. For eastward-bound travelers the trip is free, but those heading west pay a toll of $1.00 per car. If you step to the rail, you might catch a special performance by porpoises, who frequently put on a free show for ferry passengers. Back on the road in Cameron, you'll pass shrimp boats moored only a few yards from the highway. After Cameron your coastal trek takes you to Creole, Oak Grove, and Grand Chenier (*shuh-NEAR*). Along the way you'll see stranded sand and shell ridges, called cheniers, from which groves of live oaks grow despite constant contact with salt water.

To shorten the drive you can skip Grand Chenier and take Route 27 north at Oak Grove. You'll pass by rice fields and pastures of cows—some nonchalantly grazing as cattle egrets perch on their backs.

Continue east on Route 82 if you want to visit the **Rockefeller Wildlife Refuge** (337–538–2165 or 538–2276). Although a portion of the refuge is closed from December till March to provide sanctuary for wintering waterfowl, Rockefeller is open for sight-seeing and fishing year-round. At the visitor center, you'll see a display of artifacts from *El Nuevo Constant,* an eighteenth-century Spanish merchant vessel that sank off the Cameron coast. You may spot some alligators if you go exploring, especially during summer months. The refuge has an international reputation as a major alligator research center and is open daily from official sunrise to sunset.

After you leave the refuge, you'll have to do some backtracking. You can follow your trail map or choose another option. Routes 384, 385, and 14 (or variations thereof) all lead to Lake Charles. In any case, you'll be approaching the area's largest city from its southern side.

Head northwest to Lake Charles. When you arrive, you may think that the sandy beach studded with palm trees on the shore of Lake Charles is a mirage. But the artificially created North Beach is indeed real—and the only inland white-sand beach on the entire Gulf Coast. A drive over the Jean Lafitte Bridge affords a panoramic view of the beach, which borders Interstate 10.

This area was once **Jean Lafitte's** stomping ground. The "Gentleman Pirate" was a poetic sort who allegedly stashed some of his treasure in nearby watery mazes. To this day Lake Charles still plays host to pirates. Just visit in the spring when the city celebrates Contraband Days, starting with "Lafitte's invasion." The pirate's swashbuckling arrival sets off a jolly two-week round of parades, parties, pageants, boat races, and other festivities. In true buccaneering tradition, one event features local officials "walking the plank."

Lafitte's loot may be hopelessly hidden, but you'll discover treasure aplenty at the **Cottage Shops,** clustered around Hodges, Alamo, and Common Streets. Some dozen downtown specialty shops offer items ranging from antique armoires and handmade quilts to Cajun upside-down pickles and stained glass.

At 2706 Hodges Street you'll find **Nana's Cupboard** (337–433–5755), brimming over with unique gift items, antiques, and collectibles, plus a tearoom with refreshments.

If you're a coffee lover, don't pass up the **Louisiana Market** (337–439–1617) at 2710 Hodges Street. Owner Julie Vincent daily brews up a different flavor from her line of specialty coffees. You'll enjoy sipping coffee as you browse through aisles of authentic Cajun/Creole specialty foods and gifts. From hand-carved ducks to hot pepper jelly, a gift list can be taken care of here in one fell swoop.

To acquaint yourself with the history of Lake Charles, you can visit the **Imperial Calcasieu Museum** (337–439–3797), located on the corner of Ethel and Sallier Streets. The museum stands on the site of a cabin built by early settler Charles Sallier (*sal-YAY*), for whom the city was named.

Look left as you enter, and you'll see the steering wheel from the paddle wheeler *Borealis Rex*. In earlier days this ship served as the only link between Lake Charles and Cameron, located on Calcasieu Lake's southern side. Each Wednesday a crowd gathered to welcome the steamer bringing mail, freight, and passengers.

Along the museum's right aisle, you'll pass a furnished parlor, kitchen, and bedroom, all depicting scenes from yesteryear.

A collection of personalized shaving mugs adds to the decor in the museum's Gay Nineties barbershop, and a re-created country store nearby features nostalgic merchandise. A mannequin pharmacist stands ready to dispense remedies in his apothecary, an original section from a downtown drugstore. You'll see a physician's travel kit and a glass-cased display of bottles in a rainbow of colors. Be sure to notice the ornate set of ironstone apothecary jars made in France during the early sixteenth century.

A Civil War flag from the Battle of Mobile Bay is on display in the War Room. You'll also see a uniform worn by General Claire Chennault, who led the famed Flying Tigers. This exhibit includes Mrs. Chennault's wedding gown and going-away costume, books, and various items of historical significance.

A Geneva Bible, an Edison phonograph, and a stereopticon are all treasures you won't want to overlook. The museum features a fine collection of bird and animal prints by John James Audubon as well as excerpts from the diary he kept while working in Louisiana. There's an exhibit of Lafitte memorabilia with a copy of the privateer's journal, published more than a century after his death. (Maybe it contains a clue as to where he concealed his contraband.) Admission fee is modest. The adjoining artisans gallery, with local artists' work displayed, is free.

Don't leave without stepping out to the museum's backyard for a view of the venerable **Sallier Oak.** Some tree experts estimate this magnificent live oak to be about 300 years old. Whether or not the tree has weathered three centuries, it carries its age well, and its credentials include membership in the Live Oak Society. With branches dipping almost to the ground, this inviting oak would fulfill any child's tree-climbing fantasies.

Although the Sallier Oak may be visited at any time, the museum's hours are Tuesday through Saturday from 10:00 A.M. to 5:00 P.M.

A walking or driving tour of the city's historic **Charpentier Historic District** takes you through some twenty square blocks of homes dating from the Victorian era. Because many of the houses in this area were constructed before professional architects arrived on the scene, they express the individuality of their various builders. Area carpenters created their own patterns by changing rooflines, porch placements, and other exterior features. Sometimes they combined traditional design elements in new ways. A typical house constructed of native cypress and longleaf yellow pine might feature an odd number of columns with a bay on one side and a porch on the other. This distinctive look now commands an architectural category all its own—Lake Charles Style.

The Southwest Louisiana Convention and Visitors Bureau produces an illustrated brochure that outlines a walking-driving route through the historic district. You can request one by calling (337) 436–9588 or (800) 456–7952.

If you have offspring in tow, consider stopping by the **Children's Museum** (337–433–9420) while in this area. It's located at 925 Enterprise Boulevard, Lake Charles 70601. Youngsters can indulge their curiosity and creative instincts through various participatory programs. They can don uniforms and pretend to fight fires or broadcast their own news from a television-studio setting.

Changing exhibits explore areas of natural and physical science, history, art, crafts, and geography. Except for major holidays, hours are 10:00 A.M. to 5:00 P.M. Tuesday through Saturday. Modest admission.

Traveling east from Lake Charles, most drivers take Interstate 10. Route 14, however, runs south of the interstate (more in a meandering fashion than parallel) and offers some scenic vistas denied interstate travelers (albeit periodic road signs caution motorists about speeding on a substandard highway). If you do opt for Route 14, keep in mind that it takes longer, but you might see such striking vistas as entire fields white with egrets.

Persons driving through this part of the state on Interstate 10 risk possible "arrest" if they fail to take the *Jennings* exit. Typical case: Mr. L., his wife, and their two children were traveling along said route when stopped by the local sheriff. Mr. L. was not speeding or breaking any other laws. His crime? Not stopping in Jennings. Once a year the local chamber of commerce "arrests" an out-of-state driver for not stopping in Jennings. The party is charged, tried, and sentenced. Any plea-bargaining attempts by a court-appointed attorney are thrown out by presiding judges. The guilty party is sentenced to enjoy a meal before driving away with a load of gifts (plus a tank of gas) from area merchants. Also, he or she must promise to stop in Jennings if passing that way again.

Some travelers bypass highways entirely and simply fly in. An airport adjacent to the interstate attracts all sorts of "fly people"—from Cessna owners to Stearman pilots—who migrate to Jennings during a designated weekend for the annual end-of-the-season fly-in. Pilots practice formation flying in pairs and in groups because the airport allows "free flight" if sessions are performed by seasoned veterans. Pilots can taxi right up to the door of the local Holiday Inn. (From cockpit to motel room might mean a hop, skip, and jump of some 50 yards.)

Whether your visit in Jennings results from coercion or choice, all sorts of delights await you off the beaten path. Start with the *Louisiana Oil and Gas Park,* just north of town (and visible from Interstate 10). Louisiana's first oil well produced "black gold" on September 21, 1901, just 5 miles northeast of town in a rice field that belonged to farmer Jules Clement. The park, which commemorates that significant event, contains a replica of the small wooden oil rig used to drill the first well. Next to the derrick stands an early Acadian-style house where the Visitor Information Center is located.

An ideal place to take a driving break, the public recreation area includes a jogging trail, picnic facilities, playground equipment, a lake, and flocks of ducks and geese that act as a welcoming committee. You also can see *Château des Cocodries* (800–264–5521), a live alligator exhibit.

The lake is a great place to wet a fishing line and try for bluegill or largemouth bass. State law requires a fishing license. To obtain one, or some tackle, stop by More Mileage Station (337–824–2376), located at 602 North Main. Hours are 8:00 A.M. to 5:30 P.M. Monday through Friday and 8:00 A.M. to 5:00 P.M. on Saturday. Closed Sunday.

Replica of an Acadian House at Louisiana Oil and Gas Park

Select a table and spread a picnic, but save some sandwich crusts for the ducks—they consider it their duty to dispose of any leftovers. Maybe the ducks should be thanked for the trophy designating Jennings as Louisiana's cleanest city. After winning the "Cleanest City" award three years in a row, Jennings received the trophy for its permanent collection.

Jennings celebrated its first century in 1988. The town was named for a railroad contractor, Jennings McComb. When the railroad came through this section in 1880, McComb erected most of the depots, so railroad officials honored him by giving his first name to the unpopu-lated area around one of the depots. (A town in Mississippi had already claimed his last name.) Sure enough, the blank spot on the prairie began to attract settlers, mostly from the Midwest. Farmers did not have to first clear the land of trees—there were none. Homesteaders received extra land for planting trees on their property. They also planted crops they had raised in their home states of Iowa, Illinois, Indiana, and Missouri, and began to experiment with rice-farming techniques. By 1894 more than a thousand acres of rice grew on the Cajun prairie surrounding Jennings.

Later a number of Yankees who had fought in the area during the Civil War returned to settle here. The local cemetery contains quite a few more graves for the Blue than the Gray. Consequently Jennings came to be known as a "northern town on Southern soil."

Don't leave Jennings without visiting the *Zigler Museum* (337–824–0114), acclaimed for its outstanding fine arts collection. To get there from the park, take Route 26 south (going under the interstate) until you reach Clara Street, where you'll turn left. At 411 Clara Street, you'll see the museum, a white-columned structure with Colonial styling. Two gallery wings were added to the former home of Ruth and Fred Zigler to create this facility.

The central gallery, with paintings and sculpture by both state and national artists, presents a new exhibit each month. Nearby you'll see an antique handgun collection with more than fifty firearms, ranging from Colts and dueling pistols to different types of derringers.

Realistic dioramas depicting the state's southwestern wildlife fill the east wing. The museum features a facsimile of John James Audubon's *Birds of America,* an edition that was duplicated from original plates in the National Audubon Society Folio. Don't overlook the wonderful wildfowl wood carvings.

The west wing houses the museum's permanent collection of works by both European and American artists, such as Rembrandt and Whistler. From the Middle Ages to the present, the paintings take you on a journey through art history.

The Zigler's Louisiana Gallery often displays the work of state artists such as William Tolliver and George Rodrigue (*rod-REEG*). A Cajun painter, Rodrigue regularly wins international awards for his oils. His

Vive la Louisiane

*T*he year 2003 has been designated as **Louisiana Purchase Bicentennial** *year in Louisiana, with events throughout the state focused on U.S. President Thomas Jefferson's wise decision to buy the vast territory from France. to keep abreast of events, check throughout the state's Web sites, starting at louisianapurchase2003.com, or call (800) 261–9144.*

And then there's **Mardi Gras.** *In Lafayette there are large parades, rather like the New Orleans version. In the country you will find the* Courir du Mardi Gras *or Mardi Gras Run, which is a wild trail*

ride by costumed riders (sometimes with homemade masks of screen wire) who go from house to house collecting ("stealing") chickens and supplies for a giant gumbo. The riders are well fueled, the routes (complete with pickup trucks, beer, and a band) and the gumbo are all planned, and there is a big fais-do-do, *or dance, at the end. You will find this sort of event either on Mardi Gras Day or during the weekend immediately preceding it in Mamou, Iota, Church Point, and Eunice. A good place to call for information would be the Jean Lafitte Park site in Eunice (337–232–0789).*

Aioli Dinner and other paintings feature people (almost always dressed in white) portrayed against dark backgrounds. All project a haunting quality. You can see more of the artist's work at the Rodrigue Gallery in Lafayette and New Orleans.

Closed on Monday and holidays, the Zigler Museum is open Tuesday through Saturday from 9:00 A.M. to 5:00 P.M. and on Sunday from 1:00 to 4:00 P.M. Admission is modest.

Continue to the end of Clara Street, which runs into Cary Avenue. Next, turn on Second Street and go to State Street. At 710 North State Street stands **Our Lady Help of Christians Catholic Church,** one of the town's historic buildings. Step inside for a view of the windows in glowing stained glass, made in Germany. In designing the church, Father Joseph Peeters, a native of Belgium, was inspired by Notre Dame in Paris. You'll recognize some of the great Gothic cathedral's characteristics, such as the three arched entrances, in this smaller, plainer version. Constructed of homemade concrete blocks that were cast on the building site, the church was dedicated in 1916 after a building period of several years.

A short walk takes you to the **Marian Prayer Park,** located adjacent to the church on the rectory's south side. From here you'll do a bit of backtracking. While retracing your drive, you might want to take a ride along Cary Avenue for a look at the lovely old homes. Architectural features, reflecting a midwestern influence, include turrets, balconies, porches, and gables accented with gingerbread woodwork and fish-scale shingles.

Take a sentimental journey to the **W. H. Tupper General Merchandise Museum** (337–821–5532) at 311 North Main Street, Jennings 70546. The museum's stock came from a store built near Elton in 1910 by Mary and W. H. Tupper for their farm workers. Although the store closed in 1949, the contents remained intact—frozen in time for four decades. The store's original inventory consisted of toys, cosmetics, dishes, drugs, cooking utensils, seeds, fans, jewelry, denim overalls, and other items that bring back memories.

You'll also see a large selection of baskets made by members of the Chitimacha and Coushatta tribes. The Coushattas live 3 miles northwest of Elton on the northern edge of the parish. Museum hours are Monday through Saturday from 9:30 A.M. to 5:30 P.M. Admission is modest.

Take time to browse through the **Old Magnolia Gift Shoppe,** also housed here. You'll find great gifts and souvenirs such as Cajun cookbooks,

OTHER ATTRACTIONS WORTH SEEING

Cypremort Point State Park.
306 Beach Lane, Franklin; (337) 867–4510
or (888) 867–4510. Man-made beach in the
marshland on the shores of Vermilion Bay.

Cypress Island Preserve.
Off Louisiana Highway 353 between
Lafayette and Breaux Bridge. Go to Lake
Martin and look for the Nature Conservancy signs. Park at the yellow gates on
the levee. You can see virgin cypress
swamp; old-growth, live-oak ridges
(cheniers); and a huge rookery of birds,
including white ibis.

Delta Downs. 2717 Highway 3063, Vinton;
(800) 589–7441. This track offers Thoroughbred and quarter-horse races from

January into July. Quarter-horse racing
is quick and the betting is lively. Even the
food is pretty good in the clubhouse—
try the gumbo. A good place to wear
your Wranglers and your old
Tony Lama boots.

The Jeanerette Museum.
500 East Main Street, Jeanerette;
(337) 276–4408. Sugarcane history
with wildlife and Mardi Gras thrown in.

Sam Houston Jones State Park.
107 Southerland Road, Lake Charles;
(337) 855–2665 or (888) 677–7264. At the
confluence of three rivers, this woodsy park
offers boating, hiking trails, camping, and
even cabins for rent (call far in advance).

Louisiana products, jellies, children's books, toys, crafts, paintings, and antiques. In a nearby room called the Back Porch, you can watch members of the Cajun Country Quilting Guild at work and see a selection of their handiwork.

Also sharing the Tupper building, the *Telephone Pioneer Museum of Lousiana* features displays of phones from past to present with exhibits going back to switchboards and party lines.

Before leaving the area, stroll along the brick sidewalks of nearby *Founder's Park* with its fountains, landscaped patios, wrought-iron benches and chairs, and antique clock. This public park features a large hand-painted mural depicting the history of Jennings.

Afterward, stop by *Boudin King* (337–824–6593), located at 906 West Division Street in a residential district. No trip to this area would be complete without sampling boudin (*boo-dan*). The state legislature passed an act declaring Jennings the Boudin Capital of the Universe, and you would be hard-pressed to find a better place for trying this specialty. The late restaurant owner Ellis Cormier, whose customers called him the Boudin King, defined his boudin as a mixture of pork, spices, and long-grain rice. Louisiana French people have been partial to boudin for more than two centuries, and Cormier's Acadian recipe passed down in the family for generations. His widow, June, continues the family enterprise. Parsley, peppers, green onions, and rice (cooked separately) are added to the prime pork. The resulting mixture is stuffed into a sausage casing, then steamed and served warm.

A great appetizer, boudin comes in links, both mild and hot. If you can't decide which to try, you may sample each. Start with mild and work your way up to hot (my favorite).

When June and Ellis Cormier turned their neighborhood grocery store into a restaurant featuring boudin, local folks predicted a short run for the establishment because the Cormiers decided not to serve alcohol. Customers joked that it took both "a pound of boudin and a six-pack of beer to make a seven-course Cajun dinner." That was in 1974, and if you stop by the Boudin King today, you'll probably have to stand in line.

Although boudin gets star billing here, the menu offers other items such as chicken-and-sausage gumbo, fried crawfish, catfish, chicken, and red beans and rice with smoked sausage. You also can buy hogshead cheese, a sort of pâté especially good when spread on crackers.

Prices are economical to moderate. Boudin King, which closes on Sunday, operates from 8:00 A.M. until 9:00 P.M. Monday through Saturday.

Before leaving Jefferson Davis Parish, take Route 26 down to Lake Arthur, 9 miles south of Jennings. For some picturesque scenery, drive along the edge of the lake, lined with lovely old homes. Cypress trees, with swaying Spanish moss trailing from their branches, stand knee-deep in Lake Arthur. In this laid-back resort area, you can fish, hunt, or watch the cranes, egrets, herons, and other birds.

Lake Arthur Park offers a bandstand, pavilions, picnic facilities, and an enclosed swimming area. Throughout the year the town stages events at the park. The park is also the setting for a star-spangled Fourth of July Celebration and a Christmas Festival with thousands of lights. For more information on Lake Arthur events, call the Town Hall at (337) 774–2211.

If hunger pangs hit while you're in Lake Arthur, head for the *Lakeshore Restaurant* (337–774–1000), located at 40532 East Lakeshore Road. This restaurant offers seafood, steaks, and a large dance hall—which should be bouncing on weekends!

After your delectable repast, drive back to Route 26 and travel north until the road intersects U.S. Highway 90. You'll then go east, passing by acres of rice fields on your way to Crowley, the Rice Center of America.

Cajun Country

As home of the International Rice Festival, Crowley promises plenty of good food along with rice-eating contests, fiddling and accordion competitions, parades, a street fair, a livestock show, and other events.

While you're in Crowley, go by the courthouse square. Starting on Main Street you can drive through the downtown historic district, which features some 8 blocks of lovely Victorian homes. From here take U.S. Highway 90 east to reach Rayne, about 7 miles from Crowley and 13 miles west of Lafayette.

If you didn't realize that **Rayne** is the Frog Capital of the World, you will before you depart. The first clue might be big colorful murals on the sides of old buildings—all depicting frogs in one fashion or another. On your driving tour be sure to notice the interesting above-ground cemetery.

Mark Twain's jumping frog of Calaveras County would have been in his element here, happy among his peers. This town is filled not only with bona fide frogs but also with pictures of frogs, statues of frogs, literature about frogs, and even frog factories. What do frog factories export? Frog

Blue Stories

At **Crystal Rice Plantation** *(337–783–6417) you'll find the* **Blue Rose Museum,** *located at 6428 Airport Road in Crowley. The museum's name came from a variety of rice that was developed locally. Rice is the main crop in this area, and the Blue Rose Musueum covers the development of the rice industry. (Also on the premises, you can tour a rice farm and see crawfish ponds and an antique automobile collection.) Admission.*

The fictionalized version of the search for a hybrid rice (which the Blue Rose Museum commemorates) is told in the late Frances Parkinson Keyes'
1956 novel Blue Camellia. *Keyes, a New Englander, who lived from 1896 to 1970, spent years in Louisiana churning out big-selling historical novels. Her research is good, and her stories are usually long, family sagas. If you like romance novels or historical fiction, you'll enjoy her books.*

River Road *covers the sugar industry;* Crescent Carnival *describes New Orleans old-line Mardi Gras krewes (the carnival organizations that sponsor balls and parades), and dishes out generations-old gossip. Look for Keyes's books in your public library—they are mostly out of print.*

Dazzle 'Em with This

*L*ike all of Chef Roy Lyons's creations, this recipe for oysters paired with eggplant slices will wow 'em and bring 'em back for more. Chef Roy first developed this dish for a television audience and generously offered to share it with my readers.

Note: If you can't find Chef Roy's seasonings (in frog containers, of course), request that your supermarket stock them or call Chef Roy's Frog City Cafe (337–334–7913) to order your own.

Rocky Mountain Oysters Napoleon

Oyster/Tasso Wine Cream Sauce

2 tablespoons butter

2 tablespoons minced tasso

1 tablespoon minced onion

1 teaspoon each finely chopped red, yellow, and green bell peppers

1 teaspoon minced garlic

2 teaspoons flour

2 teaspoons Chef Roy's Seafood Seasoning Mix

4 oysters

2 tablespoons white wine

1 cup heavy cream

2 tablespoons grated Parmesan cheese

2 tablespoons minced green onion

1 tablespoon minced parsley

Melt butter in large skillet. Quickly add tasso, onion, bell peppers, and garlic; sauté 30 seconds. Season and flour oysters and cook in white wine until the oysters curl. Add the heavy cream and Parmesan cheese and reduce until mixture coats a spoon. Fold in the green onion and parsley.

Fried Eggplant

Cut 4 slices of eggplant, $1/2$ inch thick. Coat in seasoned egg wash then toss in Chef Roy's Oyster/Fish/Vegetable Fry mix. Fry until crispy.

Fried Oysters

Toss 5 oysters in Chef Roy's Oyster Fry Mix until coated completely. Fry oysters until they are crispy but still moist in center.

Arrange Dish:

Place a fried eggplant slice on plate. Top with a fried oyster, then add oyster/tasso sauce and repeat layers. Serves one.

legs for restaurant menus and specimens for scientific purposes, of course. Besides being the center of Louisiana's frog industry, Rayne also ranks as one of the world's largest shippers of frogs.

For fifty-one weeks of the year, Rayne could be considered off the beaten path. During Labor Day weekend, however, the world beats a path to its door for a fun-filled Frog Festival, which features fireworks, frog-cooking contests, frog derbies, and frog beauty contests.

The Lone Prairie

In Eunice, back by the old railroad tracks, there is a preserved area of prairie that encompasses several city blocks. Although Louisiana once had miles of prairie, civilization and the plow removed most of the typical deep-rooted grasses and fragile wildflowers that form the typical prairie ecosystem. Here, where some untouched land was found, grasses and plants that are original to this soil have been replanted and a true prairie has been growing. Walking trails and an interpretive center will soon be available, but the sweet smell of prairie grasses is already here. Ask for directions at the Jean Lafitte Park offices; (337) 457–8499.

Soon after arriving in town, search out **Chef Roy's Frog City Cafe** (337–334–7913) at 1131 Church Point Highway, a quarter of a mile north of Interstate 10, exit 87. Here, you'll find even more frogs—both in the cafe's frog boutique and on the menu.

Well traveled, Chef Roy Lyons has instructed chefs in Canada, Mexico, France, Belgium, Turkey, Holland, the Netherlands, and elsewhere on the preparation of Cajun cuisine. He has shared culinary tips with *Good Morning America* audiences and served as featured chef in the U.S. Senate. His peers selected him 1997's Acadiana Chef of the Year.

Chef Roy confided, "They tell me I make the best gumbo in the state." No small compliment if that state happens to be Louisiana. Start with an appetizer of his celebrated seafood gumbo or a crab cake, grilled and served with crawfish cream sauce. Blackened chicken salad features mixed greens, juicy blackened chicken strips, and the chef's fig vinaigrette dressing. Popular entrees include shrimp or crawfish enchiladas, seafood platters, and Catfish Willie, grilled and topped with crawfish herb cream sauce. And yes, you can get a fried frog leg platter or a combination with frog leg étouffée. As for dessert, popular choices include peach bread pudding with rum sauce, crème brûlée, or the turtle specialty combining chocolate cake and vanilla ice cream served in a pool of caramel.

The cafe opens daily at 11:00 A.M. and closes at 9:30 P.M. Monday through Thursday, 10:00 P.M. Friday and Saturday, and 2:00 P.M. on Sunday. Prices are moderate.

After leaving Rayne, return to Crowley and take State Route 13 north. Consider a short trip on the **Acadiana Trail** (also U.S. Highway 190), which runs through a number of interesting towns such as **Eunice,** the state's crawfish-processing center. Depending on the season you'll see acres of rice growing or thousands of crawfish traps in this area where fields do double duty. Now a major agricultural industry, crawfish farming utilizes flooded rice fields during winter and early spring.

Complement your trip to Cajun country by taking in a performance at the *Liberty Center for the Performing Arts* on the corner of South Second Street and Park Avenue in downtown Eunice. Every Saturday night from 6:00 to 8:00 P.M., *Rendezvous des Cajuns,* a live radio show, features a lineup of musicians and entertainers, with Barry Jean Ancelet serving as master of ceremonies. Ancelet announces each act in both Cajun French and English. Don't miss the outstanding exhibits at neighboring *Jean Lafitte National Historical Park and Preserve, Acadian Cultural Center* (337–232–0789), open daily (except Christmas Day) from 8:00 A.M. to 5:00 P.M. and until 6:00 P.M. Saturday.

Overnight visitors can make reservations at the *Seale Guesthouse* (337–457–3753), located 2 miles south of Eunice on State Route 13 at 123 Seale Lane. The country house with wraparound porch offers lodging options such as rooms with private baths, suites with shared baths, or a two-bedroom guest cottage. On weekdays, the breakfast is continental. Weekend fare features local (and yummy) boudin, quiche, and pastries. Rates are standard.

Each fall, Eunice hosts the Prairie Cajun Folklife Festival—a feast for the senses where you can hear Cajun, zydeco, blues, and jazz music; smell and taste tempting specialties such as boudin, gumbo, and jambalaya; and watch artisans make crafts in the tradition of their ancestors. For more information on the festival or other events, call the Eunice Chamber of Commerce at (337) 457–2565 or call Eunice City Hall at (337) 457–7389.

After visiting Eunice, head north to Ville Platte. While passing through Ville Platte, plan to stop by *Floyd's Record Shop* (337–363–2138) at 434 East Main Street (Highway 167), where you'll find not only film, photographic supplies, and regional books but a comprehensive inventory of traditional Cajun music with recordings by artists dating from the 1930s. If Floyd Soileau (pronounced *swallow*) is available, he can give you the history of the sounds he helped preserve by recording these musicians. The retail business is open Monday through Friday from 8:30 A.M. to 5:30 P.M. and Saturday from 8:30 A.M. to 5:00 P.M.

For dining, try the *Jungle Club* (337–363–9103) on Highway 167 west (1636 West Main Street), famous for its boiled crawfish trays (in season). This specialty comes in mild, hot, and super-hot choices. Although the crawfish selections including étouffée and bisque remain favorites, the restaurant offers softshell crabs, alligator, and other outstanding dishes such as its award-winning gumbo. "We won the grand championship for our gumbo at the Gumbo Festival," says owner Victor

Manuel. The Jungle Club opens for lunch Monday through Friday from 11:00 A.M. to 1:30 P.M. and for dinner beginning at 5:30 P.M. Monday through Saturday. Prices are moderate.

About 6 miles north of Ville Platte, you'll find *Chicot State Park* (888–677–2442) on State Route 3042. With 6,500 acres of rolling hills and a 2,000-acre lake, the park offers plenty of recreation opportunities. Just beyond, you can visit *Louisiana State Arboretum* (888–677–6100 or 337–363–6289) with inviting nature trails and footbridges interspersed among labeled specimens of native plants. Rambling through the forest and across hills, ravines, and creeks, you'll see birds, deer, and local flora such as pine, oak, magnolia, beech, dogwood, and papaw. The arboretum is open daily from 9:00 A.M. to 5:00 P.M.; admission is free.

In a tin shed near his Grand Prairie home, Joe Soileau practices an uncommon craft—making cowhide chair seats. From cleaning and curing the hides to producing finished products such as rockers, baby chairs, footstools, bar stools, rugs, tom-toms, vests, and even cowhide jewelry, Joe takes great satisfaction in continuing a family tradition. After studying the craft by watching his father and grandfather make chair covers from cowhide, Joe took up the business on a part-time basis. Success soon followed, forcing him to give up his job selling insurance to fill increasing orders. To observe the chair-making process or place an order, call Joe at (337) 826–3295, or check out his inventory at www.cowhiderugs.com.

Afterward, continue to Washington, one of the state's oldest permanent settlements. Located on Bayou Courtableau, Washington once bustled as a steamboat town, and you can glimpse a bit of local history at Jack Womack's *Steamboat Warehouse* (337–826–7227) at 525 North Main Street, Washington 70589, and enjoy a good meal at the same time. The large brick warehouse, built between 1819 and 1823 and restored as a restaurant in 1976, specializes in steaks and seafood. After dipping into Jack's Catfish Lizzy topped with crawfish étouffée, or a rib-eye, take time to look at lading bills and other documents displayed here. An 1870 shipment, for instance, included candles, claret, coffee, tea, table salt, pickles, apples, and nails. Except for Christmas Day and New Year's Day, the restaurant is open Tuesday through Thursday from 5:00 to 10:00 P.M., on Friday and Saturday from 5:00 to 11:00 P.M., and on Sunday from 11:00 A.M. to 2:00 P.M. Two cottages on the restaurant's grounds are available for overnight guests. For more information, tap into www.chefie.com.

Many of Washington's historic homes, plantations, and buildings were

Spice Up Your Life

W̶hile exploring Opelousas, drop by **Tony Chachere's** *(337–948–4691 or 800–551–9066) at 519 North Lombard for a free plant tour. Along with an orientation, you can sniff the ingredients that go into Tony Chachere's original seasoning, a mixture many great cooks swear by. The company store opens Monday through Friday from 8:00 A.M. to 5:00 P.M.*

At www.tonychachere.com, you can take a look at Mr. Tony's Creole kitchen and learn about this man, who became the first inductee into the Louisiana Chef's Hall of Fame. Enhance your own culinary creations with Tony Chachere's line of products and try the following recipe for a classic dish.

Look for Tony's Creole Seasoning in the bright green container at your supermarket.

Tony's Chicken and Sausage Jambalaya

This recipe comes from Tony Chachere's Second Helping.

1 3-pound fryer, cut up

Tony's Creole Seasoning, to taste

4 tablespoons margarine

4 onions, chopped

4 cloves garlic, minced

2 ribs celery, chopped

1 bell pepper, chopped

$^1/_2$ pound smoked pork sausage

3 cups uncooked rice

6 cups water

Season chicken generously with Tony's Creole Seasoning. Melt margarine in a 5-quart Dutch oven and fry chicken until brown. Remove chicken from pot and add all vegetables. Sauté for 10 minutes. Add sausage and rice, then cook for 10 minutes, mixing thoroughly. Return chicken to pot; add water and stir. Cover and simmer about 30 minutes or until rice is fully cooked. Yields 8 servings.

constructed between 1780 and 1835, and some are open for tours or as bed-and-breakfasts. For more information, contact the Washington Museum and Tourist Center at (337) 826–3627. The museum is open daily from 9:00 A.M. until 4:00 P.M.

After exploring Washington, head south to Opelousas. On U.S. Highway 190 east, you'll find the *Jim Bowie Museum* (337–948–6263), next to the tourist information center. Exhibits focus on Bowie's career, but there are also displays on Acadian culture along with old documents, photographs, farm equipment, and firearms.

During his boyhood Bowie lived here in a home that his father built on what is now the museum lawn. After serving for a while in the Louisiana

Ils Sont Parti!

In south Louisiana even the horses might speak French. At the start of each race at Evangeline Downs, the announcer does not shout "They're off!" but rather "Ils sont parti!"

legislature, Bowie moved to Texas, where he fought and died at the Alamo. While legend credits him with the invention of the bowie knife, some historians contend that this is not a fact, although Bowie may have contributed to the knife's design. The Jim Bowie Museum is open daily from 8:00 A.M. until 4:00 P.M., and there's no admission charge.

The *Opelousas Museum and Interpretive Center* (337–948–2589) at 329 North Main Street, Opelousas 70570, presents a fascinating overview of local culture back to prehistoric times. The area can be described as "a melting pot or cultural gumbo" because the settlers came from many ethnic backgrounds. Named for a Native American tribe that occupied the site earlier, Opelousas became a bayou trading post for French and Indian interchange in 1720. This fertile area also attracted the Spanish around the same time. Displays in the main exhibit room spotlight the people—their agriculture, home and family, business and professions, music, and food.

Among other things, the town pays tribute to the sweet potato's cousin, the yam, with an annual Yambilee Festival the last weekend in October. Spring and fall Folklife Festivals focus on the "olden days." A *Zydeco Festival* is staged in nearby Plaisance each September, and you'll see a presentation on zydeco (*ZI-da-ko*), which might be described as a musical merger of such sounds as rhythm and blues, jazz, rock and roll, gospel, and Cajun music. Opelousas, the birthplace of this unique style, was the home of "Zydeco King," the late Clifton Chenier. Also, before leaving the main room, be sure to notice the exhibits on Mardi Gras, the Orphan Train, and the 1914 Dunbar kidnapping case.

Another section contains the Geraldine Smith Welch doll collection. You'll see more than 400 dolls, grouped in categories from antiques and miniatures to pop culture.

The center also houses the *Louisiana Video Collection Library,* a valuable resource for delving into state history, and a section on the Civil War when Opelousas served as the state's capital for a brief period. You can visit the center (which is fully handicapped accessible) Monday through Saturday between 9:00 A.M. and 5:00 P.M.

Before leaving town, stop by the *Palace Cafe* (337–942–2142) at 135 West Landry Street (Highway 190 west), where owner Tina D. Elder carries on tradition in the family business started in 1927. Try the fried chicken salad, Grecian salad, or house specialty—baked eggplant stuffed with crab. Top off your meal with the restaurant's famous baklava, a Greek pastry made with pecan butter and honey. Prices are economical to moderate. The cafe is open Monday through Saturday from 6:00 A.M. to 9:00 P.M. Sunday hours run from 7:00 A.M. to 3:00 P.M.

Afterward, head toward **Chrétien Point Plantation** (337–662–5876, 337–233–7050, or 800–880–7050), located at 665 Chrétien Point Road in the town of Sunset about 12 miles north of Lafayette. From Opelousas get on Interstate 49 south. Take the exit for Sunset/Grand Coteau and drive through Sunset. This puts you on Route 93 south. After 3.8 miles you'll see the Bristol/Bosco Road. Turn right, go 1 block, then take another right. Go 1 mile and Chrétien Point Plantation will be on your left.

Built by Hypolite Chrétien II in 1831, this grand Greek Revival house features both a window and a staircase that served as models for those in Tara during the filming of *Gone with the Wind*. The mansion stands on land that was a wedding gift from Chrétien's father, a rich cotton planter and close friend of the pirate Jean Lafitte, who frequently visited this plantation.

When Hypolite II died soon after moving into the mansion, his wife Félicité took over the reins and ran the large farming operation. On a mansion tour, your guide will tell you more stories about Félicité, a liberated woman who smoked cigars and played poker—supposedly her aptitude for gambling doubled the plantation's size to 10,000 acres. Local lore also holds that she shot a man (perhaps a pirate from Lafitte's crew) on the stairs when he broke in and refused to halt. Bloodstains, which partially show from beneath the carpet runner, remain on the steps.

Although the house survived the Civil War's ravage, the plantation's outbuildings were destroyed. Later, after the farm failed and dilapidation set in, the mansion served as a barn where animals roamed and hay was kept. Now restored to its former grandeur and furnished with nineteenth-century pieces and portraits, it is open for daily tours from 10:00 A.M. to 5:00 P.M. except for major holidays. The day's last tour starts at 4:00 P.M. Admission is charged.

Visitors may also stay overnight here in the mansion itself and enjoy a full plantation breakfast and use the pool and tennis courts. Bed-and-breakfast guests get a mansion tour and are welcomed with mint juleps on the gallery. Rates are moderate to deluxe.

As you drive through this part of the country, tune in to local radio stations, where you'll hear the unique sounds of Cajun music and dialect. Sometimes the news is broadcast in French and sometimes in English.

For a special treat, take Route 93 (designated a Louisiana State Scenic Byway) and go back across I–49 to the little town of *Grand Coteau.* This was the center for early-nineteenth–century religious education in Acadian Louisiana, with both males and females being accommodated. *St. Charles College,* now a Jesuit seminary, began in 1837 and serves as a center for religious retreats.

The Academy of the Sacred Heart (337–662–5275), 1821 Academy Drive, began in 1821 and is still operated by the Religious of the Sacred heart, known worldwide for their elite girls' schools. The convent and grounds are open for tours by appointment only. There is a fee. The main school building was erected in 1831; fluted iron columns support its 300-foot-long galleries. Stroll in the pleasant gardens, and be sure to notice the century-old camellia plants.

The convent also has strong Catholic religious associations: One of the miracles attributed to St. John Berchmans at his canonization occurred here when a young postulant was miraculously cured.

On a secular note, the village of Grand Coteau has undergone a recent flowering as a good place for visitors to spend time: You can shop diligently, eat well, and sleep in elegant comfort! Among those to see commercial possibilities in the historic district were sisters Mae Tietz and Cecile Fontenot (both native French speakers), who in 1996 opened their antiques shop, *La Maison des Deux Soeurs* (337–662–4007), at 256 East Martin Luther King. Soon they were joined by other new businesses, including the antiques-filled *Auntie Violet's Attic* (337–662–6039) at 248 East Martin Luther King.

Oldest of the upscale stores is *The Kitchen Shop* (337–662–3500), 296 East Martin Luther King, which offers interesting cookware and gadgets—and scrumptious lunches.

Grand Coteau House Bed and Breakfast (337–662–3910), 284 East Martin Luther King, is built in Acadian architectural style, with antiques-filled rooms, galleries, and a courtyard. The upper floors look out over the grounds of St. Charles College. It also houses the *Three French Hens* gift shop (everything you purchase is gift wrapped!) and *Le 'tit Cafe* with light lunches.

Catahoula's Restaurant (888–547–BARK), Highway 93, 0.5 mile off I–49 in Grand Coteau. This restaurant overlooks the grounds of St. Charles College, features "new Louisiana cooking," and your visit is destined to be a culinary experience (according to *Gourmet Magazine* in 1999). Open Friday and Sunday for lunch or brunch from 11:00 A.M. to

2:00 P.M., Tuesday through Thursday from 5:00 to 9:00 P.M., and Saturday from 5:00 to 10:00 P.M. for dinner.

Continue south to reach Lafayette, the hub city of Acadiana. The Acadiana area, which comprises nearly one-third of Louisiana's sixty-four parishes, was settled by French Acadians who were ousted from Nova Scotia and New Brunswick by the British in 1755. Forced to leave their homes and property, families were broken up and sent to various destinations. Many eventually made their way to South Louisiana, where Acadians came to be known as "Cajuns."

Make the *Jean Lafitte National Historical Park and Preserve/Acadian Cultural Center* (337–232–0789) at 501 Fisher Road one of your first sight-seeing stops. A free forty-minute film chronicles the Cajun experience, tracing the exile from Nova Scotia to settlement in the state's Southern landscape of bayous, swamps, and prairies. Exhibits highlight Acadiana's contemporary culture. Open 8:00 A.M. to 5:00 P.M. daily.

During the 1770s a large number of Acadians settled in Lafayette (then called Vermilionville because of the nearby bayou's reddish color). In 1884 the town was renamed to honor Lafayette, the French general of American Revolutionary War fame. Now *Vermilionville* (337–233–4077 or 866–992–2968) has been reincarnated as a twenty-three-acre living-history attraction focusing on Cajun and Creole culture. Located at 1600 Surrey Street across from the airport, the complex features entertainment, craft demonstrations, and an operating farm typical of those in the eighteenth century. Also, a cooking school staff demonstrates Creole and Cajun methods of food preparation.

Geese strut about, honking at visitors, and costumed storytellers, musicians, and craftspeople re-create the folklife of bayou settlers from 1765 to 1890. As Acadian descendants, many staffers switch easily from speaking English to Cajun French. A hand-pulled ferry takes you across Petit Bayou to Fausse Pointe, where you'll meet Broussard family members such as Camille and Eliza. The couple speak and behave as people did in the 1840s and may inquire about your strange apparatus called a camera, your attire, or some unfamiliar expression. Except for Christmas Day and New Year's Day, Vermilionville is open Tuesday through Sunday from 10:00 A.M. to 5:00 P.M. There is an admission fee.

For dinner, step next door to the *Evangeline Seafood and Steakhouse* (337–233–2658), a family restaurant that dishes up Cajun specialties. Popular entrees include seafood platters and crawfish, crab, and shrimp dinners. A dish called the Evangeline features broiled snapper or flounder with shrimp-mushroom stuffing and crab cream sauce topping. Prices are moderate.

Basically French country cooking, Cajun cooking utilizes fresh indigenous ingredients such as rice, peppers, herbs, game, and fish—notably the ubiquitous crustacean called crawfish—and Lafayette boasts some great places to sample traditional specialties. For classic Cajun and Creole cuisine, stop by *Cafe Vermilionville* (337–237–0100), housed in a circa 1818 Acadian inn at 1304 West Pinhook Road. For lunch, try the bronzed shrimp and artichoke salad or crab cakes Vermilion. Dinner selections might include such specialties as smoked salmon and tasso, pecan tilapia, or tuna steak topped with seared foie gras.

Because music plays a primary role in Acadiana's culture, you might enjoy "two-stepping" to the sounds of Cajun triangles, fiddles, and accordions at one of the local Cajun dance hall/restaurants. Both *Randol's Restaurant and Cajun Dancehall* (800–YO–CAJUN) at 2320 Kaliste Saloom Road and *Prejean's Restaurant* (337–896–3247) at 3480 I–49 North specialize in Cajun cooking and feature live music. Tap into www.prejeans.com for a profile on Prejean's award-winning chef, James Graham, or to preview recipes reflective of his celebrated cuisine.

A good place to start a city tour is the *Lafayette Museum–Alexander Mouton House* (337–234–2208) at 1122 Lafayette Street. The home of Louisiana's first Democratic governor, this antebellum town house contains antiques, Civil War relics, and historic documents. Go upstairs and see the lavish hand-beaded Mardi Gras costumes and other glittering regalia. The museum's hours are Tuesday through Saturday from 9:00 A.M. until 4:30 P.M. and Sunday from 1:00 until 4:00 P.M. Admission is modest.

A walking tour from this point will take you past some of the city's landmark buildings, including the *Cathedral of St. John the Evangelist,* an interesting structure of German-Romanesque design.

Either University Avenue or St. Mary Avenue, both of which turn off Lafayette Street, will lead you to the University of Southwestern Louisiana. Look for a parking place somewhere near the student union, then head for the tall cypress trees. Right in the middle of campus, you'll see an honest-to-goodness swamp studded with cypress trees trailing their streamers of Spanish moss. Called *Cypress Lake,* the natural swamp (about the size of a city block) comes complete with native vegetation, waterfowl, migratory birds, fish, and even alligators.

Because this is a miniature swamp, you get a sense of the mysteries such an environment conceals—without the threat of danger. Visitors are welcome to stroll along the water's edge and feed the ducks. Small signs placed at intervals in the murky water invite you to PLEASE FEED THE FISH and inform you that this is an alligator habitat. (You're not supposed to feed the alligators, but if you toss half a hot dog to the fish and it's intercepted by an alligator, it's best to let him have his way.)

A must-see in Lafayette is *Acadian Village* (337–981–2364 or 800–962–9133), located on the southwest edge of town. After leaving the campus take Route 167 south until you reach Ridge Road, where you'll turn right. Next take a left on West Broussard Road. Then you'll follow the signs to Acadian Village. By the time you reach this cluster of buildings situated on a bayou and surrounded by gardens and woodlands, you'll agree it's definitely off the beaten path.

When you step through the gate, you may feel as if someone turned the calendar back about 200 years. With its general store, schoolhouse, chapel, and original steep-roofed houses, the folklife museum replicates a nineteenth-century Acadian settlement.

Stop at the general store to buy a ticket and pick up a guide sheet describing the individual buildings. Strolling along a brick pathway and crossing wooden footbridges, you'll wend your way in and out of the various vintage structures. Although the blacksmith shop, chapel, and general

Acadian Village

store are reproductions, all other structures are authentic, most dating from the early 1800s. Transported from various locations throughout Acadiana, they were restored and furnished with native Cajun household items, clothing, photographs, books, and tools. The charming village captures the spirit of early Acadiana, and commercialism is noticeably absent.

The *LeBlanc House,* birthplace of Acadian state senator Dudley J. LeBlanc, contains a display featuring the tonic Hadacol. An early elixir touted to cure all ailments, this vitamin tonic concocted by LeBlanc, fondly known as "Couzan Dud," contained 12 percent alcohol. During the early 1950s George Burns, Bob Hope, Jack Benny, Mickey Rooney, Jimmy Durante, and other entertainers performed in Hadacol caravans, updated versions of the old-time traveling medicine shows.

The *Billeaud House's* exhibits focus on spinning and weaving. You'll see looms, spinning wheels, and a display of homespun coverlets and clothes. Take a look at the cotton patch, planted behind the cottage. If you packed a picnic, this peaceful setting is the perfect spot to enjoy it as you watch villagers (wearing the traditional clothing of their ancestors) spin wool on a porch or chat by the bayou.

Acadian Village is open daily from 10:00 A.M. to 5:00 P.M. except for major holidays. Admission is charged.

From Lafayette's outskirts it's only a fifteen-minute drive northeast via Route 94 to Breaux Bridge, also known as the Crawfish Capital of the World.

If you visit *Mulate's Cajun Restaurant* (337–332–4648 or 800–422–2586) at 325 Mills Avenue (on Route 94) in Breaux Bridge, owner Goldie Comeaux promises you a Cajun *"bon temps!"* Besides a good time, you can also anticipate good food.

The restaurant's support beams came from cypress trees cut more than seventy years ago at the nearby swamp in Henderson. Local festival posters and paintings by Acadian artists line Mulate's walls, and the tables are covered with red-and-white checkered cloths. Waiters speak both French and English.

Order some stuffed mushrooms or catfish tidbits to nibble on as you soak up some of the atmosphere, best described as lively and informal. While waiting for your entree, you can take Mulate's Cajun quiz: "How to tell a full-blooded, dipped-in-the-bayous Cajun from someone who just wishes he was."

The restaurant offers dozens of fresh seafood dishes including catfish, shrimp, oysters, and frog legs. The dinner of stuffed crabs, also a house specialty, comes with jambalaya, coleslaw, homemade french fries, and garlic bread. If you order the super seafood platter, you can sample stuffed crab, stuffed bell pepper, fried shrimp, catfish, oysters, frog legs, and jambalaya. Prices are moderate.

Authentic "chank-a-chank" music sends everybody, including children, to the dance floor. Parents holding toddlers in their arms waltz round and round or dance the Cajun two-step to the beat of triangles, fiddles, and accordions. The restaurant features live music at lunch on Saturday and Sunday and seven nights a week. Mulate's hours are 11:00 A.M. to 10:00 P.M. daily.

If you visit the Breaux Bridge area during the fall, you can watch sugarcane being harvested and hauled to market. This state produces much of America's sugar. (The sugar you spooned into your morning coffee or cereal may have come from South Louisiana's cane fields.) Harvesting starts in October, before winter's first freeze, and extends through late December. When the cane reaches a height of 9 to 11 feet, it is cut by mechanical harvesters and left in rows on the ground. Then the leaves are burned off, and the cane is loaded on trailers to be taken to nearby mills for processing. In this part of the country, you'll drive along roads strewn with stalks and pass many slow-moving trucks transporting their cargoes of cane from field to mill.

Don't leave Breaux Bridge without stopping by *Cafe des Amis* (337–332–5273) at 140 East Bridge Street. Chef Cynthia Breaux presides over a kitchen that turns out scrumptious specialties such as Creole turtle soup and crawfish pie (crawfish or shrimp étouffée served in puff pastry). Get your camera out for this dish, which turns heads from tables all around. Or try the restaurant's terrific signature dish, barbecue shrimp Pont Breaux style. (Look for author James Lee Burke's autograph on the wall.) Closed Monday and Tuesday. Moderate prices.

Marked Routes

Out from St. Martinville on Louisiana Highway 96 there are small hand-painted wooden shrines, commemorating the fourteen Stations of the Cross, affixed to trees along the highway. Catholics from the church at the Isle L'Abbe community walk this route annually during Lent.

*You can see one shrine next to the historic marker at the beginning of **Oak and Pine Alley**. The marker signals the starting point of the fabulous pre–Civil War wedding procession for a bride of the locally prominent Durand family. During her wedding, the bride passed under trees that were decorated for the occasion by gold dust sprinkled on webs spun by imported spiders.*

Ask Cynthia or her husband, Dickie, about their creative country inns, Maison Des Amis and Chez Des Amis (337–407–3399).

Only a few miles east of Breaux Bridge lies one of this country's great untamed regions, the *Atchafalaya Basin* (that large uncluttered area west of Baton Rouge on your state map). In this vast wilderness swamp, an overflow area for the Atchafalaya (*a-CHOFF-a-lie-a*) River, you can step back into a pristine world, but don't venture into its depths on your own. If you're game for a guided safari, take Route 347 northeast from Breaux Bridge, then pick up Route 352 to reach Henderson, the gateway to the Atchafalaya Basin. This area features a number of boat tours designed to introduce visitors to the Atchafalaya Basin's mysteries.

Driving through various portions of South Louisiana in the spring, you sometimes see people wading in ditches of water near the roadside. They are *crawfishing*—capturing those tasty little lobster look-alikes. Now that commercially grown crawfish is so readily available, this practice is not as common as it once was. Crawfishing is still great sport, however, and if you feel the urge to engage in this activity (children especially find it fascinating), it's a simple matter to buy some set nets at a local hardware store. Next, find a nearby grocery store and buy some beef spleen, known as "melt." Then search out a deep ditch or swampy area. In this area of the state, you don't have to be a super sleuth to find one. Cut the meat into small pieces, and tie them to the centers of the nets. Spacing the nets several yards apart, place them in the water. After a few minutes grab a stick and start yanking the nets up, and presto!—dinner.

If you prefer someone else to snare and prepare your crawfish, head for Henderson and *Pat's Fisherman's Wharf Restaurant* (337–228–7110), located on Route 352 across the bridge at 1008 Henderson Levee Road. Request to be seated on the porch, and you can look directly down into Bayou Amy.

Restaurant owner Pat Huval helped put Henderson on the map. After buying the restaurant in 1954, he added crawfish to the menu. (At that time, restaurants seldom served crawfish.) The specialty proved so popular that it created a new industry for the town—raising, processing, and selling crawfish.

Here is the place to sample Hank Williams's famed "jambalaya, crawfish pie, and filet gumbo," while a Cajun band provides listening entertainment. Be sure you're hungry because the meal starts with a salad and a cup of delicious gumbo (probably the state's most famous dish and often served with a dollop of rice). When my husband and I visited, the waitress brought gumbo for us, and she gave me some rice but left none for my husband. Returning momentarily, she set down a bowl of rice, saying, "Here is for Papou" (*pa-POO*).

Afterward, a large platter (garnished with two bright red crawfishlike miniature lobsters in armor) containing crawfish étouffée, fried crawfish, *boulette* (a fried crawfish meatball), and hush puppies, arrives.

If you don't want crawfish for dinner, a delicious alternative is Pat Huval's seafood platter, a house specialty featuring a green salad, seafood gumbo, fried shrimp, oysters, catfish, french fries, and hush puppies. "Our food is so fresh," says Huval, "the catfish slept in the river last night." The restaurant is noted for its dirty rice (so called because it's cooked with chopped chicken giblets—not dropped on the floor). In season you can also order turtle soup. Rates are moderate. The restaurant is open daily from 11:00 A.M. until 10:00 P.M., until 11:00 P.M. on Friday and Saturday.

For your excursion into the Atchafalaya, you can catch a boat tour at *McGee's Landing* (337–228–2384). To get there head for 1337 Henderson Levee Road and turn left at the fourth exit. Just past Whiskey River landing, you'll see McGee's.

The ninety-minute tour takes you into a different world—a jungle of plants such as wild hibiscus, lotus, and elephant ears. Lots of trees also grow here—cypress, hackberry, willow, and oak, to name a few. The swamp serves as home to alligators, nutrias, muskrats, minks, opossums, otters, ducks, turkeys, wading birds, and other wildlife. You'll glide under the Swampland Expressway, the 18-mile span on Interstate 10, which opened up Cajun Country to the rest of the world. Building this bridge, once considered impossible because of the basin's boggy bottom, required considerable engineering ingenuity. If you encounter fog when driving on this stretch of interstate over the swamp, please exercise extreme caution. Heavy mists come with the terrain, and being suspended over a swamp magnifies the hazard. Tours are offered daily, starting at 8:00 A.M. If you arrive before or after a tour in progress, you can grab a sandwich or snack at McGee's Deli; hours are 11:00 A.M. to 5:00 P.M.

From here head south toward St. Martinville. You can either return to Breaux Bridge by way of Route 347, which continues to St. Martinville, or follow Route 31 south from Breaux Bridge. Another option is Route 96, an off-the-beaten-path road by way of Catahoula.

On the outskirts of St. Martinville in a serene park setting at 1200 North Main Street, you'll find the *Longfellow-Evangeline State Historic Site*

(337–394–3754 or 888–677–2900) on the banks of Bayou Teche. (The word *teche,* pronounced "tesh," comes from a Native American word meaning "snake" and refers to the bayou's serpentine path.)

This large complex offers facilities for picnicking. The park's main thrust, however, is to preserve and interpret the history of its early French settlers. Many Acadians who were forced by Britain to leave their Canadian "Acadie" in 1755 later made their way to South Louisiana. Henry Wadsworth Longfellow's epic poem *Evangeline,* the symbol of all Acadiana, tells the story of their long struggle to find a new home.

On the **Olivier Plantation,** an 1815 Creole raised cottage serves as the park's focal point and contains furnishings typical of that period. This plantation house and its detached kitchen and herb garden, in a setting of ancient live oaks for which Cajun country is famous, present a living history lesson. At the working livestock barn, youngsters are invited to participate in animal-feeding sessions. Stop by the visitor center for a look at the variety of exhibits related to early Acadian and Creole lifestyles. Except for Thanksgiving, Christmas, and New Year's Day, the park is open daily from 9:00 A.M. to 5:00 P.M. Admission is modest.

Continue to the charming downtown area of "Le Petit Paris," as St. Martinville was once known. The town became a haven for aristocrats escaping the French Revolution's horrors during "the worst of times." Slave rebellions in the Caribbean sent other French planters here, and French Creoles from New Orleans joined them. With a patrician population prone to staging courtly ceremonies, elaborate balls, concerts, and operas, St. Martinville developed into a cultural mecca.

The mother church of the Acadians occupies a place of prominence on the **St. Martin de Tours Church Square.** Dating from 1832, the current structure contains some original sections from its 1765 predecessor—an altar, box pews, and a chapel. Inside St. Martin de Tours Catholic Church are a silver and gold sanctuary light and carved marble baptismal font, said to be gifts from Louis XVI and Marie Antoinette. Somewhat to the side and rear of the church, you'll see a statue of Evangeline, for which actress Dolores del Rio posed when she portrayed the heroine in an early movie filmed here. Movie cast members later presented the bronze monument to the townspeople.

Le Petit Paris Museum (337–394–7334), constructed in 1861, stands on the right side of the church and contains local arts and crafts, colorful carnival costumes, Mardi Gras memorabilia, and a gift shop. Except for major holidays, the museum is open daily from 9:30 A.M. to 4:30 P.M.

Take the Scenic Route

*W*hile driving along Highway 90, watch for the Cade/St. Martinville exit and follow Louisiana Highway 182 to enjoy a picturesque drive. Along the way you'll see an old dance hall that dates back more than forty years, now renamed The Stockyard Saloon, plus inviting golf courses. Other roadside landmarks include Bruce Foods, where authentic Cajun seasoning and food are prepared for distribution, and Camp Pratt, a prisoner-of-war camp for German soldiers during World War II. Spanish Lake, a natural refuge for wildlife and waterfowl, lies adjacent to Camp Pratt. The Jean Lafitte Scenic Byway follows State Route 182 to Highway 14 in New Iberia and then continues to Holmwood.

Church Square is also the setting for the **Presbytère** (priest's home), a beautiful white-columned structure built in 1856. Restored and furnished with period antiques, the home is open for tours by appointment only.

Within easy walking distance (a block or so) from Church Square, you'll see the **Evangeline Oak** on Bayou Teche's bank. You may hear the sounds of Cajun music before you see the celebrated tree because the Romero Brothers often perform for visitors here. They "know enough songs in French to play all day long."

Like Evangeline, many Acadian refugees in pursuit of their dreams stepped ashore at this spot. According to legend, Evangeline's boat docked under the large old tree when she arrived from Nova Scotia searching for her lover. Local lore differs from Longfellow's tale, but both stories portray the heartbreak of a forced exodus. Emmeline Labiche (Evangeline's real-life counterpart), after a ten-year search, discovered her true love, Louis Arceneaux (Gabriel in Longfellow's poem), here under the Evangeline Oak, only to learn that he had since married another. It's said that Emmeline died of a broken heart, and the nearby Evangeline shrine marks her grave. (If oak trees could talk, this one might say that another tree actually witnessed the sad scene because *which* live oak is the authentic Evangeline Oak remains a topic of debate. This massive specimen nevertheless serves as a stately symbol.)

The adjacent **Acadian Memorial** (337–394–2258) at 121 South New Market Street, St. Martinville 70582, pays tribute to the memory of individual women, men, and children who came to Louisiana during the 1760s after the harsh exile from their Canadian homeland. A mural

Marais and Platins

On the southwestern prairies of Louisiana you'll find two distinct types of ponds that are referred to by terms that are French in origin. "Marais" are irregular shaped marshy spots that fill seasonally. "Platins" are on higher ground and are circular. Both occur naturally and are useful to the region's cattle ranchers.

portrays the Acadians' arrival, and in several cases, direct descendants posed for this group portrait. A Wall of Names lists some 3,000 refugees identified using early state documents. Visitors can step out back to the garden, which features an eternal flame as its focal point and overlooks Bayou Teche. This facility also serves as a genealogy and media center and is open daily from 10:00 A.M. until 4:00 P.M.

Only a few steps from the memorial and the Evangeline Oak's spreading branches, the **Old Castillo Hotel** (337–394–4010 or 800–621–3017), now a bed-and-breakfast, beckons travelers. Located at 220 Evangeline Boulevard, the galleried two-story brick structure with French doors features large rooms furnished with antiques and reproductions. Some rooms overlook Bayou Teche and the celebrated Evangeline Oak, and others offer a view of St. Martin de Tours Church Square.

Owner Peggy Hulin encourages guests to enjoy beignets or French toast with cafe au lait prepared the traditional way but also offers full American breakfasts. Standard to moderate rates.

Also housed here, **La Place d'Evangeline Restaurant** features Cajun cuisine with French flair. The corn-and-crab bisque makes a tasty beginning for a memorable meal. Seafood dinners, especially the crab and shrimp versions, prove perennial favorites. The restaurant opens daily at 8:00 A.M. It closes at 2:00 P.M. on Sunday, at 5:00 P.M. on Monday and Tuesday, and at 9:00 P.M. the remaining days. Prices are economical to moderate. In summer the restaurant may be closed on Monday.

Novelized New Iberia

The crime novels of contemporary author James Lee Burke are often set in his hometown of New Iberia. Burke's novels accurately capture the town and its people but are very violent in nature. Burke is a lyrical writer nonetheless. Try Sunset Limited *for a sample of his work.*

"I was born and raised here, and this is all part of me," says Peggy, who provides information on walking tours and tips on local attractions. "I dedicate myself to this and even though I can't travel the world, I welcome travelers from everywhere to my door and learn from them."

After exploring "Evangeline country," follow Route 31 south toward New Iberia, into Vermilion Parish. To see why Vermilion Parish has been called the most "Cajun place" on earth, head southwest on State Route 14 to **Delcambre Shrimp Boat Landing.** Known as the Shrimp Capital of

Louisiana, the picturesque Acadian town of Delcambre stands with one foot in Vermilion Parish and the other in Iberia Parish.

At the fisherman's wharf you can hear Cajun French spoken and watch the day's catch being unloaded. You can also buy shrimp—fresh, frozen, cleaned, or the do-it-yourself kind—at any of the several seafood shops here and indulge in a shrimp feast at the covered picnic area nearby.

In August Delcambre hosts a four-day shrimp festival, which includes a blessing of the fleet. During shrimping season, generally from April through June and again from August through October, you'll see shrimp boats departing from Delcambre on their way to Vermilion Bay or the Gulf of Mexico. After harvesting their bounty the shrimp trawlers return to home port, their hulls filled with iced-down shrimp to be sorted, packed, and frozen. From this small inland port, millions of pounds of shrimp are shipped annually to both American and international markets.

Afterward, continue west to nearby Erath, a sleepy French village and home of the **Acadian Museum,** also known as Musée Acadien (337–937–5468). "Probably more French is still spoken in business and on the streets of Erath than anywhere in South Louisiana," says attorney Warren Perrin, who founded the museum and maintains an office here. Housed at 203 South Broadway in the "Old Bank of Erath," exhibits offer both French and English interpretations and focus on the Prairie Bayou Acadians.

Look around You . . .

*E*nglish architect Christopher Wren's burial marker in St. Paul's Church advises those who seek a monument to "look around you." Likewise, visitors to Abbeville can look around them for "monuments" to the work of contemporary Louisiana architect A. Hays Town.

Town, who has achieved fame for his architectural restorations, began his work here in Southwest Louisiana.

For instance, St. Marie Madeleine's Church is a restoration for which Town can claim credit. Among the thousands of homes he has restored,

you'll find some along the river here in Abbeville.

Hays Town works to achieve the look of Louisiana's heritage in his restorations: warm brick, aged wood, pleasant vistas, gentle living spaces. He does so by using recycled building components: wood, shutters, doors, windows, and bricks. Town's patrons collect these items themselves, and it can take years to gather enough for a single home.

So anyone with a Hays Town house has personally put in long hours of effort to assist Town in achieving the level of perfection you'll see in Abbeville.

Here Comes the . . .

Daytime weddings in Abbeville at St. Marie Madeleine's Church provide a spectacular entrance for the bride. As the last of the wedding party, the bride and her father come in from outside the church, with the door being held open so that light streams into the dim interior and forms a halo around her.

At the wedding reception (perhaps just down the street at **Magdalen Place,** *a recently restored building on the town square) you'll witness an old Cajun custom as the occasional guest pins money to the bride's veil for the privilege of a dance.*

Some 2,000 artifacts, books, drawings, photos, maps, and models pertaining to Cajun culture back to the Acadian expulsion from Nova Scotia fill three rooms. Open Monday through Friday, the museum's hours are 1:00 to 4:00 P.M. Admission is free.

Don't miss **Abbeville,** Vermilion's parish seat. This charming French-flavored town, which served as the setting for several movies, lies west of Erath on Route 14. You'll find the beautiful Mary Magdalen Church built in 1910, lovely homes, and outstanding eateries like **Black's Oyster Bar** at 319 Père-Megret and **Dupuy's Oyster Shop** at 108 South Main; both specialize in fresh shellfish.

The town is also home to the **Abbey Players,** a local theater group that, in the words of resident Gerard Sellers, a documentary filmmaker, location scout, and performer himself, has a reputation for presenting polished performances and producing professional actors. You'll find the **Abbey Theater,** which is on the National Register of Historic Places, at the corner of Lafayette and State Streets. For information on performances, call (337) 898–4264, the Abbeville Tourist Center, or (337) 893–2442.

Steen's Syrup Mill, located at Abbeville, is one of the nation's largest open-kettle syrup mills. Here, from mid-October through December, you can smell the sweet boiling cane syrup as raw sugarcane is converted into an amber-colored substance almost as thick as taffy. For more information on the area, call the Vermilion Parish Tourist Commission at (337) 893–2491.

Abbeville also is home to the **Depot at Magdalen Place** (337–740–2112), with two restored cabooses nearby (one is wooden with a cupola, the other is steel with a bay window). You will also find a museum with local artifacts (ask about alligator products) and an assortment of regional gifts for sale. Also ask here about taking a walking tour with a local costumed tour guide—or use a handy brochure to guide yourself.

For a unique gift or souvenir from Abbeville, consider one of Kathy Richard's Swamp Ivory Creations. Kathy, nicknamed "the head hunter," collects about 500 alligator skulls a year from a local processing plant and spreads them outside her studio to season. She later turns the alligator teeth into striking jewelry—earrings, pins, necklaces, and bolos. Nearby, Kathy's husband, Johnny, runs a saddle shop and does leathercrafting in an old livestock sale barn. To see his antique saddle collection and memorabilia or to visit Kathy's workshop, call ahead at (337) 893–5760.

Return to Delcambre and take Route 675 into New Iberia, a Spanish stronghold in the midst of French territory. The town was named for Europe's Iberian Peninsula.

Don't miss *Shadows-on-the-Teche* (337–369–6446 or 877–200–4924), a white-pillared plantation house located at 317 East Main Street. Visitors park along a well-traveled street in front of the mansion. Once on the lovely grounds, however, one forgets traffic and other modern distractions. Statuary, camellias, wisteria, magnolia trees, and magnificent live oaks festooned with Spanish moss form a serene backdrop for Shadows-on-the-Teche. The mansion's name was inspired by the interplay of lights and darks across the lawn, created by sunlight filtering through the trees.

Built in 1834 for sugar planter David Weeks, the manor house stands on Bayou Teche's bank. (You don't see the bayou until you step into the backyard.) Slaves collected mud from the bayou's banks to make the house's coral-colored bricks. All the Shadows' main rooms open onto galleries, and there is no central hall. An exterior flight of stairs in front of the house, concealed by a lattice, leads to the second floor.

When William Weeks Hall (the original owner's great-grandson) took over the mansion during the early 1920s, he found it in an advanced state of deterioration. An artist, Hall lived in Paris before relocating to New Iberia to accept his lifetime challenge of restoring the Shadows to its former grandeur. Throwing himself into the restoration project, he also threw open his doors to extend Southern hospitality to such celebrities as Mae West, Henry Miller, W. C. Fields, and H. L. Mencken. In the pantry you'll see a door covered with signatures scribbled by Hall's houseguests—Cecil B. DeMille, Arleigh Burke, Tex Ritter, Walt Disney (along with his alter ego, Mickey Mouse), and others. Hall's friends referred to him as "the last of the Southern gentlemen."

Hall, who died in 1958, willed Shadows-on-the-Teche to the National Trust for Historic Preservation. When researchers discovered the mansion's original inventory of furnishings filed in an adjoining parish, they used it as a mandate to furnish the house as authentically as possible. The mansion's accessories include everything from indigo-dyed trousers and pier tables to finger bowls and foot warmers.

Except Thanksgiving, Christmas Eve, Christmas Day, and New Year's Day, the mansion is open daily from 9:00 A.M. until 4:30 P.M. Admission is charged.

Directly across the street at 314 East Main, you'll see the lovely flower-filled gardens of *leRosier Country Inn Bed & Breakfast* (337–367–5306). Mary Beth and Hallman Woods restored an 1870 home to house leRosier's restaurant, and behind it replicated an Acadian raised cottage for guests. They furnished the inn with antiques and floral prints, which echo the place's name. A vintage rosebush that refused to die—even when covered by the iron fence's concrete foundation—inspired the inn's name. That former lone survivor now keeps company with many varieties of antique roses.

Hallman, who has been an avid cook and "chef" for thirty years, handles the duties of kitchen master on Friday and Saturday evenings for inn guests and the lucky few who secure dinner reservations. (No reservations are needed for lunch, Tuesday through Friday.) The dinner menu, a culinary tour de force, might include crawfish spring rolls, award-winning grilled duck with wild rice/tasso dressing, or tasty spring lamb. Each presentation is personally prepared by the chef. Check out www.lerosier.com for more information. Both lodging rates and restaurant prices fall in the moderate range.

Take an after-dinner stroll to the nearby *Iberia Savings Bank* and see the spotlighted statue of Hadrian, the only full-length rendering that dates from the Roman emperor's lifetime. (Someone at leRosier will point you in the right direction.) Created by an unknown Roman sculptor around A.D. 130, the statue of white marble stands 7 feet tall and weighs about 3,000 pounds. After departing Italy, the statue commanded a post at an English castle prior to its arrival in New Iberia.

During your visit, plan to stop by *Lagniappe Too Cafe* (337–365–9419) for lunch. Located nearby at 204 East Main Street, this delightful little restaurant lives up to its name. *Lagniappe* translates to "a little something extra," which is exactly what you get at this eatery, owned by Elaine and Al Landry.

No matter which entree you select, you can't go wrong. I had the mirliton (a type of tropical squash) stuffed with shrimp and beef, and it was delicious. There's also an eggplant version; each comes with a salad, vegetables, and special Lagniappe bread rounds. Another popular item is the shrimp and avocado salad. Don't forgo dessert here. If you miss Tante Mouth's W. B. ("World's Best") Bread Pudding with hot rum sauce, you'll leave hating yourself. Al's original art, a feast for your eyes, lines the walls. Some works are serious and others whimsical.

Lagniappe Too serves lunch Monday through Friday and is open from 10:00 A.M. until 2:00 P.M. The cafe also serves dinner on Friday and Saturday from 6:00 to 9:00 P.M.

The *Estorge-Norton House* (337–365–7603), a charming three-story structure of cypress that dates from about 1912, offers bed-and-breakfast accommodations. Located at 446 East Main Street in the heart of New Iberia's historic district, the home makes an ideal place to headquarter while taking in the local attractions, which should definitely include a walking tour of the historic district.

On the second floor a variety of accommodations is offered. An apartment on the third floor sleeps four and offers a kitchen and private bath. Guests can enjoy a full breakfast in the sunroom, kitchen, or dining room. Standard rates. For more information, visit www.bbhost. com/estorgenortonhouse.

At 309 Ann Street, you'll find the *Konriko Rice Mill and Company Store* (337–364–7242 or 800–551–3245), offering tasty treats and another interesting tour. Sip a cup of coffee while you watch a twenty-minute slide presentation on Cajun culture and the history of rice harvesting and milling. Afterward you can tour America's oldest working rice mill and browse in the Konriko Company Store (a replica of an actual company store). You might be given a rice cake to munch on and a sample of artichoke rice or other Konriko specialty. The store, which carries local foods, craft items, and gifts, is open Monday through Saturday from 9:00 A.M. until 5:00 P.M. Modest tour charge.

From New Iberia it's only about 6 miles south on Route 329 to *Avery Island* (800–634–9599). Chances are your kitchen cabinet already contains the island's famous export, Tabasco sauce. The red sauce comes in a small bottle for a very good reason: It is meant to be used sparingly, unless Cajun blood runs in your veins.

Not only is the sauce hot, but so is the temperature (most of the time) on this lush island, the home of the *McIlhenny Tabasco Factory.* An introductory movie explains how Tabasco peppers are grown, aged, and made into the fiery sauce. The peppers are pulverized, put into oak barrels, and covered with a thick layer of salt (which is mined in tunnels beneath the island's surface) for three years of fermentation. You can observe the bottling process from behind a glass window. You'll also receive a miniature bottle (the ⅛-ounce size is in such demand by airlines and restaurants that orders cannot be filled fast enough) of the celebrated hot pepper sauce to take back home. Hours are 9:00 A.M. to 4:00 P.M. daily. Free admission. Afterward, stop by the Tabasco Country Store. Tap into www.tabasco.com for some great recipes, history, or a shopping spree.

While here, take time to explore the island's 250-acre bird and animal sanctuary, *Jungle Gardens* (either by car or on foot). If you packed a lunch, head for the picnic tables under massive bearded live oak trees. You'll be entertained by prancing peacocks and nesting egrets against a backdrop of exotic vegetation from all over the world. Wasi orange trees, Chinese bamboo, South American papaya trees, and Egyptian papyrus all grow here as well as a profusion of other trees, shrubs, and blooming plants. Don't miss the ancient statue of Buddha, originally commissioned for a Chinese temple, sitting atop a lotus throne in a glass pagoda overlooking a lagoon.

Another must in this wildlife paradise is *Bird City,* one of the country's largest egret rookeries. During the latter part of the nineteenth century when the great demand for feathers to adorn women's hats almost led to the egret's extinction, conservationist Edward Avery McIlhenny (son of Tabasco's creator, Edmund McIlhenny) caught seven young egrets and raised them in a flying cage that he built on the island. The snowy egrets were later released to fly south for the winter, but they returned to Avery Island the next spring. Their descendants continue the practice—to the tune of some 20,000 birds each year.

Proceed on your safari with caution. Alligators slither all around. (How close they get is up to you.) They love to be tossed marshmallows (a practice frowned on by the management). To alligators, marshmallows look like egret eggs, and they gobble up both with gusto. Jungle Gardens (337–369–6243) can be visited seven days a week; hours are from 8:00 A.M. to 5:00 P.M. Admission is charged.

While in this area, consider a visit to *Franklin.* A lovely town founded in 1808, Franklin features several plantation homes as well as the nearby *Chitimacha Tribal Museum* (337–923–4830) in Charenton. Admission is free.

Settled mainly by the English, the town (said to be the only one in the state that sided with the North during the Civil War) was named for Benjamin Franklin.

Located at 3296 East Oaklawn Drive, off Irish Bend Road, *Oaklawn Manor* (337–828–0434) makes an interesting stop. The home was built in 1837 by Judge Alexander Porter, an Irish merchant who founded the state's Whig Party and also served as a United States senator.

Once the center of a large sugar plantation, the three-story Greek Revival house, which faces Bayou Teche, is splendidly furnished and contains many European antiques and extensive collections of Audubon prints and hand-carved game birds of Louisiana. The house's bricks were made from clay on the premises. Magnificent live oaks and lovely gardens provide a perfect setting for the mansion, now owned by Louisiana governor Mike Foster.

"We have oak trees that were here when Columbus discovered America," says guide Mamie Broussard. An aviary, a gift from Warner Brothers following the filming of a movie here, is home to an assortment of birds, including fifteen parrots. Be sure to visit the mansion's original milk and butter house on the grounds.

Except for major holidays, Oaklawn is open daily (even on Monday, when many area plantations close) from 10:00 A.M. until 4:00 P.M. Admission is charged.

Continuing south on U.S. Highway 90 takes you to Morgan City, a commercial fishing center and home of the *Louisiana Shrimp & Petroleum Festival.* Now nearing its seventh decade, this annual Labor Day weekend celebration features a Blessing of the Fleet ceremony on Berwick Bay and a water parade of shrimp boats, pleasure craft, and the king's and queen's big vessels. With much music and merriment, the boats bearing royalty meet and greet in a bow-to-bow "kiss" (a feat requiring skillful navigation), and the king and queen lean forward from their respective decks for the traditional champagne toast. Along with shrimp eating, other events include a Cajun cook-off, a gala street parade, fireworks, arts and crafts, and children's activities. In the downtown Historic District, festival-goers can enjoy music under the oaks at *Lawrence Park.*

Before leaving Morgan City, consider taking a guided walking tour through the *Original Swamp Gardens* (985–384–3343) at 725 Myrtle Street, Morgan City 70380, and visiting a cypress home called *Turn of the Century House and Mardi Gras Museum* (985–380–4651) at 715 Second Street, Morgan City 70380. Tours take place Tuesday through Saturday from 10:00 A.M. to 4:30 P.M. and Sunday from 1:00 to 5:00 P.M.

About 3 miles north of town on Route 70 at Lake Palourde, you'll find *Brownell Memorial Park* (985–384–2283), a pleasant place to take a driving break. The Brownell Carillon Tower houses sixty-one bronze bells, which chime on the hour and half hour. The park offers picnicking facilities and is open daily from 9:00 A.M. to 5:00 P.M. Admission is free.

If you continue traveling southeast on U.S. Highway 90, you'll arrive in Houma, a perfect place to begin exploring the toe portion of Louisiana's boot.

PLACES TO STAY IN SOUTHWEST LOUISIANA

IMPERIAL CALCASIEU
Best Western Richmond Suites Hotel,
2600 Moeling Street,
Lake Charles,
(337) 433–5213 or
(800) 643–2582.

Hampton Inn Sulphur,
210 Henning Drive,
Sulphur,
(337) 527–0000 or
(800) 426–7866.

Inn on the Bayou,
1101 West Prien Lake Road,
Lake Charles,
(337) 474–5151 or
(800) 642–2968.

Travel Inn Motor Hotel,
1212 North Lakeshore Drive,
Lake Charles,
(337) 433–9461 or
(888) 436–2580.

CAJUN COUNTRY
Best Western of Crowley,
9571 Egan Highway,
Crowley,
(337) 783–2378 or
(800) 940–0003.

Best Western
Hotel Acadiana,
1801 West Pinhook Road,
Lafayette,
(337) 233–8120 or
(800) 874–4664.

Chrétien Point Plantation,
665 Chrétien Point Road, Sunset,
(337) 662–5876,
(337) 233–7050, or
(800) 880–7050.

Comfort Inn Opelousas,
4165 I–49 South Service Road,
Opelousas,
(337) 948–9500 or
(800) 228–5151.

Days Inn Lafayette,
1620 North University,
Lafayette,
(337) 237–8880 or
(800) 329–7466.

Estorge-Norton House,
446 East Main Street,
New Iberia,
(337) 365–7603.

Hilton Lafayette,
1521 West Pinhook Road,
Lafayette,
(337) 235–6111 or
(800) 33–CAJUN.

Holiday Inn Holidome,
2032 N. E. Evangeline Thruway, Lafayette,
(337) 233–6815 or
(800) 942–4868.

La Quinta Inn,
2100 Northeast Evangeline Thruway, Lafayette,
(337) 233–5610 or
(800) 531–5900.

LeRosier Country Inn Bed & Breakfast,
314 East Main Street,
New Iberia,
(337) 367–5306.

Old Castillo Hotel,
220 Evangeline Boulevard,
St. Martinville,
(337) 394–4010 or
(800) 621–3017.

Seale Guesthouse,
123 Seale Lane,
Eunice,
(337) 457–3753.

PLACES TO EAT IN SOUTHWEST LOUISIANA

IMPERIAL CALCASIEU
Boudin King,
906 West Division Street,
Jennings,
(337) 824–6593.

Steamboat Bill's,
Broad and Highway 14,
Lake Charles,
(337) 494–1700.

For More Information

Acadia Parish Convention and Visitors Commission
401 Tower Road, Crowley 70526; (337) 783-2108

Allen Parish Tourist Commission
8904 Highway 165, Oberlin 70655; (337) 639-4868 or (888) 639-4868

Beauregard Parish Tourist Commission
Box 1174, DeRidder 70634
(800) 738-5534

Breaux Bridge Bayou Teche Visitor Center
314 East Bridge Street, Breaux Bridge 70517; (337) 332-8500

Cajun Coast Visitors & Convention Bureau
112 Main Street, Patterson 70392; (800) 256-2931

Cameron Parish Tourist Commission
P.O. Box 388, Cameron 70631; (337) 775-5222

Iberia Parish Convention & Visitors Bureau
2704 Highway 14, New Iberia 70560; (337) 365-1540 or (888) 9-IBERIA
www.iberiaparish.com

Jefferson Davis Parish Tourist Commission
Louisiana Oil and Gas Park, P.O. Box 1207, Jennings 70546; (800) 264-5521

Lafayette Convention and Visitors Commission
P.O. Box 52066, Lafayette 70505; (800) 543-5340

Southwest Louisiana Lake Charles Convention and Visitors Bureau
1211 North Lakeshore Drive, Lake Charles; 70601; (800) 456-7952

St. Landry Parish Tourist Commission
131 West Bellevue Street, Opelousas 70570; (337) 948-8004
or (877) 948-8004

St. Martinville Parish Tourist Information Center
215 Evangeline Boulevard, St. Martinville 70582; (337) 394-2233

Area newspapers include the *Daily Advertiser* and *Times of Acadiana* in Lafayette. Both will have entertainment listings. The weekly *Times of Acadiana* will be trendier and also covers Cajun music venues well. Other local newspapers are the *Lake Charles American Press* in Lake Charles (which has a very good Web site: www.americanpress.com), the *Breaux Bridge Banner* in Breaux Bridge, the *Cameron Parish Pilot* in Cameron, the *Crowley Post Signal* in Crowley, and the *Daily World* in Opelousas.

Put your radio on in Cajun country—in Ville Platte you can catch the music show from Fred's on Saturday morning from 9:00 to 11:00 on KVPI at 1250 AM. KRVS at 88.7 FM in Lafayette will have Cajun music on the early show every morning and zydeco on Sunday. You will also hear newscasts in French on AM stations throughout the area from time to time. Also, if you want to really hear the local accent, just listen to the TV spots in Lafayette.

CAJUN COUNTRY
Black's Oyster Bar,
319 Père-Megret,
Abbeville,
(337) 893–4266.

Cafe des Amis,
140 East Bridge Street,
Breaux Bridge,
(337) 332–5273.

Cafe Vermilionville,
1304 West Pinhook Road,
Lafayette,
(337) 237–0100.

Charley G's,
3809 Ambassador Caffery
Parkway, Lafayette,
(337) 981–0108.

Chef Roy's Frog City Cafe,
1131 Church Point
Highway,
Rayne,
(337) 334–7913.

Don's Seafood and
Steak House,
301 East Vermilion Street,
Lafayette,
(337) 235–3551.

Dupuy's Oyster Shop,
108 South Main,
Abbeville,
(337) 893–2336.

Evangeline Seafood
and Steakhouse,
Southeast Evangeline
Thruway, Lafayette,
(337) 233–2658.

Judice Inn Restaurant,
3134 Johnston Street,
Lafayette,
(337) 984–5614.

Jungle Club,
1636 West Main Street,
Ville Platte,
(337) 363–9103.

LaFonda Restaurant,
3809 Johnston Street,
Lafayette,
(337) 984–5630.

Lagniappe Too Cafe,
204 East Main Street,
New Iberia,
(337) 365–9419.

La Place d'Evangeline
Restaurant,
220 Evangeline Boulevard,
St. Martinville,
(337) 394–4010 or
(800) 621–3017.

Mulate's Cajun Restaurant,
325 Mills Avenue,
Breaux Bridge,
(337) 332–4648 or
(800) 422–2586.

Palace Cafe,
135 West Landry Street,
Opelousas,
(337) 942–2142.

Pat's Fisherman's Wharf
Restaurant,
1008 Henderson Levee
Road,
Henderson,
(337) 228–7110.

Prejean's Restaurant,
3480 U.S. Highway 167
North,
Lafayette,
(337) 896–3247.

Randol's Restaurant and
Cajun Dancehall,
2320 Kaliste Saloon Road,
Lafayette,
(800) YO–CAJUN.

Rice Palace,
2015 North
Cherokee Drive,
Crowley,
(337) 783–3001.

Steamboat Warehouse,
525 Main Street,
Washington,
(337) 826–7227.

Southeast Louisiana

Southeast Louisiana—the toe of the boot—has incredibly diverse landscapes to charm any traveler. And there have been many visitors, from the early Europeans who marveled at the almost bank-to-bank alligators in the rivers to the stars of the 1967 film *Easy Rider* on their high-flying quest for the perfect Mardi Gras.

North of Lake Pontchartrain lie the piney Florida Parishes, where local heritage is more likely English than French. This area was not part of the 1803 Louisiana Purchase but was a section of Spanish, then English, west Florida, hence the name.

Plantation homes can be found along the River Road between New Orleans and the Feliciana Parishes (the "happy land" of the painter John James Audubon) east of the capital city Baton Rouge, itself a town of great charm.

The heart of Southeast Louisiana is, of course, New Orleans. The Crescent City, founded on a "beautiful crescent" of the river by French Canadians in 1718, is cosmopolitan, hard-edged urban, and utterly bewitching.

The area below New Orleans is marked by waterways, fishing and shrimping industries, and the oil business—and small communities known for fun-filled festivals and good times.

Swampland

Entering Terrebonne (*TER-a-bone*) Parish from the west, take State Route 182 to reach Houma (*HOME-uh*). Between Morgan City and Houma, this road follows Bayou Black. Driving along, you'll notice portions of the dark water covered by a bright green film. This substance, known as duckweed, may look like slime to you, but to ducks, it's dinner. A close examination of the plant reveals a mass of tiny four-petaled flowers. One of the world's smallest flowering plants, duckweed makes a tasty salad for ducks and geese.

Because of its many waterways, Houma is sometimes called the Venice

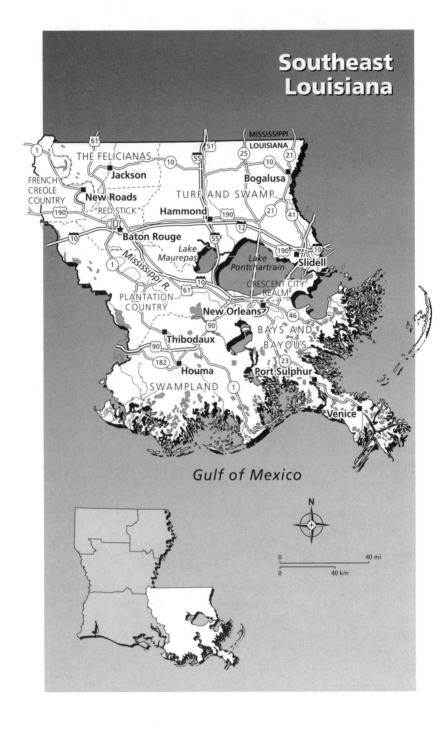

Southeast Louisiana

THE FELICIANAS

Jackson

Bogalusa

FRENCH CREOLE COUNTRY

New Roads

TURF AND SWAMP

"RED STICK"

Hammond

Baton Rouge

Lake Maurepas

Lake Pontchartrain

Slidell

CRESCENT CITY REALM

Mississippi R.

PLANTATION COUNTRY

New Orleans

BAYS AND BAYOUS

Thibodaux

Houma

Port Sulphur

SWAMPLAND

Venice

Gulf of Mexico

MISSISSIPPI
LOUISIANA

N

0   40 mi
0   40 km

GAY'S FAVORITES IN SOUTHEAST LOUISIANA

A Cajun Man's Swamp Cruise, Houma

Feliciana Cellars Winery, Jackson

French Quarter, New Orleans

Garden District, New Orleans

Grand Isle State Park, Grand Isle

Laura, A Creole Plantation, Vacherie

Louisiana State University, Baton Rouge

Ponchatoula Country Market, Ponchatoula

Rural Life Museum and Windrush Gardens, Baton Rouge

Town of Jean Lafitte

of America. Its navigable bayous and canals serve as streets for shrimp boats and various vessels that glide by the town's backyards. The parish was established in 1834 on the banks of Bayou Terrebonne (which means "good earth"), and more than half of it is water. Houma is named for a Native American tribe that settled here during the early eighteenth century. Later Cajun settlers arrived and were joined by English, German, and Irish families.

A delightful way to acquaint yourself with the local flora and fauna is to take a swamp cruise, and the region offers several choices. For a swamp tour with a unique slant, try *A Cajun Man's Swamp Cruise* (985–868–4625), headquartered on State Route 182, about 10 miles west of Houma and 20 miles east of Morgan City.

Black Guidry, a French-speaking Cajun singer who dishes up music with his commentary and tour, serves as captain for this trek into a beguiling wilderness. "Folks, if you want to know something, ask me," he says. "If I don't know the answer, I'll tell you a lie, and you won't know the difference." It's obvious that he knows this lush area well, and he often checks his crab traps along the way. Black sometimes brings along Gatorbait, his Catahoula cur. As is characteristic of the breed, Gatorbait is a patchwork of mottled colors—almost a genetic explosion, in fact.

Black will take you through a surrealistic world of cypress trees adorned with swaying Spanish moss. You'll see elephant ears, palmettos, muscadine (wild grape) vines, and pretty purple water hyacinths (which rob the water of oxygen and are extremely difficult to control). Black will point out bulrush, which provides nesting areas for snowy egrets, black-crowned night herons, and other birds. You'll probably see cormorants, ibis, blue herons, ducks, cranes, red-tailed hawks, and perhaps bald eagles and pelicans. You may also spot nutrias (fur-bearing members of the rodent family), otters, turtles, snakes, alligators, and other creatures that populate this eerie realm.

Black's "pet" alligators recognize the sound of his boat and come when he calls (unless they're hibernating). Papa Gator, who is 14 feet long, and other members of his family may put in an appearance.

After the boat tour Black will play his guitar and sing for you. A gifted musician, he composes songs and appears on national television. Maybe he'll sing "Crawfish, Crawdads, Mudbugs, and Other Things" (from one of his albums) or a Hank Williams favorite like "Jambalaya," whose famous line "Son of a gun, we're gonna have big fun on the Bayou!" takes on added relevance in this setting.

During the musical session Black will show you his Cajun accordion made from part of a wooden chest, diaper pins, and other materials of opportunity. Cajuns are noted for their resourcefulness; they are also known for their friendliness, zest for life, strong family ties, and cooking skills. "Most Cajun men cook," says Black's wife, Sondra, "and are *good* cooks."

The swamp cruise, narrated in either French or English, takes about two hours and costs $15 per adult and $10 per child (ages three through twelve). Kids younger than three get free rides. Telephone ahead because tour times vary, and reservations are required. Click on www.cajunman.com for more background.

While in Cajun country try to take in a *fais-do-do (FAY-doe-doe)*, a sort of Acadian hoedown with lots of dancing, talk, and laughter. Ask Sondra or Black about any local shindigs that may be going on. Houma's warm and friendly folks will make you feel right at home.

If you're game for another tour, visit **Wildlife Gardens** (985–575–3676) at 5306 North Bayou Black Drive in Gibson 70356. North Bayou Black Drive runs parallel to State Route 182. Owned by Betty Provost and her son, Joseph, the preserve is populated with some 500 animals from

Getting Grounded

*I*n Southeast Louisiana there is rich powdered loess soil and some remaining mixed hardwood bottomland forest in the area just east of Baton Rouge in the Feliciana Parishes.

Just north, or east of the Mississippi River, the shallow and brackish Lake Pontchartrain is the largest of a chain of lakes leading into the Gulf of Mexico. North of Lake Pontchartrain the land rises to the sandy soil region of the piney woods.

The land along the Mississippi on the West Bank and nearing the Gulf of Mexico on the East Bank is cut by slow-flowing bayous winding through swamps and marshes. Highland occurs on natural levees along watercourses and on old shoreline ridges called cheniers for the oak trees (des chenes) growing there.

SOUTHEAST LOUISIANA

TOP ANNUAL EVENTS IN SWAMPLAND

Thibodaux Fireman's Fair,
Thibodaux, first weekend in
May. (877) 537–5800.

International Grand Isle
Tarpon Rodeo,
Grand Isle, last full weekend
in July. (985) 787–2997.

Cajun Heritage Festival,
205 West Seventy-Ninth Street,
Cut Off, second weekend in
September. (877) 537–5800.

Downtown on the Bayou,
Houma, second weekend in
October. (800) 688–2732.

French Food Festival,
307 East Fifth Street, Larose,
late October.
(985) 693–7355.

South Louisiana. The Provosts' pets range from otters, nutrias, bobcats, raccoons, and deer to ducks and black swans. The natural swamp setting in Gibson is also home to great horned owls, pheasants, exotic chickens, alligators, and alligator loggerhead turtles.

Here you can give bread to the white-tailed deer, perhaps scratch their velveteen horns, and watch their fawns being bottle-fed. Watch out for Clarence, a 90-pound alligator loggerhead turtle. The Provosts also operate an alligator farm, and visitors can touch the babies and observe the different stages of alligator growth.

On a guided tour, you'll see an authentic trapper's cabin with furnishings. A gift shop on the premises sells native crafts. Except for Sunday and major holidays, tours are given daily from 9:00 A.M. to 3:00 P.M. Admission is charged.

The Provosts also offer bed-and-breakfast. "Guests can stay in one of our four little rustic cabins nestled in the swamp," says Betty. Moderate rates.

After your encounter with the local wildlife, continue on State Route 182 east to Houma. At 809 Bayou Black Drive, you'll find one of Black Guidry's favorite hangouts, *A-Bear's Cafe* (985–872–6306). Owner Jane Hebert (pronounced *ay-bear* in this area, the cafe's name thus reflecting its ownership), assisted by family members, dishes up some good Cajun cooking here. Her hearty breakfasts, popular with the local crowd, feature homemade biscuits, eggs, grits, and a choice of sausage, ham, or bacon.

The cafe's best-selling lunch is sausage, red beans, and rice with potato salad. Another delicious entree is catfish A-Bear, a fried fillet of catfish topped with homemade crab sauce. This meal comes with a salad, gumbo, white beans, French bread, and pie. Prices are economical. The homemade lemon meringue and coconut pies made by Curly, Jane's husband, will make you forget your diet. His pecan, pumpkin, and sweet potato pies are also great hits with the restaurant's customers.

Closed on Sunday, A-Bear's Saturday hours are 11:00 A.M. to 2:00 P.M. The weekday schedule runs from 7:00 A.M. to 3:00 P.M. except on Friday when the cafe also is open from 5:30 to 9:30 P.M. for dinner and musical entertainment. People also bring their own instruments and join in the fun.

While in Houma, take time to drive along Route 311 on the city's western outskirts to see several lovely plantation homes situated along Little Bayou Black.

Stop by **Southdown Plantation House** (985–851–0154), located about 3 miles southwest of town on the corner of Route 311 and St. Charles Street at 1208 Museum Drive, Houma 70360. This grandiose pink Victorian mansion, trimmed in green, also serves as the Terrebonne Museum. Inside the twenty-one-room structure, you'll see a colorful Mardi Gras exhibit. Be sure to notice the hall doorways with inserts of stained glass in a sugarcane motif. There is also an exhibit on the Houmas Indians, with handicrafts and photographs.

Other interesting exhibits focus on local history and the state's native peoples. You'll also see a re-creation of the Washington, D.C., office of the late Allen J. Ellender from Houma, who served almost thirty-six years in the U.S. Senate. Autographed pictures of familiar political personalities line the wall. Senator Ellender's colleagues acknowledged him as the Senate's master chef, and his original gumbo recipe is still prepared in the U.S. Senate dining room. You can pick up a brochure featuring some of Senator Ellender's Creole recipes such as gumbo, shrimp Creole, jambalaya, oyster stew, and pralines.

Guided tours take about forty-five minutes, and the day's last tour starts at 3:00 P.M. Except for holidays, Southdown is open Tuesday through Saturday 10:00 A.M. to 4:00 P.M. Admission.

At this point, anglers might want to venture south on State Route 56 to

Hot Weather Tip

Keep your bathing suits and a towel in the car to be ready for a quick dip. North of Lake Pontchartrain, ice-water creeks with local swimming holes can be found— ask at a busy filling station, especially if you see inner tubes hanging around. Pushepatappa Creek, north of Bogalusa near Varnado, and Big Creek, outside Amite off Highway 16, are both local favorites. Or check out a "tubing" company—you rent a tube, float down a river, and the service picks you up. Try near Franklinton on Highway 25 from Folsom.

You might also find swimming opportunities on the beach at Grand Isle or around False River. Only swim where it is allowed—Louisiana has serious water pollution problems and you don't want to take a risk.

Feeling Crabby?

O*ne of the simplest outdoor pastimes Louisiana folks enjoy is crabbing. Any hardware store or bait shop can supply you with white twine and crab nets.*

Tie an old chicken neck (crabs like smelly food) into the center of a net and lower it into salt or brackish water from a pier. Have ready a wooden bushel basket with top to hold your scuttling crabs. A set of tongs to pick them out of the net saves fingers.

Buy some crab-boil mix (a bag of spices; Zatarain's brand is good). Boil a huge pot of water, steep the mix plus salt and lemon, and add crabs. Twenty minutes later you have a free feast (not counting your net and seasoning costs).

Cocodrie. At *Coco Marina* (985–594–6626 or 800–648–2626), about 26 miles south of Houma, Johnny Glover promises good fishing year-round at his facility on the Gulf of Mexico's fruitful fringes. Here you can charter a boat (the marina currently operates ten boats, ranging from 25 to 38 feet in size) for fishing expeditions. A day's catch might include black drum, redfish, speckled trout, sheepshead, cobia, red snapper, flounder, and mackerel. The marina has recorded daily catches of more than twenty-six different species, and a typical weekend haul might bring in a sampling of ten to fifteen species.

Celebrate your catch at the *Island Oasis Bar* while enjoying a wetlands sunset. Afterward, you can dine at the *Lighthouse Restaurant,* which offers seafood specialties. Or you can feast on your own catch in the privacy of your condo. The complex offers accommodations from motel units to studio apartments, and all buildings stand on 12- to 14-foot pilings. Except for major holidays, the marina is open daily. Rates are standard to moderate.

While in Cocodrie visit the *Louisiana University Marine Consortium* (LUMCON, 985–851–2800). This working research facility also welcomes tourists for free. You will find exhibits on the environment and some aquarium displays and, best of all, a viewing tower that lets you have a gull's-eye view of Louisiana's wetlands. The dying cypress forests were caused by saltwater intrusion from the Gulf, and you can see the straight lines of petroleum industry canals.

Afterward, return to Houma and follow Route 24 east until you reach Route 1 in Lafourche Parish. Then head south on Route 1, which runs parallel with Bayou Lafourche, known locally as the "longest street in the world." This waterway, busy with the traffic of barges, shrimp boats, and a variety of other vessels, extends to the Gulf of Mexico. A number of Cajun fishing communities line the shore.

Slow down when you reach the little town of **Golden Meadow** (actually you should slow down *before* you get here because the speed limit means what it says). Watch for a small shrimp boat, the *Petit Caporal,* moored beside Route 1. Named for Napoleon Bonaparte, the century-old boat serves as a monument to the area's shrimping industry. Driving through the area south of Golden Meadow and all the way down to the coast, you'll see a variety of birds—gulls, terns, shorebirds, and such.

Located on the Gulf of Mexico at the end of Route 1, you'll discover **Grand Isle.** A bridge links the narrow 8-mile barrier island to the mainland. You'll drive past fishing camps, homes built on tall pilings, and stretches of empty beaches. Grand Isle is noted for its excellent bird-watching, especially during spring and fall when migrating flocks follow the flyway (the migratory interstate for birds from Canada to Mexico), which crosses the island.

Grand Isle State Park (985–787–2559 or 888–787–2559), at the island's eastern tip, offers many seashore recreation opportunities such as fishing, surfing, crabbing, picnicking, and camping. A swimming beach, visitor center with observation tower, and fishing jetties also attract vacationers. Be sure to bring along your fishing gear because

For the Birds

*G*rand Isle is for the birds—at least just before and after their great migration over the Gulf of Mexico. In early spring, just after a cold snap, the trees of the island are filled with warblers and songbirds taking their ease after their long trek.

Grand Isle is also a site for the Audubon Society Christmas Bird Count, the annual census of birds that takes place all over the United States. The Grand Isle count is always high.

You can see interesting species at any time. Check out the gulls and terns

for some western strays. Keep an eye out for scissor-tailed flycatchers (that tail is remarkably long: you can't miss them). You probably won't see an albatross, but one dedicated birder did add one to his life list here.

On the Internet go to www.audubon. org, look for Louisiana in the state lists, then go to the map. You can download a map for birding on Grand Isle, showing which of the small residential streets might lead you to a good venue.

Shrimp Boats

you can catch some big fish from the park's 400-foot pier. The superb fishing brings many folks this far off the beaten path. Grand Isle is also a headquarters for charter boats and deep-sea fishing. (Both a regular and a saltwater fishing license are required if you fish in Louisiana's coastal waters.) Park hours are 7:00 A.M. to 9:00 P.M. (till 10:00 P.M. on Friday and Saturday).

You'll have to return north after you've finished fishing and sunning because Grand Isle is the end of the line.

At Golden Meadow once more, you can vary your route by switching from Route 1 to Route 308 (which also runs parallel to the waterway) on the eastern bank of Bayou Lafourche. Continue driving north toward Thibodaux (*TIB-a-doe*). Two miles before reaching Thibodaux, just off Route 308 on Route 33, you'll find ***Laurel Valley Plantation*** (504–446–7456). Dating from the 1840s, this complex is America's largest surviving sugar plantation. Head first for the General Store and Museum where you'll see a couple of locomotives, old machinery, and a pen filled with chickens, ducks, sheep, and goats. The store carries prints depicting Laurel Valley Plantation as it looked during the nineteenth century, as well as local arts and crafts. You'll also see vintage items: iron pots, churns, crocks, smoothing irons,

---

OTHER ATTRACTIONS WORTH SEEING IN SWAMPLAND

Annie Miller's Swamp Tours.
100 Alligator Lane, Houma;
(504) 879–3934. Best known locally, this
swamp tour has the usual pleasant patter,
as well as comfortable seats and alligators
who appear on cue. Kids will enjoy this.

Edward Douglass White Historic Site.
2295 St. Mary Street, Thibodaux;
(985) 447–0915. White, U. S. Supreme
Court chief justice from 1910 to 1921, was
born in this raised cottage, now maintained
as a historic site by the state of Louisiana.

View of Grande Terre Island.
From the easternmost tip of Grand Isle you
can see across to the onetime location of U.S.
Army Fort Livingston. After Jean Lafitte
vacated his pirate lair here in 1814, the
military fortified his old camp.

Wetlands Acadian Cultural Center.
Jean Lafitte National Historical Park
and Preserve, 314 St. Mary Street,
Thibodaux; (985) 448–1375. This
multisited national park offers a glimpse
into the life of those Acadians (Louisiana
immigrants from French Canada, evicted
by the conquering English in the late
1700s) who settled along the waterways
of the state. Here they trapped, fished, and
hunted while developing their own unique
crafts. The center, which often features
local craftspeople and experts, houses a
theater for video presentations as well as
detailed displays and artifacts. This is a
good place to check up on what's happen-
ing locally: festivals, performances, even
how the fishing is.

---

farm implements, and pirogues. Laurel Valley Village consists of some
seventy weathered structures, including a manor house, school,
blacksmith shop, and barns. A cane-lined drive takes you past rows of
workers' cabins. Pick up a leaflet at the museum and go exploring on
your own. The complex closes on Monday; otherwise, hours are 10:00
A.M. to 3:00 P.M. daily.

After leaving Laurel Valley, drive on into **Thibodaux** (about five minutes
away) to see the town's fine group of Victorian homes and other interesting buildings such as the courthouse, St. Joseph's Catholic Church,
and St. John's Episcopal Church. Dating from 1844, St. John's is the oldest Episcopal church west of the Mississippi River. Nearby **Nicholls
State University** also features an interesting boat-building facility.
After touring Thibodaux take Route 308 north toward Napoleonville.

Plantation Country

About 2 miles south of Napoleonville, a town founded by a former soldier of the Little Corporal, you'll find **Madewood**
(985–369–7151 or 800–375–7151). Dating from the 1840s, this magnificent white-columned Greek Revival mansion features a huge ballroom, handsome walnut staircase, and ornate plasterwork. The home

is furnished with period antiques, fine paintings, Oriental rugs, and crystal chandeliers.

"We're the least commercial of the area plantations," says Keith Marshall, "and some of our guests have returned four and five times." He and his wife, Millie, make their lovely plantation home on Bayou Lafourche available for both day tours and overnight lodging. On the grounds you'll see an interesting old cemetery, several plantation outbuildings, and lovely landscaping complete with live oak trees and swaying Spanish moss.

Overnight guests are greeted with wine and cheese. A house tour, an elegant dinner (with candlelight and wine) followed by after-dinner coffee and brandy in the parlor, and a full plantation breakfast are included in the price of a mansion room or the nearby raised bay cottages. Rates are deluxe. With the exceptions of Thanksgiving, Christmas Day, and New Year's Day, Madewood is open daily from 10:00 A.M. to 4:00 P.M. Admission is charged.

Depending on your time frame and interests, you can travel farther east to do some plantation hopping along the **Great River Road** (actually composed of several state highways), which parallels both sides of the Mississippi River between New Orleans and Baton Rouge. Along the way you'll see lovely scenery—magnolia, oak, pecan, and willow trees and many of the South's most beautiful plantation homes. Several of the plantation homes are patterned after Greek temples and feature long oak-lined approaches. Many of these magnificent old mansions offer both tours for daytime visitors and bed-and-breakfast accommodations for overnight guests.

Among the homes you can visit along River Road are **San Francisco,** with its elaborate Steamboat Gothic design, and the impressive Greek Revival–style **Oak Alley,** with its grand canopy of live oaks.

For a rare glimpse into the past, stop by **Laura, A Creole Plantation** (225-265-7690) at 2247 Highway 18 near Vacherie 70090. Located on the west side of the Mississippi River, this multicolored manor house built in 1805 was named for Laura Lacoul, whose memoirs provide firsthand

German Coast

When Louisiana was a young French colony, it was difficult to attract settlers. Finally some German farmers were enticed and given land along the Mississippi River in the 1760s. This area became known as the German Coast. Soon the Germans intermarried with the French-Acadian exiles who arrived a bit later. That is the reason that Schexnayder is a typical "French" Louisiana name. The name Hymel (pronounced HEE-mel, or EE-mel) probably began as "Himmel." The little community of Des Allemands (usually pronounced des-AL-muns) is just inland on the West Bank of the German Coast—the name des Allemands is French for "Germans."

Laura, A Creole Plantation

accounts of a thriving, hard-driving sugar and wine importation business managed for eighty-four years by women—no languorous hours spent sipping mint juleps on Laura's verandas.

To make Laura's colorful, sometimes cruel history come alive for visitors, general manager Norman Marmillion and staff tracked down and studied some 5,000 pages of documentation from several states and as far afield as the National Archives in Paris. People find Laura captivating "not because of our ancient moss-draped oaks or a few pieces of furniture," Marmillion notes, "but because our stories transport visitors into the fascinating world of Creole Louisiana." Throughout the house and wine cellar, life-size "paper dolls" depict Laura, various family members, and servants. From baby teeth to voodoo charms, Laura's family artifacts, clothing, photo albums, business ledgers, and slave records reinforce accounts of "the good, the bad, and the ugly" shared by staff members.

Historians regard Laura as the American home of the Br'er Rabbit stories. "Here in our remaining slave quarters, the centuries-old tales of the West African folk hero [Compair Lapin] were first written down in North America, later to be translated, adapted, and become widely known as the American legend, Br'er Rabbit," Marmillion says. Slaves from Senegal brought the stories to Louisiana during the early 1700s.

Plantations in the Movies

Louisiana appears on the silver screen with great regularity. Fans of Anne Rice might recognize Destrehan Plantation as the scene for parts of the film Interview with a Vampire. *The Bette Davis–Olivia deHavilland vehicle* Hush, Hush, Sweet Charlotte *took place at Houmas House. Nearby Ashland (also called Belle Helene) was the setting for* The Beguiled *with Clint Eastwood. Oak Alley appears in* Primary Colors.

Other Attractions Worth Seeing in Plantation Country

Destrehan Plantation.
13034 River Road, Destrehan; (985) 764–9315. Built in 1787, this is a fine example of the Louisiana French Colonial–style plantation house. Careful restoration is ongoing, supported by a fall festival and other events. Besides a resident ghost, you will also find a nice museum shop for souvenirs.

Houmas House.
40136 Highway 942, Darrow; (888) 323–8314. Built in 1840, this grand plantation home boasts fourteen Doric columns. The thick-walled rear wing, attached by an enclosed carriageway, is most likely of early construction. With its spacious rooms and comfortable antiques, this is the plantation most appealing to contemporary tastes in interior design.

River Road.
From Houmas House, ride up the River Road to view Bocage Plantation (in 2 miles), Hermitage Plantation (3 miles), and Belle Helene or Ashland Plantation (7.5 miles). You can actually get to Baton Rouge (37 more miles) by taking the River Road (part of the way is gravel). You eventually get to the campus of LSU, and you will pass through the community of Carville, which at one time housed the American treatment center for Hansen's disease (leprosy). Carville is named for the family of James Carville, outspoken political operative.

Sunshine Bridge.
Donaldsonville. The Sunshine Bridge over the Mississippi River commemorates the song written by Louisiana governor Jimmie Davis, "You are My Sunshine." Davis was a prolific songwriter and performer, also penning such favorites as "That Silver Haired Daddy of Mine," but "Sunshine" was his greatest hit.

Texcuco Plantation.
3138 Highway 44, Darrow; (225) 562–3929. The main house recently burned, but outbuildings and bed-and-breakfast cottages remain. There is also the River Road African-American Gallery and Museum, featuring exhibits concerning life of the plantation workers and their culture, plus African and African-American art.

Except for major holidays, Laura is open daily from 9:00 A.M. to 5:00 P.M. The day's first tour starts at 9:30 A.M. and the last one at 4:00 P.M. Pay a virtual visit to www.lauraplantation.com. Admission is charged.

From Laura, follow the River Road (Highway 18) west to Donaldsonville. First settled in 1750, this little city was a thriving port in the nineteenth century and served as the Louisiana state capital in the 1830s. Donaldsonville is now best known as the home base of Chef John Folse.

Lafitte's Landing at Bittersweet Plantation, 404 Claiborne Street, is Folse's restaurant, and his imaginative take on native Louisiana foods (and a good following from television shows and cookbooks) has made this is a popular spot for diners. Hours are 6:00 P.M. Tuesday through Saturday and 11:00 A.M. to 3:00 P.M. Sunday. This is gourmet fare, priced

Top Annual Events in Plantation Country

Gonzales Jambalaya Festival,
Gonzales, last weekend in May. (225) 647-2937 or (800) 680-3208.

Louisiana Catfish Festival,
Des Allemands, second weekend in July. (985) 758-7542.

Donaldsonville Sunshine Festival,
Louisiana Square, Donaldsonville, late October to early November. (225) 473-4814.

Destrehan Plantation Fall Festival,
13034 River Road, Destrehan, second full weekend of November. (985) 764-9315.

Festival of the Bonfires,
P.O. Box 247, Lutcher, December. (800) 367-7852.

accordingly. Call (225) 473-1232 for reservations. An added bonus: Rooms at Bittersweet Plantation are available for bed-and-breakfast.

Also in Donaldsonville check out **Russo's Custom Framing and Gallery,** Sandra Imbraguglio's emporium in an old five-and-dime. Featured is primitive painter Alvin Batiste (view his work at www.alvinbatiste.com). Hours are 8:30 A.M. to 5:00 P.M. Monday through Friday, till 3:30 P.M. on Saturday, and from 10:00 A.M. to 3:00 P.M. Sunday. **Rossi's** is at 510 Railroad Avenue. (Also on Railroad Avenue are the **Railroad Cafe** at 212 Railroad Avenue, with simple po'boys and plate lunches, and the **Grapevine Restaurant** at 211 Railroad Avenue, offering good Cajun cooking from the people who run Cafe des Amis in Breaux Bridge.)

Check out Donaldsonville's museum, the old B. Lemann department store building, and the Fort Butler historic site—a Union Army fortification where African-American soldiers served in the Civil War. You can continue following the Mississippi west toward White Castle to visit Nottoway Plantation.

Nottoway (225-545-2730) is the biggest plantation house of all. It, as well as several other great plantation homes, can be visited via steamboat on the Mississippi River. Nottoway visitors who use this mode of transportation simply walk across the levee and through the gate to the mansion's front door. If you wish to arrive in this grand manner, you have to climb aboard in New Orleans.

Nottoway, sometimes called the White Castle, is a splendid interpretation of the Italianate style. The three-story mansion with sixty-four rooms, once the centerpiece of a 7,000-acre plantation, was designed by acclaimed architect Henry Howard. Sugar baron John Hampden Randolph commissioned the house, which was completed in 1859. The 53,000-square-foot home provided plenty of space for the Randolphs' eleven children, staff, and visitors. Cornelia, one of the Randolph daughters, wrote a book about life at Nottoway entitled *The White Castle of Louisiana*. You can buy a copy at the gift shop. Nottoway is now owned by Paul Ramsay of Sydney, Australia.

Perhaps the home's ornate interior, the setting for exquisite antiques and art, is best exemplified by the grand White Ballroom. This immense room, with its white marble fireplace and Corinthian columns, is a vision in varying shades of white. With its gleaming floor (covered by three layers of white enamel), vanilla-colored walls, and lofty ceiling, this room made an elegant backdrop for both balls and weddings. Six of the Randolph daughters were married in the White Ballroom, and during the past decade some 500 weddings have also been performed here.

At Nottoway, unlike some mansions, visitors are told they may explore after the tour and go through any door that's not closed. Overnight guests are free to stroll through the mansion after hours between 5:00 and 10:00 P.M.

Dinner may be served either in Randolph Hall, an elegant restaurant on the grounds, or in the mansion's first-floor Magnolia Room (formerly a three-lane bowling alley original to the house).

Overnight guests are served sherry and nuts on arrival and receive a wake-up call on the intercom. A prebreakfast pot of coffee, juice, and tasty sweet potato muffins are delivered on a silver platter. Afterward, guests can enjoy a full plantation breakfast.

Nottoway is open daily for lunch from 11:00 A.M. until 3:00 P.M. and for dinner from 6:00 to 9:00 P.M. Nottoway closes at 3:00 P.M. on Christmas Eve and reopens on December 26. Otherwise, the mansion can be visited daily from 9:00 A.M. to 5:00 P.M. Admission is charged. Rates are moderate to deluxe. Visit the mansion via your computer at www.nottoway.com.

Political Louisiana

*T*he marble halls of the Louisiana State Capitol building (tallest in the country) have heard their share of political gossip. Political aficionados can watch the legislature in action from the galleries and, in the area near the elevators toward the rear of the main floor, speculate on whether the holes in the marble really date from the assassination of Huey Long. Long's statue stands atop his grave, just in front of the capitol. His son, former

U.S. Senator Russell Long, posed for the statue.

Also on the capitol grounds is a plaque commemorating Louisianian Zachary Taylor, who was commandant of the U.S. Army barracks here when he was named president in 1848. Supposedly, the letter telling him of his election sat at the post office for several days before Taylor paid the postage due.

LSU Sports

When the legislature is not in session, the best games in Baton Rouge are usually on the Louisiana State University campus. The Tigers field teams in every possible sport, and they do very well in most. Tiger Stadium earns its nickname "Death Valley" for the steep sides and the roaring hometown crowds. The baseball and basketball teams have gained national honors.

The Marching Tiger Band puts on spectacular halftime shows. It is said that the late governor Huey Long, who was a big LSU booster, wanted LSU to have a band big enough to spell out the full name of opponent Virginia Polytechnic Institute on the field. He got it.

When you leave Nottoway (assuming you arrived by car instead of boat), you will exit near the gift shop. To see the world's smallest church (quite a contrast to the South's largest mansion), turn left when you drive out of Nottoway's parking lot. This puts you on Route 405, also called River Road, which runs in front of the mansion and beside the levee. Proceed toward Bayou Goula and watch for the ***Chapel of the Madonna*** on the left. (My car clocked the distance at 4.3 miles.) A green sign on the road's right side announces: SMALLEST CHURCH IN THE WORLD/MADONNA CHAPEL. Unfortunately there's no place to park except on the roadside in front of the church, but at the time of my visit some members of a utility crew at work nearby assured me that this was quite all right.

You may feel a bit like Gulliver approaching a Lilliputian chapel as you open the gate of the fence surrounding this miniature church, which is about the size of a large closet. Mounted on the wall to the right of the door, you'll see a wooden box, which should contain a key to unlock the front door. If the key is not there, check the top of the door frame or ask at the house next door.

When I visited, several candles were burning, and three straight wooden chairs flanked each side of the altar. I was told that the church was built in 1890 by a devout woman to fulfill a vow she had made during her daughter's critical illness. An annual Mass is held here on August 15. You can sign a register and make a donation if you wish.

After this brief detour return to Route 1 (there's a cut-through near Bayou Goula) and head north toward Baton Rouge. A few miles north you may want to stop in downtown Plaquemine to see the locks, built in 1900, which once provided the only access to waterways west of the Mississippi. ***Plaquemine Locks*** (no longer in use) linked the navigable Bayou Plaquemine with the Mississippi River. Here you'll see the original lockhouse with exhibits on the river's traffic and history. The facility also features picnic grounds and an observation tower that affords a sweeping view of the Mississippi River. After visiting Plaquemine continue to Baton Rouge, about 15 miles north.

"Red Stick"

A ccording to legend, *Baton Rouge's* name came from a notation on a map used by French explorer Pierre le Moyne, sieur d'Iberville, and his brother, Jean Baptiste le Moyne, sieur de Bienville, who led an expedition up the Mississippi River in 1699. Iberville spotted a tall cypress pole smeared with animals' blood, which apparently marked the dividing line between the hunting grounds of the Bayou Goula and Houmas Native American tribes who shared this area. When Iberville jotted *"le bâton rouge"* (French for "red stick") on his map, little did he know that he had named what would become Louisiana's capital city.

Baton Rouge offers many attractions, but most of them hardly qualify as off the beaten path, particularly the State Capitol or a major college campus like Louisiana State University. You'll miss some unique places, however, if you bypass them. Many of the city's historic sites are clustered close to the *State Capitol,* which stands on the north side of the downtown area. You can't miss it—it's thirty-four stories high, the tallest state capitol in the United States. The observation tower on the twenty-seventh floor affords a panoramic view of the city. A special project of Governor Huey P. Long, the Capitol was completed in 1932. (Ironically, Long was later shot on the first floor of this building.)

Don't miss the *Old State Capitol,* which Mark Twain called "an atrocity on the Mississippi." Located at 100 North Boulevard in Baton Rouge, this Gothic Revival castle houses Louisiana's Center for Political and Governmental History (225–342–0500). Hours are 10:00 A.M. to 4:00 P.M. Tuesday through Saturday and noon to 4:00 P.M. Sunday. Tours take one hour and admission is charged. You may also want to visit the **U.S.S. Kidd** (225–342–1942), a World War II destroyer, located downtown on the riverfront at the foot of Government Street. Hours are 9:00 A.M. to 5:00 P.M. daily, and admission is charged.

After your downtown sight-seeing tour, head toward the city's southwestern corner for a visit to *Louisiana State University.* LSU offers interesting attractions ranging from museums and a live Bengal tiger to Indian mounds and a Greek amphitheater. You'll find the campus 1.5 miles south of downtown Baton Rouge, between Highland Road and Nicholson Drive.

Stop first at the Visitor Information Center, located on the corner of Dalrymple Drive and

Baton Rouge Stars

Joanne Woodward and critic Rex Reed both attended LSU. Filmmaker Steven Soderburgh, whose Sex, Lies and Videotape *won a Palm award at the Cannes Film Festival, was also a Baton Rougean.*

Highland Road, where you can pick up a parking permit (required Monday through Friday) and a campus map. Consider headquartering at nearby **Pleasant Hall** (225–387–0297), which offers attractive accommodations at reasonable rates. This campus hotel, also the Continuing Education Center, makes a handy base within easy walking distance of LSU attractions and several eateries. A local dining guide is available at the lobby desk.

The concierge level offers lovely suites, decorated in French Colonial style, along with complimentary continental breakfast and evening snack. Rooms and suites come with private baths, cable TV, telephones, and daily maid service plus convenient parking. Preference is given to accommodate those with business on campus.

While on campus, stop by the **LSU Faculty Club** (225–578–2356) for lunch. Located on Highland Road across from the Parade Ground, the eatery is housed in an attractive building reminiscent of a French salon. The Faculty Club offers soups, salads, and sandwiches along with seafood, chicken, beef, and pasta entrees and desserts in an attractive setting, enhanced by live piano or harp music. Popular choices include the shrimp salad, gourmet burger, or glazed crabmeat sandwich on an English muffin with cheese and fruit. The praline sundae makes a fitting finale. Serving hours are Monday through Friday from 11:30 A.M. to 1:30 P.M. Prices are economical to moderate.

Afterward you can visit Memorial Tower, built in 1923 as a monument to Louisianians who died in World War I. Housed in the tower, the **LSU Museum of Art** (225–578–4003) features a series of furnished rooms illustrating early English and American interiors. Various exhibits

Casinos

*S*ince Louisiana legalized gambling, there have been numerous gambling boats docked throughout the state. As is usual in Louisiana, the introduction of legal gambling was all very exciting, very political, and very controversial. If you like the constant electronic clamor of slot machines and you relish sitting in a room without clocks or windows, you're going to enjoy Louisiana casinos. The ones in Baton Rouge are on the Mississippi River (they are boats, but they seldom cruise) in the Catfish Town vicinity of restored, old-wharf area buildings.

Greater Baton Rouge Zoo.
Thomas Road; (225) 775–3877. Spend
a pleasant afternoon on the zoo's
walkways, then treat yourself to a
miniature train ride.

Louisiana Naval War Memorial.
305 River Road South, Baton Rouge;
(225) 342–1942. In addition to the U.S.S.
Kidd, the memorial on the riverfront
holds the largest collection of ship models
in the South. There is a replica of the gun
deck of Old Ironsides (the U.S.S. Constitution) and the pilothouse of an 1880s
steamboat, as well as a restored jet. Be
sure to take a look at the Mississippi
River while you're there.

Louisiana State Capitol grounds.
Near the capitol is a sunken rose garden.
The Pentagon Barracks, dating from
1819, once served as dormitories for LSU

students back when the school was all-
male and had a somewhat military
regimentation—one of LSU's nicknames
is "The Old War Skule." By 1906 the Pentagon housed female students and today
it holds apartments for legislators. Those
privileged to stay here can enjoy the
Christmas spectacle at the capitol with
long strings of colored lights adorning it.

Louisiana State University Campus.
Highland Road and Nicholson Drive,
Baton Rouge. The old part of the campus
invites strolling, especially in spring when
the azaleas are in bloom. This campus
has been rated one of the ten most attractive in the country, and the warm red tile
roofs and stuccoed loggias of the Italianate complex of core campus buildings
has an inviting atmosphere. The cam-
panile chimes the hours.

demonstrate England's enduring contribution to American culture. Among the museum's holdings are a number of impressive collections ranging from the seventeenth to mid-nineteenth centuries, including several etchings and engravings by English artist William Hogarth. Also housed here are the largest public collection of New Orleans–made nineteenth-century silver, a fine Newcomb crafts collection, and a comprehensive grouping of prints—dating from 1932 to 1980—by internationally acclaimed Louisiana printmaker Caroline Durieux. While on campus, inquire about current shows because the LSU Museum of Art and Hill Memorial Library sometimes sponsor joint exhibitions.

Admission to the museum is free; you can either browse on your own or take a group tour for a modest fee. Except for holidays, the museum is open from 9:00 A.M. to 4:00 P.M., Tuesday through Friday. On Saturday you can visit from 10:00 A.M. to noon and 1:00 to 4:00 P.M. Sunday hours are 1:00 to 4:00 P.M.

Afterward you can stroll to nearby Foster Hall, home of the *Museum of Natural Science,* to see dioramas depicting Louisiana's wildlife. On display are mounted specimens of birds, reptiles, and animals, including LSU's original Bengal tiger mascot. (You also can visit the current mascot,

Alligator Bayou Swamp Tours

Alligator Bayou *(225–642–8297 or 888–3–SWAMPS), a wilderness tucked away into Baton Rouge's outskirts at 35019 Alligator Bayou Road, Prairieville, offers boat excursions complete with local flora and fauna. Hours vary by season. Frank Bonifay, Jim Ragland, Shiner (the black Lab), and other animal friends will treat you to an informative session combining history and ecology sprinkled with humor. Call for information on guided swamp tours, canoe rentals, and weekend concerts. For a virtual visit, check out www.alligatorbayou.com.*

And That's Not All

Chef Michael Thomas, who dishes up his specialties for group events at Alligator Bayou, shared his mouthwatering recipe for White Chocolate Bread Pudding and White Chocolate Sauce with readers.

White Chocolate Bread Pudding

4 large eggs

1 stick butter, melted and cooled

1 1/4 cups granulated sugar

1/2 cup brown sugar, loosely packed

2 1/4 cups half-and-half

1/8 teaspoon cinnamon

1/8 teaspoon vanilla extract

8 cups stale French bread cubes

1/4 pound white chocolate, grated

Whisk eggs. Add melted butter and blend into eggs. Add sugars, half-and-half, cinnamon, and vanilla; whisk well. Add bread cubes and mix. Let stand for about one hour. Add chocolate and mix. Pour into buttered 9-by-13-inch baking pan. Bake for 40 minutes in 350°F oven. Reduce temperature to 250°F and bake for 20 minutes. Rest for 15 minutes to allow center to firm up. Pudding should be spongy to touch.

White Chocolate Sauce

1 stick butter

1/2 cup flour

2 cups half-and-half

1/3 cup spiced rum

1/2 pound powdered sugar

1/4 pound white chocolate, grated

Over a medium-low flame, melt butter. Add flour and blend well. Simmer for a couple of minutes and whisk often at reduced heat. Add 1 cup half-and-half; whisk, whisk, whisk. Add another cup of half-and-half; whisk. Add rum (or liqueur of choice) and whisk well. Add powdered sugar and blend well. Add chocolate and stir until melted. Spoon over bread pudding.

Mike IV, who resides in an environmentally controlled home outside Tiger Stadium—a nearby sign reads GEAUX TIGERS!)

Before leaving campus make a point of seeing the 3,500-seat Greek amphitheater; the avenue of stately oak trees, planted as memorials for

The Wandering River

*T*he reason there is a Pointe Coupee (or "cut point") is that the Mississippi River, in its ceaseless fight to make a beeline to the Gulf, lopped off a turn and created a lake here. Think of the river as a garden hose whipping around on the grass. The force of water is seldom a steady pulse. Also consider the varying composition of the river's bed and its banks—some areas more firm than others, with soil constantly washing away. You can then begin to understand the quandary of the U.S. Army Corps of Engineers as it tries to tame this monster.

The most important building near here is the Old River Control Structure, which keeps the Mississippi from moving into the bed of the Atchafalaya and going south to Morgan City instead of proceeding eastward toward New Orleans. In the great flood of 1927, the Atchafalaya River basin was subject to dreadful flooding from the Mississippi.

LSU alumni killed in World War II; and two intriguing Indian mounds believed to date from 3300 to 3800 B.C.

A short distance northwest of the campus, you'll find *Magnolia Mound* (225–343–4955), one of the state's oldest plantations. Located at 2161 Nicholson Drive, this 1791 home serves as a lovely example of French Creole architecture. Surrounded by a grove of live oak and magnolia trees, the house stands on a ridge facing the Mississippi levee.

Magnolia Mound, authentically restored, is made of large cypress timbers joined by wooden pegs and packed with *bousillage.* Be sure to notice the quaint iron latches and the carved woodwork. In the dining room you'll see an unusual buffet with locked wine compartments and a Napoleon mirror over the mantel. Other interesting furnishings include an overseer's desk in the plantation office, a pianoforte in the parlor, and an old rope bed. According to the museum's guide, the familiar expression "Good night; sleep tight" originated because some old-fashioned beds used rope-supported mattresses that had to be pulled taut periodically. Mattresses made with Spanish moss were used on plantation beds during summer months and were replaced by feather mattresses for winter.

On the grounds you'll see both a kitchen garden and a crop garden and several outbuildings typical of early plantation life—a detached kitchen, a *pigeonnier,* and an overseer's house.

Quilting exhibits, holiday candlelight tours, and weekly open-hearth cooking demonstrations are scheduled to acquaint visitors with the

Colonial Africans

Recent historical research has revealed that Louisiana has a rich African-connected past. Historian Gwendolyn Midlo Hall's book Africans in Colonial Louisiana *traces how, in the early years of French domination, Africans retained tribal ties, names, and language to a greater extent than realized, especially in this area. The Pointe Coupee district was headquarters for an unsuccessful revolt in 1795—organized not just by African slaves, but also by their white allies, Europeans holding the beliefs of French revolutionaries.*

lifestyle of colonial Louisiana. Magnolia Mound opens at 10:00 A.M. Tuesday through Saturday and at 1:00 P.M. on Sunday. The day's last tour starts at 3:15 P.M. The museum closes on Monday and holidays. Admission is modest.

If you want to step back into the nineteenth century, drive to the junction of Interstate 10 and Essen Lane, where you'll find the entrance to an outdoor complex called **Rural Life Museum and Windrush Gardens** (225–765–2437).

The museum's grounds occupy part of a family plantation that the late Steele Burden and his sister Ione Burden donated to Louisiana State University. The 450-acre tract serves as a setting for the museum as well as an agricultural research station.

The folk museum consists of more than twenty old buildings collected from farms and plantations throughout the state. Instead of a "big house" (most farm families could not afford extravagant residences), you'll see a brick-front overseer's cottage with a parlor, dining room, and two bedrooms. The rooms are furnished with authentic utilitarian pieces. Nearby stands a kitchen, detached from the main house because of the danger of fire.

A row of slave cabins and other rustic buildings paint a picture of austerity. In the sick house, the plantation's infirmary, you'll see rope beds, a tooth extractor (circa 1800), and a shock-treatment machine from the 1850s (which generated mild electrical charges for treating arthritis, nervous twitches, and other ailments).

You can also visit a commissary, smokehouse, schoolhouse, blacksmith's shop, gristmill, cane grinder, and sugarhouse. Other structures include a country church, pioneer's cabin, corncrib, potato house, shotgun house, Acadian house, and dogtrot house. The museum's big barn contains hundreds of items, including a voodoo exhibit, a 1905 Edison phonograph, plantation bells, bathtubs, irons, oxcarts, trade beads, an African birthing chair, and pirogues.

TOP ANNUAL EVENTS IN FRENCH CREOLE COUNTRY

July 4th Boat Parade, *New Roads, July 4. (225) 638–3500.*

Noel sur la Fausse Riviere, *New Roads, first Saturday in December. (225) 638–3500.*

Call ahead for a one- to two-hour guided tour for ten or more persons. The museum is open from 8:30 A.M. to 5:00 P.M. daily. Admission is charged.

To see an impressive collection of European antiques and architectural elements, head for **Fireside Antiques** (225–752–9565) at 14007 Perkins Road. Shop hours are Monday through Saturday from 10:00 A.M. to 5:00 P.M.

Afterward, follow U.S. Highway 190 west to Livonia and into the French Creole country of Pointe Coupee Parish.

French Creole Country

Don't miss **Joe's "Dreyfus Store" Restaurant** (225–637–2625) at 2741 Maringouin Road West (also State Route 77 south) in Livonia. Bright, noisy, and popular, this jeans-and-Keds kind of place offers creative Creole cuisine in an old general store/pharmacy. The interior features displays of old-fashioned pharmaceutical products and nostalgic items, and Cream of Wheat posters line the walls. Try the marinated crab claws or turtle soup au sherry. Other specialties include crawfish entrees (seasonal), angel hair pasta with shrimp and crabmeat, stuffed eggplant, crab and spinach au gratin, and pork loin. For dessert, order the bread pudding with rum sauce. Prices are moderate. Restaurant hours are Tuesday through Saturday from 11:00 A.M. to 2:00 P.M. and 5:00 to 9:00 P.M. (11:00 A.M. to 2:00 P.M. on Sunday).

OTHER ATTRACTIONS WORTH SEEING IN FRENCH CREOLE COUNTRY

West Baton Rouge Museum. *845 North Jefferson Avenue, Port Allen; (225) 336–2422. A plantation cabin, an 1830 French Creole cottage, and a 1904 sugar mill can all be seen and enjoyed here.*

West Baton Rouge Parish Tourist Commission Office. *2855 I–10 Frontage Road, Port Allen; (800) 654–9701. Take a break and enjoy a video and some displays on this mostly rural area across the river from Baton Rouge.*

Afterward, follow State Route 78 north until it intersects State Route 1. You'll take a left here for **New Roads,** stopping first at nearby **Parlange Plantation** (225–638–8410), on State Route 1 just north of the State Route 78 intersection. Overlooking False River, a lovely oxbow lake created when the mighty Mississippi River changed its mind, this galleried West Indies–type home built by the Marquis Vincent de Ternant dates from 1750. A National Historic Landmark (a status attained by few structures), Parlange is still a working plantation of 2,000 acres and home to descendants of the original family. On a house tour, you'll see eight generations of Parlange and Brandon family possessions, rare antique furnishings, china, and crystal.

The main salon features unusual corner-hung family portraits. The guide will tell you about one forebear, Virginie (Mme. Pierre Gautreau), who posed for John Singer Sargent's then-startling *Portrait of Madame X* now housed in New York's Metropolitan Museum of Art. A house tour includes the wine cellar, which contains wooden brick molds used in the home's construction, and *pigeonniers* flanking the entrance. Parlange is open daily by appointment from 9:30 A.M. to 4:30 P.M. Admission is charged.

Continue north to the charming town of New Roads, where you should consider making *Jubilee!* (225–638–8333) your base. Virginia and Ovide De Soto offer bed-and-breakfast with a big serving of warm hospitality in their lovely 1840 Creole cottage on three acres facing the Mississippi River. Located at 11704 Pointe Coupee Road (Highway 420) near the ferry, the home is furnished with antiques, including many unusual accessory pieces. Architectural features include walk-through windows and eight fireplaces complete with original cypress mantels.

Virginia serves a full country breakfast and will share some of the home's history with you. Ovide (a descendant of Spanish explorer Hernando de Soto) can direct you to some interesting off-the-beaten-path spots. At several nearby points, you can drive up the levee via a single-lane dirt-gravel road for a sweeping view of the river. Amenities include a pool and sometimes calliope music from passing paddle wheelers. Both private and shared baths are available, and rates are moderate.

After exploring Pointe Coupee Parish, head for the St. Francisville Ferry.

Into the Hills

*T*he soil in this region is loess—a rich but powdery mix that tends to form deep gorges. This formed the **Tunica Hills** region near Angola, where the deep ravines around Little Bayou Sara are the haunt of a large number of bird species, some of the last bottomland hardwood forest, and some buried treasure.

The treasure in question was in the form of grave goods of the Tunica-Biloxi Indian tribe. The Native American group lived in this region in the 1700s and traded extensively with the French. Their graves, with contents of precious objects, contained an assortment of French trade goods, ceramics, beads, and metal, as well as handcrafted items. Ownership of the treasures passed from the person who dug them up to Harvard University and finally to the Tunica-Biloxi tribe, who now house the collection in a museum on tribal land near Marksville.

Except for the period between midnight and 4:00 A.M., the ferry leaves twice hourly, at a quarter past and a quarter to the hour. While waiting, you'll see people standing around chatting or perhaps an enterprising youngster going from car to car selling bags of parched peanuts.

The Felicianas

*A*fter crossing the Mississippi River, follow the ferry road (State Route 10, which soon becomes Ferdinand Street) up a hill into St. Francisville, a picturesque town in a tranquil setting of live oak, magnolias, and pine trees. A fascinating place to visit, this quaint village in West Feliciana Parish retains its nineteenth-century charm. Many plantation houses, built during the early 1800s, lie tucked away in the surrounding countryside.

About a mile from the ferry, you'll see a sign for *Shadetree Inn* (225–635–6116) on your right. Perched on a hill at the corner of Ferdinand and Royal Streets, Shadetree offers bed-and-breakfast in three romantic hideaways: The Loft, Sun Porch, and Gardener's Cottage, each with its own ambience. Enticements include a treetop deck along with hammock and swings on the grounds—perfect for sipping coffee, reading, and listening to the birds (whose avian ancestors attracted John James Audubon to this area named Feliciana). A cicada chorus also provides evening music. A continental breakfast of juice, coffee, and pastries with an assortment of jams, jellies, and lemon curd awaits. Moderate to deluxe rates. Visit this retreat on-line at www.shadetreeinn.com.

Even though you'll want to linger at Shadetree, the village begs to be explored and lends itself beautifully to walking.

Clustered along Ferdinand and Royal Streets, you'll pass lovely houses, antique shops, offices, banks, and churches. The National Historic District contains 146 structures.

At 11621 Ferdinand Street, you'll see *Grace Episcopal Church,* an English Gothic–style structure surrounded by a canopy of moss-covered oak trees. Fighting came to a halt for the funeral of Union naval officer John E. Hart during the Civil War. Hart had asked for a Masonic burial, and his fellow Confederate Masons honored the deathbed request. A granite slab in the churchyard cemetery tells his story.

The *Emporium* (225–635–0113) at 11931 Ferdinand Street carries children's classic toys, framed prints, gourmet coffees and teas, and a variety of unique gift items. Except on Sunday, when hours start at noon, owner

Battle on the Bluffs

The State Historic Site at **Port Hudson,** *756 West Plains-Port Hudson Road, Zachary (225–654–3775 or 888–677–3400), marks the site of a Civil War battle, one in which African-American troops fighting in the Union Army acquitted themselves well in their first outing. Union troops besieged the Confederate defenders of the high bluffs from May until July 1863, when starvation forced them to surrender.*

The site today includes a museum, guided trails, and a picnic area. There are often reenactments with authentically clothed and outfitted soldiers of both sides.

Judy Decoteau opens daily at 10:00 A.M. and closes at 5:00 P.M.

Housed in a 1905 bank building at 9814 Royal Street, you'll find the **Grandmother's Buttons** (225–635–4107) retail shop with unique bracelets, brooches, earrings, cuff links, and watches. You can browse through the **Button Museum,** which features multitudes of intricate buttons in pearl, glass, enamel, brass, cut steel, jet lustre glass, celluloid, horn, and pewter—all with pertinent identification.

When owner Susan Davis stepped into her grandmother's sewing room one afternoon more than a decade ago, she had no notion that the buttons she saw there would change both her life and that of her husband, Donny, a former farmer and wildlife biologist. The button jewelry that Susan crafted in an upstairs bedroom blossomed from a budding supplemental income into a booming business for both of them. The couple subsequently hired a designer and production staff and started showing jewelry at major markets across the country. Prominent stores, museum shops, boutiques, and catalogs now carry the Grandmother's Buttons line nationwide.

"Our museum star is the rare George Washington inaugural button," said Susan. "We're also doing more reproductions now, like perfume buttons."

Next, continue to the **West Feliciana Historical Society Museum** (225–635–6330) at 11757 Ferdinand Street, St. Francisville 70775, for a map detailing a driving-walking tour of St. Francisville. While here take time to see the museum's dioramas, displays of vintage clothing, documents, maps, and other interesting exhibits. The museum is open from 9:00 A.M. to 5:00 P.M. Monday through Saturday. Sunday hours are 9:30 A.M. to 5:00 P.M. Admission to the museum is free.

Take a sight-seeing break by stopping for lunch at the **Magnolia Cafe** (225–635–6528), housed in a former gas station downtown at 5687 East Commerce Street. The eatery features homemade pizzas, salads, sandwiches, and Mexican entrees. Try the turkey pita with Swiss cheese, guacamole, sprouts, and tomato or the muffuletta made with

Italian bread, salami, ham, mozzarella, lettuce, and original olive oil mix. Prices are economical. The cafe opens daily until 4:00 P.M. as well as Wednesday through Sunday evenings.

Continue to the *Myrtles* (225–635–6277), an elegant home located at 7747 U.S. Highway 61, 1 mile north of Route 10. The plantation's name comes from the many crepe myrtles on the grounds. The oldest portion of the house was built around 1796 by General David Bradford, leader of the Whiskey Rebellion in Pennsylvania. Later owners enlarged the Myrtles and added wide verandas trimmed in "iron lace," one of the house's trademarks. Inside, you'll see Italian marble mantels, mirrored doorknobs, and Irish and French crystal chandeliers. The house is also noted for its elaborate interior plasterwork—and its resident ghosts.

Overnight accommodations feature beautifully furnished bedrooms and a continental breakfast. Rates are moderate to deluxe. A restaurant on the grounds offers lunch Tuesday through Sunday 11:30 A.M. to 2:00 P.M. and dinner Tuesday through Saturday 5:00 to 9:00 P.M. Except for major holidays the mansion is open for tours from 9:00 A.M. to 5:00 P.M. daily. Mystery tours are given on Friday and Saturday evenings. Admission is charged.

The State Pen

*W*ant to see an electric chair? *The Louisiana State Penitentiary Museum has one, and you can see it from 8:00 A.M. to 4:30 P.M. Monday through Friday, from 9:00 A.M. to 5:00 P.M. Saturday, and from 1:00 to 5:00 P.M. Sunday. Call (225) 655–2592 for information. The museum is located at* **Angola State Penitentiary,** *at the end of Highway 66.*

Also on view are exhibits of confiscated prisoner-made weapons, the script of the movie Dead Man Walking *(the protagonist was an Angola resident), and various guns and paraphernalia, including photos of all those who sparked a firsthand acquaintance with the seat in question. Grim but unique.*

The penitentiary hosts an interesting fund-raising event, the Prison Rodeo, held at the prison each year on a Sunday in October.

One of the best-known prisoners ever to reside at Angola was Huddie "Leadbelly" Ledbetter, twelve-string guitarist, Louisiana native, and incomparable blues artist. Leadbelly is best known for his composition "Goodnight Irene." His song was good enough to win him a reprieve from Governor O. K. Allen and get him out of Angola.

The prison newspaper, the Angolite, *often wins awards but has not won a pardon or commutation of sentence for its longtime editor, Wilbert Rideau.*

Afterward, continue to **Butler Greenwood** (225–635–6312), a plantation located 2.2 miles north of town at 8345 U.S. Highway 61. Watch for a sign on the left marking the tree-canopied drive that leads past a sunken garden and through a parklike setting. Before Hurricane Andrew blew in, says owner Anne Butler, one could not see sky through the arching live oaks—many of which grew from acorns brought from Haiti in 1799 by a planter's family.

A prolific writer whose published works span both fiction and nonfiction, Anne sandwiches in sentences between family responsibilities and guests. Her children Chase and Stewart make the eighth generation of the same family to live on this working plantation established during the 1790s.

On a tour of the English-style house, you'll see a formal Victorian parlor with a twelve-piece matched set of Louis XV rosewood furniture uphol-

A Classic Creation

*W*hen Madeline Nevill created this dish as a young bride, she did not expect it to become a classic. Appealing year-round, the recipe makes a tasty side dish for holiday feasts. In fact, the grocery stores in St. Francisville often sell out of spinach and jalapeño cheese during Thanksgiving and Christmas.

Spinach Madeleine

2 packages frozen chopped spinach

4 tablespoons butter

2 tablespoons flour

2 tablespoons chopped onion

1/2 cup evaporated milk

1/2 cup reserved vegetable liquor

1/2 teaspoon black pepper

3/4 teaspoon celery salt

3/4 teaspoon garlic salt

Salt to taste

6-ounce roll of jalapeño cheese

1 teaspoon Worcestershire sauce

Red pepper to taste

Cook spinach according to package directions. Drain and reserve liquor. Melt butter in saucepan over low heat. Add flour, stirring until blended and smooth but not brown. Add onion and cook until soft but not brown. Add liquids slowly, stirring constantly to avoid lumps. Cook until smooth and thick; continue stirring. Add seasonings then cheese, which has been cut into small pieces. Stir until melted. Combine with cooked spinach. This may be served immediately, but the flavor improves if it is put into a casserole and topped with buttered bread crumbs, then refrigerated overnight. May also be frozen. Serves 5 to 6.

stered in its original red velvet. A Brussels carpet, French pier mirrors, and floor-to-ceiling windows topped by gilt cornices echo the room's elegance. Other treasures include a Prudent Mallard bed and dresser, oil portraits, and an extensive collection of vintage clothing. House tours are offered Monday through Saturday from 9:00 A.M. to 5:00 P.M. and from 1:00 to 5:00 P.M. on Sunday. Admission.

Accommodations, which include a house tour and continental breakfast, range from the plantation's original detached kitchen of slave-made brick dating from 1796, when Spain ruled the region, and the cook's nineteenth-century cottage to several new cottages against a lovely backdrop of greenery and a pond where ducks frolic and deer come to drink. Rates are moderate to deluxe. Preview the property at www.butler greenwood.com.

For serious birders, artist-naturalist Murrell Butler offers bird and nature walks. Currently, his local checklist contains 138 species, and 78 of these nest on his property.

After leaving Butler Greenwood, continue north on U.S. Highway 61 to visit nearby *Catalpa* (225–635–3372 or 225–635–6721). The home brims over with exceptional antiques such as rosewood Mallard parlor pieces, a Pleyel piano, a Sèvres whale-oil lamp, crystal cranberry champagne glasses, antique china, porcelain, and silver. Except for December and January, Catalpa is open for tours by appointment only. Admission is charged.

Afterward, you may want to visit the *Cottage Plantation* (225–635–3674) at 10528 Cottage Lane. To reach the Cottage continue north on U.S. Highway 61. Watch for a turnoff sign on the right side of the road, then follow the narrow lane that winds through the woods. You'll cross a small wooden bridge just before you reach the plantation complex.

Definitely off the beaten path, the main house is located in an idyllic setting, thick with trees draped in Spanish moss. If you have trouble locating the Cottage, you might be interested in knowing that Andrew Jackson found it when he and his officers stayed here on their way home after the Battle of New Orleans—without today's road signs.

The 1795 galleried two-story cottage contains most of its original furniture. Outbuildings include the original detached kitchen, one-room school, smokehouse, slave cabins, and other dependencies from bygone days.

Except for holidays, the home opens daily for tours from 9:30 A.M. to 4:30 P.M. and offers bed-and-breakfast. Rates are moderate.

Afterward, return to U.S. Highway 61, turning south to St. Francisville. Watch for State Route 66 on the right, just past Afton Gardens. Turn here to visit **Green Springs Inn and Cottages** (225–635–4232 or 800–457–4978), where Madeline Nevill offers bed-and-breakfast in a lovely 1800s replica of a West Feliciana cottage at 7463 Tunica Trace. It took three years and three architects to achieve the look that prompts people to ask, "Is this a new house that looks old or an old house that looks new?" Built on Madeline's family plantation, the home stands on extensive grounds with flower gardens, woodland trails, and a 2,000-year-old Indian mound. Six cottages are also available for guests.

An avid gardener, Madeline used her love and knowledge of plants to leap from homemaker to entrepreneur with a venture called the Corporate Jungle, which proved wildly successful, just as did her original recipe for Spinach Madeleine, first published in the Baton Rouge Junior League Cookbook. Guests can anticipate a hearty plantation breakfast with homemade biscuits and sometimes the owner's famed culinary creation. Rates are moderate.

Madeline offers information on local attractions and, for interested guests, provides a map of the nearby Tunica Hills, where some of the country's most diverse forests thrive. For more background, visit www.greensprings-inn.com.

Consider wandering farther off the beaten path to **Greenwood Plantation** (225–655–4475) at 6838 Highland Road, St. Francisville 70775. Now the home of the Richard Barnes family, this replica of an 1830 Greek Revival mansion rose from its 1960 ashes to reclaim the area within its twenty-eight surviving columns. Beautifully restored to original specifications with a copper roof, period furnishings, and silver doorknobs and hinges, Greenwood Plantation served as the setting for six movies, including *North and South*. Visitors can choose from historical, agricultural, or movie tours. Admission is charged. The plantation also offers bed and breakfast. Call (225) 655–3850. Moderate rates.

Afterward, return to St. Francisville and **Rosedown Plantation and Gardens** (225–635–3332) at 12501 Highway 10, St. Francisville 70775. A live-oak avenue leads to the 1835 classic Greek Revival house set among twenty-eight acres of formal gardens. Ranked among the nation's most significant historic gardens, Rosedown showcases vintage plantings with its early varieties of azaleas, camellias, rare trees, and shrubs. Rosedown is now a Louisiana State Historic Site, and the 1835 mansion is open seven days a week, 9:00 A.M. to 5:00 P.M., for tours. Admission.

The property also offers bed-and-breakfast lodging (225–784–2337). Rates are moderate.

To learn about artist John James Audubon, visit **Oakley House** (225–635–3739 or 888–677–2838), the focal point of the **Audubon State Commemorative Area** located at 11788 Louisiana Highway 965. West Feliciana's location on the Mississippi Valley flyway lures migrating birds, and Audubon created many of his bird studies while working here as a tutor. Numerous first-edition Audubon prints line the walls at Oakley, restored as a museum with

Savvy Eating

North of Lake Pontchartrain the menus reflect Southern specialties. Look for barbecue and fried catfish and ask for sweetened iced tea.

One of the enduring restaurant phenomena in the Florida Parishes is the popularity of the all-you-can-eat catfish place. They dot the highways and all offer the same dining experience: seats at communal tables and endless trips to the buffet for an array of fried seafood, side dishes, and desserts, all served with sweet iced tea or cold drinks (beer is sometimes available).

To experience this at its apex, drive up Highway 21 north of Covington to Bush.

The House of Seafood Buffet *huddles in a gray cement-block building surrounded by a vast parking lot that quickly fills. For less than $20 you get catfish plus everything from barbecued ribs to alligator with fried okra and some boudin thrown in. Hours are 4:00 to 10:00 P.M. Thursday and Friday and 3:00 to 10:00 P.M. Saturday.*

surrounding formal gardens, nature trails, and wildlife sanctuary. Each year during the third weekend in March, St. Francisville hosts an **Audubon Pilgrimage** featuring tours of area plantation homes and gardens. Modest admission.

Afterward, follow Route 965 to **The Bluffs** on Thompson Creek (225–634–3410 or 888–634–3410) with suites within walking distance of golf, tennis, pool, and restaurant. Rates are moderate. Travelers can enjoy a casual meal in the grill or lunch or dinner featuring Louisiana and European cuisine at the Clubhouse Restaurant.

Designed by Arnold Palmer, the championship golf course continues to collect accolades. Hundreds of azaleas and native dogwoods supplement the sylvan setting and enhance sweeping swaths of greenery punctuated by high bluffs. Advance tee times are required; call (225) 634–5551.

From the Bluffs, follow State Route 10 east to Jackson, which offers a host of historical attractions and a combination winery and brewery. In a colonnaded Spanish mission-style structure at 1848 Charter Street (also State Route 10), travelers can stop by the **Feliciana Cellars Winery** (225–634–7982) for free tours and tastings. Under the direction

One Big Fair

*A*t the King Cabin a mess of greens is simmering on the back of a woodstove and a pone of corn bread is in the oven. All's fine at **Mile Branch Settlement** and the rambling community of log buildings, assembled from throughout Washington Parish. It is inhabited by folks in nineteenth-century clothes who cook, make soap, grind corn, fuss over chickens, and in general live a pioneer lifestyle for the four days (Wednesday through Saturday) of the **Washington Parish Free Fair,** held the third week in October.

The largest free country fair in the nation, this annual event brings to Franklinton an enormous number of visitors and depopulates the rest of the

parish. There's entertainment on an outdoor stage (amateurs mostly, but with country stars at night) as well as a rodeo, 4-H animals (don't miss the judging of squealing little pigs), and prizes for the best pies, roses, and art. At the Mile Branch Settlement area there is a spelling bee, plus a country store with a big wheel of cheese for slicing, and a log church where you're invited to sing hymns all day. Have a barbecue chicken lunch at the Bowling Green School booth.

Take Highway 25 north from Covington to Franklinton and step back in time. It's probably the best (and one of the few) alcohol-free festivals in the state as well.

of Tim Jobe, the winery currently makes several muscadine vintages plus a sparkling wine.

In the gift shop, decorated with big, bright banners, you'll also find muscadine grape jellies, jams, and bar supplies. Except for major holidays, the facility opens daily, closing at 5:00 P.M. From Monday through Friday, hours start at 10:00 A.M., on Saturday at 9:00 A.M., and on Sunday at 1:00 P.M.

Nearby at 1740 Charter Street, the **Old Centenary Inn** (225–634–5050) offers rooms and suites furnished with antiques and equipped with whirlpool baths. Owner Leroy Harvey imported the life-size statue of a Scottish Highlander from the British Isles to symbolize the parish's Anglo-Saxon heritage. The handsome mahogany bar embellished with stained glass and brass once served an English pub, and the grilled lift that takes you to the upstairs guest rooms also came from England. Rates are moderate.

Stroll to **Milbank Historic House** (225–634–5901), a circa 1836 classic Greek Revival town home that housed Jackson's first bank. Located at 3053 Bank Street, the home boasts museum-quality antiques such as the gentleman's elaborate dressing table with grooming accessories in the Thomas Jefferson bedroom. Milbank offers bed-and-breakfast accommodations, and rates are moderate. The home is also open for tours from 9:00 A.M. to 4:00 P.M. Monday through Friday, Saturday 9:00 A.M. to 2:00 P.M., and Sunday by appointment. Admission is charged.

Don't miss the **Republic of West Florida Museum,** in Old Hickory Village at 3406 College Street, Jackson 70748. Curator Earl Smith will show you around. "This isn't like a job," he says. "It's like coming to a toy shop every day." For more information contact the Feliciana Chamber of Commerce at (225) 634–7155.

Exhibits include vintage cars, horse-drawn carriages, a restored cotton gin from the 1880s, and a working theater pipe organ from the 1920s. Hours are 10:00 A.M. to 5:00 P.M. Tuesday through Sunday. Admission is modest. On weekends, a narrow-gauge train transports visitors from the museum to various local sites.

Continue to **Centenary State Historic Site** (225–634–7925 or 888–677–2364) at the corner of College and Pine Streets for a tour of the restored 1800s home of a former professor with exhibits on pre–Civil War education in Louisiana. Guides interpret early college life and conduct walks across campus. On the way to West Wing Dormitory (complete with historical graffiti), you'll see the remains of several

Nature Walks

St. Tammany Parish has the **Northlake Nature Center,** *with a pleasant marked nature trail through varying terrain, on Highway 190 near the entrance to Fontainebleau State Park. There is also a nature trail boardwalk (with the possibility of seeing bald eagles) at The Nature Conservancy's* **White Kitchen Preserve,** *near Slidell by the intersection of Highways 90 and 190.*

buildings. The site is open daily from 9:00 A.M. to 5:00 P.M., and admission is modest.

In Clinton, which became the parish seat in 1824, you'll see the ***East Feliciana Parish Courthouse.*** This stately Greek Revival structure, with twenty-eight columns and a domed, octagonal cupola atop a hipped roof, serves as the town's centerpiece. Be sure to walk around to the back of the courthouse, where you'll see a row of Greek Revival buildings that date from 1840 to 1860. These cottages, collectively known as Lawyers' Row, have also been designated a National Historic Landmark.

From Clinton take Route 10 east until you intersect Interstate 55. Travel south toward Hammond and then take the Springfield exit.

Turf and Swamp

Near Hammond you can visit ***Kliebert's Alligator & Turtle Farm*** (985–345–3617), an interesting stop (unless you're traveling during winter when alligators hibernate). Located at 41067 West Yellow Water Road, this unique facility is the world's largest working alligator farm. Harvey Kliebert and his son-in-law, Bruce Mitchell, operate the reptile farm.

The family has been raising alligators for a long time. You'll probably see Big Fred, now 16 feet long, who was hatched here more than four decades ago. The farm's alligators surpass wild alligators in size because they're well fed. Feeding more than 5,000 alligators, a number of which measure from 9 to 14 feet long, requires plenty of food. The alligators eat chicken, nutria, fish, and everything Harvey, who traps in winter, brings home.

During June and July, you may observe a procedure called "taking the eggs," whereby two staff members, using long sticks, retrieve the alligators' eggs. Because these reptiles do not relish relinquishing their eggs, the collection process can prove quite challenging. The eggs are then placed in incubators and hatched to restock the farm.

In addition to alligators, you'll see thousands of turtles as well as a snake pit and a bird rookery. During spring, flocks of egrets and herons nest at the farm. In the gift shop, you can buy alligator and turtle meat, sausage, and reptile novelties.

A guided walking tour of the farm takes about forty-five minutes. Except for the period from November 1 through March 1, the farm is open daily. Tours are offered starting at noon. Admission.

After visiting the alligators, head southeast to nearby **Ponchatoula**— population 5,475. Already recognized as "Strawberry Capital of the World," the town flaunts a new title, "America's Antique City." Located at the junction of U.S. Highway 51 and Route 22, Ponchatoula takes its name from Choctaw Indian words for "hanging hair" (a reference to the ubiquitous Spanish moss dangling from area trees).

Ponchatoula's rebirth as an antiques mecca happened in less than three years. "We went from twenty-four vacant downtown buildings to total occupancy," says local Realtor and Main Street Program manager Charlene Daniels, one of the driving forces in the town's restoration. The transformation required a committed community effort plus plenty of paint, chosen from a palette of historical colors. Painters from New Orleans Sheriff Charles Foti's Prison Art Program freshened up storefronts throughout the heart of town, a 2-block National Historic District.

Well over 120 dealers offer their wares for shoppers who love poking among yesterday's treasures, antiques, crafts, bric-a-brac, and collectibles. Strolling along the sidewalk, you see changing still-life compositions—a barber pole balanced against an antique pie safe, a rocking chair draped with a crazy quilt, or a hobbyhorse, doll, and vintage buggy.

Stop by the **Ponchatoula Country Market** (985–386–9580) in the heart of town. Housed in an 1854 historic depot, this bazaar offers booths of handcrafted items, antiques, collectibles, homemade jellies, and pastries. Hours are 10:00 A.M. to 5:00 P.M. Monday through Saturday and noon to 5:00 P.M. on Sunday. Beside the railroad station, you can visit the Mail Car Art Gallery, a restored baggage-mail car featuring the work of local artists. You may want to say hello to the town's mascot, "Old Hardhide." Not your average alligator, this one boasts his own bank account and local newspaper column (in which he espouses opinions that others dare not). He lives in a large wire cage in front of the railroad station.

Across the street, you'll find the **Collinswood School Museum.** This old-fashioned schoolhouse, which dates from around 1876, contains artifacts and memorabilia pertaining to the area's history. On West Pine Street browse through **Ponchatoula Feed and Seed** (985–386–3506),

Mardi Gras, Country Style

Mardi Gras, the Tuesday before Ash Wednesday, six weeks before Easter, is celebrated in Covington, Slidell, Mandeville, and Bogalusa. Even Bush has a truck parade the prior Saturday. Parade schedules will be in The Times-Picayune *and in local papers. Bogalusa's parade is the Saturday before Mardi Gras and draws a huge crowd. If you have kids and want to catch lots of throws, consider going to Bogalusa.*

an old-fashioned store that carries farm and garden supplies, baby chicks, hardware, and bedding plants.

While continuing your exploration in downtown Ponchatoula, stop for lunch or dinner at *C'est Bon* (985–386–4077), a restaurant at 131 Southwest Railroad Avenue. Try the bourbon pecan chicken—scrumptious. Prices are moderate.

Except for a spirited Saturday night antiques auction, town hours generally run from 11:00 A.M. to 9:00 P.M. Monday through Saturday and from 11:00 A.M. to 3:00 P.M. on Sunday. (About half the shops close on Monday, and a few close on Tuesday.)

On your way out, stop by *Taste of Bavaria,* a bakery and restaurant on the town's western outskirts. You can pick up some great German breads and pastries to go or enjoy a meal on the premises.

From Ponchatoula take Route 22 east to Madisonville, a charming little town on the northern shore of Lake Pontchartrain in St. Tammany Parish.

Madisonville offers several fine restaurants and shops, plus a small museum with artifacts from the town's boat-building era, all within a stroll of the riverfront.

Don't miss *Friends on the Tchefuncta* (985–845–7303), located at 407 St. Tammany Street. The seafood is scrumptious, and you can look out over the Tchefuncta River as you dine.

The restaurant opens at 11:00 A.M. Tuesday through Sunday. Seatings are taken until 9:00 P.M. on weeknights and until 10:00 P.M. on weekends. Prices are moderate, and reservations are recommended.

Two miles east of Madisonville on Route 22, you'll find *Fairview-Riverside State Park* (985–845–3318 or 888–677–3247), which offers great fishing, camping, and picnicking, as well as an old summer home available for touring. Continuing on to Mandeville, almost within shouting distance, be sure to drive along the town's lovely lakefront.

A short distance southeast of Mandeville at 67825 Highway 190, you'll discover *Fontainebleau State Park* (985–624–4443 or 888–677–3668), which covers 2,700 acres on the shores of Lake Pontchartrain. The park features the brick ruins of an old sugar mill, covered picnic

---

Top Annual Events in Turf and Swamp

Amite Oyster Festival,
Amite, late March to early April.
(985) 748–5161.

Ponchatoula Strawberry Festival,
Ponchatoula, early April. (985) 386–6677
or (800) 542–7520.

The Great Louisiana Bird Fest,
Covington, mid-April. (800) 634–9443.

Independence Italian Festival,
Highway 40 East at Pine Street,
Independence, third weekend in April.
(800) 542–7520.

Slidell Pirogue Races,
Slidell, first Saturday in June.
(800) 634–9443.

Wooden Boat Festival,
Madisonville, late June.
(800) 634–9443.

Tangipahoa Parish Fair,
Amite, first weekend in October.
(800) 542–7520 or (985) 748–8632.

Washington Parish Free Fair,
Franklinton, third week in October.
(985) 735–5731.

Fanfare,
Southeastern Louisiana University,
Hammond, October.
(985) 549–2333.

Kentwood Dairy Festival,
Kentwood, November.
(985) 229–6400.

---

pavilions, and nature trails. Hours are 7:00 A.M. to 9:00 P.M. (till 10:00 P.M. Friday and Saturday) year-round.

Before leaving the area, make a short excursion north to Covington. In the town's historic district, you may want to stop by some of the *Lee Lane Shops.* These Creole cottages, dating from the nineteenth century, have been converted to specialty shops, which carry antiques, art, gifts, clothing, and other items.

At 221 Lee Lane, Carolyn Gray and Kathy Ferguson offer yesteryear's treasures at **Walker House, Ltd.** (985–893–4235). Furniture, china, crystal, and home accessories fill room after room. Step out back and wander about the patio area brimming with plants, topiaries, statuary, and accent pieces for the garden enthusiast. Hours are 10:00 A.M. to 5:00 P.M. Monday through Saturday and 1:00 to 4:00 P.M. Sunday.

Don't miss **H. J. Smith's Son General Store** (985–892–0460), located at 308 North Columbia Street in downtown Covington. This old-time country store, which also features a museum, sells everything from ox yokes and cast-iron stoves to plantation bells. On the front porch you'll see a buckboard and an inviting swing. Other merchandise consists of cypress swings, oak rockers, wood-burning stoves, and various hardware and farm supplies. Inside the store a corncrib more than 150 years old serves as a display area for kerosene lamps, crockery, and cast-iron cookware.

"There are not a lot of stores like ours left," says Jack Smith, who remembers the "old guys sitting in rocking chairs on the front porch and spinning yarns." Jack, his brothers, and their father carry on a family business that started in 1876.

The museum contains hundreds of items from yesteryear, such as an old metal icebox, a century-old cypress dugout boat, and a cast-iron casket. A hand-operated wooden washing machine, old cotton scales, and various vintage tools are also on display.

St. Tammany Parish boasts the country's largest llama breeding ranch and a number of Thoroughbred horse farms. But the area's most remote and mysterious spot, as far as getting off the beaten path goes, is **Honey Island Swamp** on the eastern edge of the parish between Louisiana and Mississippi.

To reach Honey Island Swamp, head toward Slidell in the state's southeastern corner. A good way to explore this pristine wilderness is to take one of **Dr. Wagner's Honey Island Swamp Tours** (985–641–1769 or 504–242–5877). Tours depart from Crawford Landing, about 5 miles east of Slidell on the West Pearl River. Dr. Paul Wagner is a wetlands ecologist, and he or one of his staff will introduce you to this wild 250-square-mile region.

Because it attracted large swarms of honeybees, early settlers called the place Honey Island. One of America's least explored swamps, this area is home to a large variety of plants and wildlife—and maybe even the mysterious swamp monster, Wookie. Some hunters and anglers swear that they've seen the creature, which they consistently describe as about 7 feet tall and covered with short hair, longer at the scalp. Wookie supposedly walks upright and leaves four-toed tracks. So far nobody on the tours has spotted said creature, but if it exists, then this wild and dense area seems an appropriate environment.

Although you may miss Wookie, you'll see some of the swamp's resident and migratory birds: herons, ibis, egrets, bald eagles, owls, and wild turkeys. Crawfish, turtles, alligators, wild boar, deer, and otter also live here.

Dr. Wagner, his wife, Sue, and a staff of naturalist native guides serve as stewards of the Louisiana Nature Conservancy's White Kitchen Tract, and the tour includes a visit to this beautiful area, teeming with wildlife. This "microcosm of a swamp," as Dr. Wagner puts it, contains a rookery, a wood duck roost, and an active bald eagle nest where generations of eagles have come for some fifty years.

Other Attractions Worth Seeing in Turf and Swamp

Global Wildlife Center.
26389 Highway 40, Folsom;
(985) 796–3585. Guided covered-wagon
tours over 900 acres and a variety of
species to see. Kids will enjoy the visit.

Greensburg.
Take Highway 16 off I–55 west to Greensburg (stop off at the Bear Creek Steakhouse
in Montpelier for music and a meal if you
like). At Greensburg you can see an old
jail and the original Florida Parishes
land office, where claims were settled after
the area joined the state of Louisiana.

Highway 51.
Tangipahoa Parish was only formed in
1867, carved out from adjoining parishes
to form a corridor along the Illinois Central
Railroad. Towns are dotted at 10-mile intervals along Highway 51, which follows the
train route. Ponchatoula has antiques
stores; Hammond has the campus of Southeastern Louisiana University; Independence

has a rich Italian heritage; Amite has a
pleasant residential section and a bed-
and-breakfast mansion, Blythewood.
Near Tangipahoa is Camp Moore, a Civil
War military camp with museum exhibits.

Military Road, Highway 21.
This highway north of Covington going
toward Bogalusa is lovely in spring.
Azaleas bloom along the fences and
wisteria and Cherokee roses climb along
the pine trees for what seems like miles.

The Tammany Trace.
This biking and hiking path on an old
railroad right-of-way is a good venue for
getting out in the country for a stroll. Start
in Abita Springs (and have a sip of the
famous spring water before you begin).

Zemurray Gardens.
23115 Zemurray Garden Drive, Loranger;
(985) 878–2284. Azalea garden is glorious
in spring. Wander among the trees and
shrubbery on the trail around the lake.

A number of visitors return to see the swamp's seasonal changes. In spring
and summer, the place becomes lush like a rain forest, but cool weather
months offer improved visibility. Regular tours are offered morning and
evening, by appointment. Additional tours are available, and reservations
are required. A typical tour takes about two hours. The Wagners also offer
a hotel pickup service from New Orleans—complete with a narrated tour
of the city. Credit cards are not accepted. Call the Wagners for tour rates
and reservations.

After exploring Honey Island, proceed to nearby Slidell. Allow time to
browse through **Olde Town,** a charming area of century-old cottages
brimming over with antiques and gifts.

After leaving Slidell, you will be on the threshold of New Orleans (*Noo or-
LYUNS*). New Orleans cannot be considered off the beaten path; however,
it offers some unique sites and cityscapes that you may want to include
on your itinerary. If so, take nearby Interstate 10 and cross the twin-span
bridge over the end of Lake Pontchartrain into America's Paris.

Crescent City Realm

New Orleans, famous for its food, music, festivals, architecture, history, and carefree atmosphere, is a city like no other. New Orleans has been described as magical, rambunctious, debonair, flamboyant, seductive, and, yes, decadent—but most of all, it's fascinating.

Spring is an ideal time to visit New Orleans—it's no secret that summer days can fall in the sweaty and sweltering category.

Before beginning your exploration of the Crescent City, throw away your compass. New Orleans's confusing geography takes a while to master. Natives refer to upriver as uptown and downriver as downtown; the two other major directions are lakeside (toward Lake Pontchartrain) and riverside. You can get a good view of the crescent from *Moonwalk,* a promenade that fronts the French Quarter and overlooks the Mississippi River.

A word of warning: As you explore New Orleans, it's best to stick to the beaten path, avoiding any questionable areas. New Orleans can appear deceptively safe, so don't forget to exercise the same caution that you would in any major city.

If New Orleans is your exclusive destination, consider coming by plane or train. An Amtrak excursion with sleeping car, which includes meals and other amenities, will allow you to arrive rested and ready to tackle the Big Easy. For reservations and information call (800) 872–7245. In this city of precious parking (not to mention the French Quarter's narrow streets), a car has definite drawbacks. United Cabs offer reliable and courteous service; call (504) 522–9771. Also, the St. Charles Streetcar, listed on the National Register of Historic Places, affords an entertaining and inexpensive way to get about. You may want to purchase a pass for a day of unlimited rides.

For comfort and convenience with some marbled opulence thrown in for good measure, plan to stay at *Le Pavillon Hotel* (800–535–9095 or 504–581–3111). Fronted by large columns and ornamented with sculptures and cast terra-cotta garlands, Le Pavillon stands at 833 Poydras Street on the corner intersecting Baronne. A member of Historic Hotels of America, this 1907 architectural classic offers spacious rooms and suites along with friendly service. The lobby's crystal chandeliers came from Czechoslovakia and its marble railings from the Grand Hotel in Paris. Each of the hotel's seven deluxe suites features a different decor. From antique to Art Deco, all furnishings, paintings, and accents carry out the room's theme.

Guests can take a dip in the rooftop pool and relax on the patio with its sweeping view of the Mississippi River. After a night on the town, stop by the lobby for a complimentary late-night snack of peanut butter and jelly sandwiches (made with homemade bread) with a glass of milk. You can compensate for the fat grams with free sessions in the fitness center. Rates are moderate to deluxe.

After settling in, start your sight-seeing session in the nearby French Quarter with beignets and cafe au lait at *Cafe du Monde* (504–587–0840). Located in the French Market at 800 Decatur Street, the eatery is open twenty-four hours daily (except Christmas Day). Afterward, stroll through the Vieux Carré (*view-ka-ray*), as the old French Quarter also is known. Save some time to watch the street performers in Jackson Square with its famous artists' fence. Clopping through the quarter, straw-hatted mules pull surreys and carriages—a relaxing way to see the stately tri-towered *St. Louis Cathedral,* outdoor cafes, and "frozen lace" galleries.

While in the French Quarter with its many enticements, consider touring the *Beauregard-Keyes House* at 1113 Chartres Street just across from the Old Ursuline Convent. Frances Parkinson Keyes (*kize*), author of fifty-one books, lived here while writing *Dinner at Antoine's, Blue Camellia,* and other novels. Docents, dressed in period costume, give guided tours Monday through Saturday, from 10:00 A.M. to 3:00 P.M. on the hour. The gift shop offers a wide selection of the author's books. Admission is modest.

Afterward, take a break at nearby *Napoleon House* (504–524–9752). This interesting old building at 500 Chartres Street houses a bar and cafe. You can study the menu, printed on fans with faces of Napoleon and Josephine, while listening to classical music in the background. Try the house specialty, an Italian muffuletta—a great sandwich with meats, cheeses, and olive salad. The eatery is open daily. Hours run from 11:00 A.M. to midnight except on Friday and Saturday, when closing time is 1:00 A.M., and on Sunday, when it closes at 7:00 P.M.

Bienville House Hotel (504–529–2345 or 800–535–7836) makes a convenient and cozy base for exploring the French Quarter. You'll find it at 320 Decatur Street, only a short stroll or cab ride away from antiques shops, jazz showcases, blues clubs, and great restaurants, including the hotel's own Gamay Bistro & Bar, presided over by Chef Greg Sonnier and his wife, Mary. (Try the Gumbo Ya Ya.)

Created from two eighteenth-century warehouses, this intimate inn, elegantly appointed with hand-painted murals, exudes an old-world

ambience. Check out upcoming events and make bookings via www.
bienvillehouse.com/reservations.

After browsing through the French Quarter's antiques shops, art galleries,
and boutiques, consider taking a stroll along Riverwalk and visiting
Aquarium of the Americas (504–565–3033), where you can get nose to
nose with a shark, see white alligators, and hold a parrot in the Amazon
rain forest. The aquarium opens at 9:30 A.M. daily; closing hours vary.

Afterward, head for Canal Street, a few blocks away. This wide avenue
divides the French Quarter from "American territory" in uptown New
Orleans. On Canal you can catch the St. Charles Streetcar—one rattles by
every ten minutes—for a ride through the *Garden District.* Bumping
along you'll see handsome nineteenth-century villas, Greek Revival mansions, and raised cottages surrounded by magnolias and ancient live
oaks. This lovely area, with its lush landscaping and extravagant gardens
dotted with statuary and fountains, makes a fine place to stroll. By walking you can better admire the ornamental iron fences with their geometric and plant motifs.

Even better, sign up for a walking tour by a ranger from the French Quarter Visitor Center–Jean Lafitte National Historical Park. Tours last about
ninety minutes, so wear your walking shoes. Except for Christmas Day
and Mardi Gras, the tours take place daily and are free. Reservations are
required. Call (504) 589–2636.

You can catch the *St. Charles Streetcar* for more sight-seeing or take a
short stroll to *Commander's Palace* (504–899–8221), one of the city's
many wonderful restaurants. Housed in a Victorian mansion at 1403

Outdoor Living in the City

*O*ne of Louisiana's most popular
state parks is **Bayou Segnette** (suh-
NET), 7777 Westbank Expressway
in Westwego (888–677–2296 or
504–736–7140). In addition to a
wave pool, boat launches, and picnic
areas, Bayou Segnette has twenty
furnished rental cabins on the bayou,
with boat docks and screen porches.
There are also one hundred campsites
with water and electricity and group

camping cabins. Reserve early if
you're interested—it's about thirty
minutes from here to downtown
New Orleans.

The St. Bernard State Park, Poydras
(888–677–7823 or 504–682–2101),
also offers campsites just 19 miles
south of the city. Picnic areas and
fishing are also available on the
park's 358 acres.

Tujague's Tantalizing Tastes

Something about New Orleans spells food, and while you're exploring the French Quarter, stop by 823 Decatur Street. The city's second oldest restaurant, **Tujague's** (504–525–8676) opened its doors in 1856 and soon became a favorite spot for workers from the nearby French Market. Be sure to step into the antique bar to see the massive ornate mirror, shipped from Paris in 1856.

Presidents Franklin Roosevelt, Truman, Eisenhower, and France's de Gaulle have enjoyed Tujague's hospitality, and so can you. From appetizer through dessert, today's owners carry on the Tujague family's tradition of serving fine fare in the Creole manner. The restaurant's seven-course meals evolve from such staples as shrimp remoulade and a superb brisket of beef presented with a red horseradish sauce.

Straight from this classic New Orleans neighborhood restaurant to you, here's Tujague's signature dish:

Tujague's Boiled Brisket of Beef

6–7 pounds choice brisket of beef

2 onions, quartered

1 1/2 ribs celery, quartered

1 head garlic, peeled

1 bay leaf

1 tablespoon salt

15 black peppercorns

2 green onions, quartered

1 carrot, quartered

1 bell pepper, quartered

Note: Here are the two most important steps to produce a tender, juicy, tasty brisket:

1) Buy a quality, well-trimmed brisket, never frozen.

2) Simmer the meat (not a hard boil).

Place the brisket in a large soup pot, cover with cold water, add the remaining ingredients, and simmer for 3–4 hours until beef is tender. Remove beef and slice. Serve with a sauce made by combining 1 cup ketchup, 1/2 cup prepared horseradish, and 1/4 cup Creole mustard.

For vegetable soup, skim and strain the beef stock. Add 3 tablespoons tomato paste, 2 sliced tomatoes, and your favorite vegetables. Cook until tender and serve. We have found a little okra adds a distinctive taste to the soup. Cut and cook okra first in the oven or a saucepan to remove slime.

Any stock left after soup is made can be frozen and stored for future soups and sauces. Makes approximately 1 gallon soup.

Washington Avenue, the famous eatery features spectacular Creole cuisine and superb seafood. Start with a Commander's specialty, tasty turtle soup. For an entree, you might order roasted Louisiana quail filled with crawfish and crabmeat, roast rack of lamb, or tournedos done to your taste. Don't skip dessert here. (You can walk it off later.) Try Commander's Creole bread pudding soufflé.

Fishing

Everyone who fishes in Louisiana and is between the ages of sixteen and sixty is required to have a fishing license. They are available at most sporting goods stores and bait shops, and there is a one-day license available for about $5.00 (add $15.00 for salt water) for out-of-state visitors.

Except for Mardi Gras, Christmas Eve, and Christmas Day, Commander's Palace is open from 11:30 A.M. to 2:00 P.M. and 6:00 to 10:00 P.M. Monday through Friday. On Saturday you can enjoy a Dixieland jazz brunch starting at 11:30 A.M. Sunday brunch begins at 10:30 A.M. Prices are expensive.

For another delightful place to hang your hat in this area, head to the *Josephine* (504–524–6361 or 800–779–6361), located just at the edge of the Garden District. Owned by Mary Ann Weilbaecher and husband, Dan Fuselier, this guest house stands at 1450 Josephine Street at the corner of Prytania. The Italianate-style home dates from 1870 and houses such striking antiques as "the jewel of the Josephine," an ornate ebony bed with inlaid ivory designs of dancing nymphs. The bed, which Dan calls "a bit on the risqué side," has been featured in a bridal magazine.

Mary Ann, who studied cookery in Paris, makes fresh breads, which she serves with juice and cafe au lait on Wedgwood china and presents on a silver tray. The couple offers recommendations and makes reservations for guests. "We like to help dock our guests," says Dan. Rates are moderate to deluxe.

On St. Charles Avenue you may want to visit *Audubon Park* in a pretty setting with ancient live oaks, flower-filled gardens, and wandering lagoons. The 400-acre urban park also offers a golf course, tennis courts, and picnic facilities as well as walking and jogging paths. At Cascade Stables in the park, you can rent a horse and go galloping off along a tree-shaded trail that offers glimpses of St. Charles Avenue.

A free shuttle transports visitors from the streetcar line to nearby *Audubon Zoo* (504–861–2537). Noted for its simulated barrier-free natural habitats, the zoo also makes a delightful outing, complete with peanuts, popcorn, and more than 1,800 animals. The zoo opens at 9:30 A.M. daily; closing hours vary.

Afterward, you can either walk back to St. Charles for the streetcar or catch the bus on *Magazine Street.* Located at 2051 Magazine Street, *Bep's Antiques, Inc.* (504–525–7726) features an interesting inventory of old tools, pharmaceutical items, bottles, pottery, and gasoliers. Hours are 9:30 A.M. to 5:00 P.M. Monday through Saturday. At 3033 Magazine Street, *As You Like It Silver Shop* (504–897–6915) offers strictly estate silver and specializes in matching flatware patterns for both discontinued and active patterns. You'll also find sterling silver tea services, tureens, goblets, bowls, and other hollowware items. Hours are 10:00 A.M. to 5:00 P.M. Monday through Saturday. At 5415 Magazine Street you can browse through **British Antiques** (504–895–3716). Hours are 11:00 A.M. to 5:00 P.M. Monday through Friday and till 6:00 P.M. on Saturday.

You'll come across some excellent buys in both English and French antiques along Magazine Street's 6 miles of shops, arcades, and galleries

Making Groceries

*N*ew Orleans is a city that, like Napoleon's army, moves on its stomach. To get in the spirit of things, learn to "make groceries"—a local expression that's a rough translation of the French faire le marche.

There is a farmers' market every Saturday from 8:00 A.M. to noon on the corner of Girod and Magazine Streets featuring fresh produce, a local chef using market goods to prepare dishes for tasting, lots of baked goods, jellies, and more. There's also coffee so you can make this a breakfast. There is an uptown farmers' market Tuesday from 10:00 A.M. to 1:00 P.M. at Broadway at Leake Avenue and a mid-city version on Thursday evening from 4:00 to 6:00 P.M. at Orleans Avenue by Bayou St. John.

Langenstein's, uptown on the corner of Pitt and Arabella Streets off St. Charles Avenue (take the streetcar), is the uptown grocery of choice. It has good meats, seafoods, and produce and a deli department that prepares lots of local specialties: boiled seafood, gumbo, red beans and rice, oyster dressing for your turkey, and pies. They will ship for you.

Most eccentric supermarket? **Dorignac's,** 710 Veterans Boulevard, Metairie. Although the late "Mr. Joe" Dorignac no longer sits in the coffee shop consulting the Racing Form (at one point he owned a good string of runners), his all-inclusive inventory still holds. The aisles are jam-packed, and you can find one of every local product here first. There's an incredible array of vegetables, including things like those hard-to-find artichoke stalks that make a special dish around St. Joseph's Day. Good butchers, too.

For health food try the **Whole Food Market,** 3135 Esplanade Avenue. It is a full-size grocery with organic vegetables and meat and a deli with fresh-made New Orleans specialties, albeit in healthful form. For wines consult Martin's Wine Cellar for a huge selection and a regular schedule of tastings with a local chef each Saturday. Two locations: 3827 Baronne Street uptown and 714 Elmeer at Veteran's Boulevard in Metairie.

Not enough? Then tune your radio to WSMB, 1350 AM, around 3:00 on weekday afternoons for critic Tom "Mr. Food" Fitzmorris. You can call in with questions (504–260–9762). And check Gambit Weekly or The Times-Picayune's Friday "Lagniappe" section for restaurant reviews.

The *Delta Queen*

filled with furniture, paintings, china, crystal, silver, collectibles, and souvenirs. You'll also pass brass dealers, bookstores, restaurants, and specialty shops. Even though most of the stores don't have fancy facades (some even resemble junk shops), you can find some quality merchandise at bargain prices.

For a delectable dinner, try *Gautreau's* (504–899–7397), a small uptown restaurant at 1728 Soniat Street. Two and a half blocks from St. Charles Avenue, the eatery occupies a former neighborhood drugstore. Notice the antique pharmacy cases, reincarnated as wine cabinets, and the ceiling of embossed tin. A previous owner and descendant of Mme. Pierre Gautreau, the subject of artist John Singer Sargent's *Portrait of Madame X,* named the restaurant in honor of this celebrated beauty of nineteenth-century Paris. A reproduction of the Sargent portrait hangs on one of the restaurant's burgundy-colored walls. Hours are 6:00 to 10:00 P.M. Monday through Saturday. Prices are moderate to expensive. Reservations are required.

At some point during your visit, schedule a boat ride to experience the mighty Mississippi's romance and majesty. Describing the Mississippi, Mark Twain called it "not a commonplace river, but in all ways remarkable." For a taste of Mr. Twain's river, you can choose a short ferry trip or a longer excursion on the *Creole Queen,* the *Natchez,* or another of the local riverboats. Some cruises combine sight-seeing with jazz, dinner, or Sunday brunch.

For a real taste of the river, grab your bag and head for the *Delta*

Queen Steamboat Company (800–543–1949), located at 30 Robin Street Wharf about 2 blocks from the Convention Center. Here you can set off on an overnight luxury cruise from New Orleans aboard the *Delta Queen,* the *Mississippi Queen,* or the new *American Queen,* the biggest steamboat ever built.

Excursions range from two to twelve nights. Rates based on double occupancy vary depending on boat and cabin size. The price includes all onboard meals and entertainment. Rates are deluxe. For more information, write to the Delta Queen Steamboat Company, Number 30 Robin Street Wharf, PXR1, New Orleans 70130.

Bays and Bayous

You can take the Jackson Avenue ferry (when available; call 504–376–8100 to check schedule) from the edge of New Orleans' Garden District over the river to *Gretna,* once a small community of railroad workers and German immigrants. Near the river is the City of Gretna Visitor Center in the old depot area (888–4–GRETNA). There is a railroad exhibit there and nearby is the Gretna Historical Society, 209 Lafayette Street, which encompasses three nineteenth-century cottages, properly furnished, and the David Crockett Fire Company, now a museum. The pumper wagon still shines, and even if the Dalmatian on board is ceramic, the costumed volunteer firemen are real—most are current or former volunteer firemen. At the back of the property, you'll find a blacksmith shop, and nearby is the *German American Culture Center* (504–363–4202). The Gretna October Festival takes place here as well.

When it's time for a break from boisterous New Orleans, head for the banks of Bayou Barataria, about 30 miles south. The little fishing village of *Jean Lafitte* "where there be dragons" (just like the kind bordering the unknown on ancient maps), makes an excellent escape. The local dragons must be the gentle sort, because people in Lafitte don't feel the need to lock doors and often leave keys in their cars. The year's big crime might involve a shady aluminum-siding deal.

For your own dragon-embellished map with directions on how to find Lafitte, call Dale or Roy Ross at *Victoria Inn* (504–689–4757 or 800–689–4797) on Highway 45. Dale welcomes guests to her West Indies–style cottage with refreshments on arrival. The inn's fourteen rooms in three buildings are all named for flowers, reflecting her love of gardening. Roy, who owns a construction company, built the lovely guest houses as well as the couple's nearby home.

TOP ANNUAL EVENTS IN CRESCENT CITY REALM

Mardi Gras.
The Carnival season runs from January 6 (Feast of the Epiphany, Three Kings Day) to Mardi Gras. There are lots of street parades throughout the area. Endymion on Saturday night, Baccchus on Sunday, and Orpheus on Monday are big, glitzy parades with giant floats and Hollywood kings. For a glimpse of the old-fashioned, small-float type of parade, catch Thoth on Sunday afternoon, uptown on Henry Clay Avenue or Magazine Street. This is what New Orleans Mardi Gras used to look like: very human-sized and still fun.

Saints' Days.
St. Patrick's Day, March 17, is celebrated with parades and green beer. St. Joseph, patron saint of Italians, is celebrated on his feast day, March 19, with parades and with altars piled high with special foods and displayed to the public. There will be one at St. Alphonsus Church on Constance Street. (Writer Anne Rice is very active at St. Alphonsus and you may see her there.) African-Americans who costume as Mardi Gras Indians also parade on St. Joseph's Day. All Saints Day, November 1, is the day for cleaning and decorating graves, so New Orleans cemeteries will be filled with families bearing chrysanthemums. All cemeteries have guards then, so it's a good day to visit.

Tennessee Williams Festival.
225 Baronne Street, mid- to late March. Literary happenings—panel discussions, walking tours, performances—all concerning writing and writers with an emphasis

on Williams. Don't miss the Stanley-Stella yelling contest in Jackson Square. (504) 581–1144.

French Quarter Festival.
100 Conti Street, mid-April. Food and music all over the French Quarter. (504) 522–5730.

Jazzfest.
New Orleans Jazz and Heritage Festival, 1205 North Rampart Street, last weekend of April, first weekend of May. If you can only get to one New Orleans event in a lifetime, make it Jazzfest. The weekend music and crafts festival at New Orleans Fair Grounds racetrack has lots of stages, booths, big-name musicians, all sorts of bands, and lots of food. A crowd of 90,000 is not unusual, yet it is a safe and remarkably mellow occasion. Anyone of any age will find something to enjoy. Plus, there are concerts in the evenings, and all the musicians will be sitting in at clubs around town. (504) 522–4786; www.nojazzfest.com.

New Orleans Film and Video Festival.
225 Baronne Street, second week of October. Showcases new and experimental films and videos. (504) 523–3818; www.neworleansfilmfest.com.

Christmas in New Orleans.
December. Besides holiday events, this includes special room rates at many hotels. Ask for the "Papa Noel" rate. Also, many restaurants serve a prix-fixe Reveillon Dinner, which can be a good value. Be sure to ask.

Early risers will find coffee in the kitchen from 6:00 A.M. on. Roy prepares breakfast, and his specialties range from a wonderful interpretation of eggs Benedict made with local hand-picked lump crab to pecan waffles, crabmeat omelette, and "mosquito toast" (inspired by cuisine in his native Belize) accompanied by bacon and a fruit compote.

OTHER ATTRACTIONS WORTH SEEING IN CRESCENT CITY REALM

Art.
The New Orleans Museum of Art in City Park at the end of Esplanade Avenue (504–488–2631) has interesting holdings, especially in decorative arts, with a good selection of European as well as South American and African work to complement its American collections. There is also a Contemporary Arts Center, at 900 Camp Street (504–523–1216), in what is fast becoming New Orleans's art district, just a few blocks above the French Quarter. The C.A.C. hosts theater as well as art exhibits. Be sure to stroll the galleries of Julia Street—New Orleans has a vibrant and active art community. Soon to locate in the area will be the Ogden Museum of Southern Art, displaying a collection that spans centuries and styles. The big art event, Art for Arts Sake, takes place the first Saturday in October at all galleries.

Battle of New Orleans Site.
The Chalmette Battlefield is now part of the many-sited Jean Lafitte National Park. Military history buffs will enjoy this one: Here's where the Duke of Wellington's brother-in-law, General Pakenham, came to his end during the British defeat. This is what started Andrew Jackson on the road to the White House.

From the French Quarter go east on Rampart Street, then on St. Claude Avenue, which actually becomes St. Bernard Highway and leads you right to the park. A few miles farther is the Isleños Center, also in Jean Lafitte National Park. Here you can learn the history of the Canary Islanders who settled the area. Sometimes the local docent demonstrates how to skin a nutria or coypu, a local wild rodent. Warning: It's not for the squeamish.

House Museums.
New Orleans has such a rich stock of nineteenth-century housing, it can offer the very best in accurately furnished period homes. Try Gallier House, 1133 Royal Street, home of architect James Gallier, or the Hermann-Grima House, 820 St. Louis Street (both at 504–525–5661).

There is also one in-town plantation, the Pitot House on Bayou St. John, 1440 Moss Street (504–482–0312).

Music.
Traditional jazz can be heard nightly at Preservation Hall at 726 St. Peter Street (504–522–2841) where fans sit on benches and pay a modest fee for pure music. Visit the Louisiana State Museum's Jazz and Mardi Gras displays in the Old Mint Building on Esplanade Avenue at the Mississippi River to ground yourself in history. (Louis Armstrong's first horn is there.)

If you decide to hit the clubs, expect to be out late—New Orleans music hits its stride after midnight. There is sometimes a van service that operates between clubs; ask at a club to see if it is still rolling.

So varied is Roy's repertoire that guests can stay two weeks and enjoy a different breakfast every day. Rates are moderate.

Both Gulf and inland fishing charters are available locally, and Dale can arrange pickup from the Rosses' back dock. Other local attractions include swamp tours and a Sunday *fais-do-do* at nearby Bayou Barn with live music, food, and Cajun dancing.

Top Annual Events in Bays and Bayous

Louisiana Iris Festival,
Jean Lafitte Park and
Lafitte, mid-March.
(800) 689-3525.

**Blessing of the
Shrimp Fleet,**
Lafitte, last Sunday in April.
(800) 689-3525.

Only ten minutes away you'll find the *Jean Lafitte National Park Barataria Unit,* 6588 Barataria Boulevard, Marrero 70072 (504–589–2330). You'll see an interpretive center with a good video on Cajuns and extensive displays on the local environment and the cypress timber industry (which decimated the indigenous trees in the area). Other enticements include several hiking trails, all of them enjoyable. There is also a canoe trail, and close by are canoes for rent. Rangers guide regular free tours.

The most popular trail is the Bayou Coquille–Marsh Overlook, especially spectacular when ringed with iris in spring. It ends on high ground with an aerial view of the marsh and the skyscrapers of New Orleans in the background—and perhaps an alligator nearby. Those little black "pickles" you see are nutria droppings. Watch for the rooting armadillos with their little piggy ears. If you have one afternoon to go to the country, go here.

Hungry? On the West Bank of the Mississippi and downriver from New Orleans, look for boiled seafood such as shrimp, crabs, and crawfish. You may have to be shown how to pick a boiled crab, but it's worth it. Add some crackers and cold beer and you have an instant picnic.

Stop at small bakeries for fresh French bread. Look for homemade hoghead cheese (Creole Country is a good New Orleans brand). Be on the lookout for roadside stands that sell "Creole" (home-grown) tomatoes or strawberries in season.

A po'boy sandwich on French bread can be ordered dressed (with lettuce and tomato) and with gravy (for roast beef). Po'boy Nirvana? Softshell crab.

At *Voleo's Seafood Restaurant* (504–689–2482) on Nunez Street, about 1 mile past Goose Bayou Bridge, you can sample either German or Cajun cuisine. Consider ordering the stuffed eggplant with fish, shrimp, oysters, and jambalaya. The restaurant opens at 11:00 A.M. daily, but closing times vary. Prices are moderate.

Other local eateries include *Boutte's Bayou Restaurant* (504–689–3889) overlooking Bayou Barataria and *Restaurant des Familles* (504–689–7834), which specializes in authentic Cajun cuisine and serves local seafood.

**PLACES TO STAY IN
SOUTHEAST LOUISIANA**

SWAMPLAND
Cajun Holiday Motel,
2002 Highway 1,
Grand Isle,
(985) 787–2002.

Coco Marina, Cocodrie,
(985) 594–6626 or
(800) 648–2626.

Holiday Inn–Holidome,
210 South Hollywood
Road, Houma,
(800) HOLIDAY.

Howard Johnson Motel,
201 North Canal Boulevard,
Thibodaux,
(985) 447–9071 or
(800) 952–2968.

PLANTATION COUNTRY
Holiday Inn LaPlace,
3900 Main Street, LaPlace,
(985) 652–5544.

Madewood,
4250 Highway 308,
Napoleonville,
(985) 369–7151 or
(800) 375–7151.

Nottoway,
30970 Highway 405,
White Castle,
(225) 545–2730.

"RED STICK"
Baton Rouge Marriott,
5500 Hilton Avenue,
Baton Rouge,
(225) 924–5000 or
(800) 842–2961.

Hampton Inn,
4646 Constitution Avenue,
Baton Rouge,
(800) HAMPTON.

Pleasant Hall, Louisiana
State University Campus,
Baton Rouge,
(225) 387–0297.

FRENCH CREOLE COUNTRY
Holiday Inn Express,
I–10 and Highway 415,
Port Allen,
(225) 343–4821 or
(800) HOLIDAY.

Jubilee!,
11704 Pointe Coupee Road,
New Roads,
(225) 638–8333.

Ramada Inn,
722 Lobdell Highway,
Port Allen,
(800) 732–1280.

THE FELICIANAS
Asphodel,
4626 Highway 68,
Jackson,
(225) 658–8808.

Best Western St. Francis
Hotel on the Lake,
Highway 61,
St. Francisville,
(225) 635–3821 or
(800) 826–9931.

Butler Greenwood,
8345 Highway 61,
St. Francisville,
(225) 635–6312.

Cottage Plantation,
10528 Cottage Lane,
St. Francisville,
(225) 635–3674.

Green Springs Inn
& Cottages,
7463 Tunica Trace,
St. Francisville,
(225) 635–4232 or
(800) 457–4978.

Greenwood Plantation,
6838 Highland Road,
St. Francisville,
(225) 655–3850.

Hemingbough,
10101 Highway 965,
St. Francisville,
(225) 635–6617.

Milbank Historic House,
3045 Bank Street, Jackson,
(225) 634–5901.

Myrtles, 7747 Highway 61,
St. Francisville,
(225) 635–6277.

Old Centenary Inn,
1740 Charter Street,
Jackson,
(225) 634–5050.

Rosedown Plantation
and Gardens,
12501 Highway 10,
St. Francisville,
(225) 784–2337.

Shadetree Inn,
Ferdinand and Royal
Streets,
St. Francisville,
(225) 635–6116.

TURF AND SWAMP
Best Western
Northpark Inn,
625 North Highway 190,
Covington,
(985) 892–2681 or
(877) 766–6700.

The Dansereau House,
506 St. Philip Street,
Thibodaux,
(985) 447–1002.

Holiday Inn,
2000 South Morrison
Boulevard,
Hammond,
(985) 345–0556 or
(800) HOLIDAY.

Land–O–Pines Family
Campground,
17145 Million Dollar Road,
Covington,
(800) 443–3697.

La Quinta Inn,
794 East I–10 Service
Road, Slidell,
(985) 643–9770 or
(800) 531–5900.

CRESCENT CITY REALM
Bienville House Hotel,
320 Decatur Street,
New Orleans,
(504) 529–2345 or
(800) 535–7836.

Grand Victorian,
2727 St. Charles Avenue,
New Orleans,
(504) 895–1104.

Hampton Inn,
3626 St. Charles Avenue,
New Orleans,
(800) 426–7866.

Josephine,
1450 Josephine Street,
New Orleans,
(504) 524–6361 or
(800) 779–6361.

Le Pavillon Hotel,
833 Poydras Street,
New Orleans,
(504) 581–3111 or
(800) 535–9095.

The Monteleone,
214 Royal Street,
New Orleans,
(800) 535–9595.

St. Charles Guest House,
1748 Prytania Street,
New Orleans,
(504) 523–6556.

Sully Mansion,
2631 Prytania Street,
New Orleans,
(504) 891–0457.

BAYS AND BAYOUS
Best Western Westbank,
1700 Lapalco Boulevard,
Harvey,
(504) 366–5369 or
(800) 528–1234.

Travelodge Hotel Westbank,
2200 Westbank
Expressway,
Harvey,
(504) 366–5311 or
(800) 578–1878

Victoria Inn,
Highway 45,
Lafitte,
(504) 689–4757.

**PLACES TO EAT IN
SOUTHEAST LOUISIANA**

SWAMPLAND
A-Bear's Cafe,
809 Bayou Black Drive,
Houma,
(985) 872–6306.

The Jolly Inn,
1507 Barrow Street,
Houma,
(985) 872–6114.

Lighthouse Restaurant,
Coco Marina,
Cocodrie,
(985) 594–6626 or
(800) 648–2626.

1921 Seafood Restaurant,
1522 Barrow Street,
Houma,
(985) 868–7098.

Politz's Restaurant, 535 St.
Mary Street, Thibodaux,
(985) 448–0944.

PLANTATION COUNTRY
The Cabin Restaurant,
Corner of Highways
44 and 22, Burnside,
(225) 473–3007.

Lafitte's Landing
Restaurant at Bittersweet
Plantation,
404 Claiborne Avenue,
Donaldsonville,
(225) 473–1232.

Madewood,
4250 Highway 308,
Napoleonville,
(985) 369–7151 or
(800) 375–7151.

Nottoway,
30970 Highway 405,
White Castle,
(225) 545–2730.

Oak Alley Plantation
Restaurant and Inn,
3645 Highway 18,
Vacherie,
(225) 265–2151 or
(800) 44–ALLEY.

"RED STICK"
Drusilla's,
3482 Drusilla Lane,
Baton Rouge,
(225) 923–0896.

LSU Faculty Club,
Highland Road,
Baton Rouge,
(225) 578–2356.

Mike Anderson's,
1031 West Lee Drive,
Baton Rouge,
(225) 766–7823.

FRENCH CREOLE COUNTRY
Joe's "Dreyfus Store"
Restaurant,
2741 Maringouin Road
West, Livonia,
(225) 637–2625.

Morel's,
210 Morrison Parkway,
New Roads,
(225) 638–4057.

Oxbow Restaurant,
6813 False River Road,
Oscar,
(225) 635–6276.

THE FELICIANAS
The Bluffs on Thompson
Creek,
Route 965,
St. Francisville,
(225) 634–3410 or
(888) 634–3410.

Magnolia Cafe,
5687 East Commerce
Street,
St. Francisville,
(225) 635–6528.

St. Francisville Inn,
5720 North Commerce
Street,
St. Francisville,
(225) 635–6502.

TURF AND SWAMP
Abita Brewing Company,
72011 Holly Street,
Abita Springs,
(800) 737–2311.

C'est Bon,
131 Southwest Railroad
Avenue,
Ponchatoula,
(985) 386–4077.

Coffee Rani,
234–A Lee Lane,
Covington,
(985) 893–6158.

Friends on the Tchefuncta,
407 St. Tammany Street,
Madisonville,
(985) 845–7303.

The House of
Seafood Buffet,
Highway 21,
Bush,
(985) 886–2231.

Middendorf's,
30160 Highway 51,
Manchak (Akers),
(504) 386–6666.

CRESCENT CITY REALM
Arnaud's,
813 Bienville Street,
New Orleans,
(504) 523–5433.

Brennan's,
417 Royal Street,
New Orleans,
(504) 525–9713.

Bruning's,
1922 West End Parkway,
New Orleans,
(504) 282–9395.

Café du Monde,
800 Decatur Street,
New Orleans,
(504) 587–0840.

Commander's Palace,
1403 Washington Street,
New Orleans,
(504) 899–8221.

Emeril's Restaurant,
800 Tchoupitoulas Street,
New Orleans,
(504) 528–9393.

Galatoire's,
209 Bourbon Street,
New Orleans,
(504) 525–2021.

Gautreau's,
1728 Soniat Street,
New Orleans,
(504) 899–7397.

K–Paul's Louisiana Kitchen,
416 Chartres Street,
New Orleans,
(504) 596–2530.

Napoleon House,
500 Chartres Street,
New Orleans,
(504) 524–9752.

Tujague's,
823 Decatur Street,
New Orleans,
(504) 525–8676.

BAYS AND BAYOUS
Boutte's Bayou Restaurant,
Lafitte,
(504) 689–3889.

Copeland's Restaurant,
1700 Lapalco Boulevard,
Harvey,
(504) 364–1575.

Restaurant des Familles,
Lafitte,
(504) 689–7834.

Voleo's Seafood Restaurant,
Nunez Street,
Lafitte,
(504) 689–2482.

For More Information

SWAMPLAND

Grand Isle Tourist Commission
3240 Highway 1, Grand Isle 70358
(985) 787–2997
www.grand-isle.com

Houma–Terrebonne Tourist Commission
1702 St. Charles Street, Houma 70361
(800) 688–2732

Lafourche Parish Tourist Commission
P.O. Box 340, Raceland 70394
(985) 537–5800 or (877) 537–5800

Local newspapers: *Houma Daily Courier* (owned by The New York Times Corporation) and the *Thibodaux Daily Comet.* Check both for events.

PLANTATION COUNTRY

Ascension Parish Tourist Commission
6470 Highway 22, Sorrento 70778
(225) 675–6550 or (888) 775–7990

Gonzales Welcome Center
1006 West Highway 30, Gonzales 70737
(225) 647–9566

St. Charles Parish Economic Development Department
P.O. Box 302, Hahnville 70057
(985) 783–5140

St. James Historical Society
P.O. Box 426, Gramercy 70052
(800) 367–7852

St. John Parish President's Office
1801 West Airline Highway, LaPlace 70068
(985) 652–9569

Local newspapers: *The Donaldsonville Chief, Gonzales Weekly, L'Observateur* in LaPlace, *Lutcher News–Examiner, The Enterprise* in Vacherie, *Plaquemine Post/South.*

RED STICK

Baton Rouge Area Convention and Visitors Commission
730 North Boulevard, Baton Rouge 70802
(800) LA ROUGE
www.batonrougetour.com

Newspapers: *Baton Rouge Advocate.* Check the Friday "Fun" section for events, restaurant reviews, etc. Also, check the LSU student paper, *The Daily Reveille.*

For More Information

FRENCH CREOLE COUNTRY

Pointe Coupee Chamber of Commerce
2506 False River Drive, New Roads 70760
(225) 638–3500

West Baton Rouge Tourist Commission
2855 I–10 Frontage Road, Port Allen 70767
(225) 344–2920 or (800) 654–9701

Newspapers: The *Pointe Coupee Banner* of New Roads, the *West Side Journal* of Port Allen. Check the Friday "Fun" section of the *Baton Rouge Advocate* for events.

THE FELICIANAS

East Feliciana Chamber of Commerce
P.O. Box 667, Jackson 70748
(225) 634–7155

West Feliciana Parish Tourist Commission
P.O. Box 1548, St. Francisville 70775
(225) 635–6330

Newspapers: *St. Francisville Democrat, Zachary Plainsman–News, The Watchman* in Clinton. The *Baton Rouge Advocate* Friday "Fun" section will cover events.

TURF AND SWAMP

Bogalusa Chamber of Commerce
608 Willis Avenue, Bogalusa 70427
(985) 735–5731

St. Tammany Tourist & Convention Commission
68099 Highway 59, Mandeville 70471
(800) 634–9443

Tangipahoa Parish Tourist Commission
42271 South Morrison Boulevard, Hammond 70403
(985) 542–7520 or (800) 542–7520

Newspapers: *Bogalusa Daily News, Franklinton Era Leader, Amite Tangi–Digest, Hammond Daily Star, Slidell Sentry–News, St. Tammany Farmer, Covington News–Banner, Kentwood News–Ledger, St. Helena Echo* in Greensburg, and *The Ponchatoula Times*. The *Times–Picayune* puts out a Northlake edition with local events. The Friday "Lagniappe" (*lan-yap*—a little something extra) section also covers this area.

For More Information

CRESCENT CITY REALM
New Orleans Metropolitan Convention and Visitors Bureau
1520 Sugar Bowl Drive, New Orleans 70112
(800) 672–6124
www.nawlins.com

Newspapers: *The Times–Picayune* has a daily calendar of events and on Friday has a "Lagniappe" section with lots of news on entertainment and music. *The Gambit Weekly* has another event calendar. *Off–Beat* newspaper has music listings. WWOZ community radio (FM 90.7) sponsors a phone line for recorded information on performances: (504) 840–4040.

BAYS AND BAYOUS
Jean Lafitte National Park
Barataria Unit, 6588 Barataria Boulevard, Marrero 70072
(504) 589–2330

Jean Lafitte Tourist Commission
City Hall, Highway 45, Lafitte 70067
(800) 689–3525

Jefferson Parish Tourist Office
1221 Elmwood Park Boulevard, Suite 703, Jefferson 70123
(504) 780–1909 or (877) J–PARISH

Newspapers: *The Times–Picayune* covers this area. Check Friday's "Lagniappe" section for events.

General Index

Entries for Bed-and-Breakfasts, Plantation Homes, Restaurants, and Recipes appear in special indexes on pages 173–74.

A

Abbeville, 102
Abbey Players, 102
Abbey Theater, 102
Academy of the Sacred Heart,
    The, 90
Acadian. *See* Cajun.
Acadian Memorial, 99
Acadian Museum, 101
Acadian Village, 93
Acadiana Trail, 84
Afton Villa Gardens, 140
Alexandria Museum of Art, 57
Alexandria National Cemetery, 58
Alexandria Zoological Park, 57
Arna Bontemps African-American
Alligator Bayou Tours, 130
American Queen, 156
American Rose Center, 6
Annie Miller's Swamp Tours, 120
Antique Alley, 29
Aquarium of the Americas, 152
Ark-La-Tex, 1
Ark-La-Tex Antique and Classic
    Vehicle Museum, 8
Arna Bontemps African-American
    Museum and Cultural Arts
    Center, 57
As You Like It Silver Shop, 154
Atchafalaya Basin, 96
Audubon Park, 154
Audubon Pilgrimage, 140, 142
Audubon State Commemorative
    Area, 141
Audubon Zoo, 154
Auntie Violet's Attic, 90
Authentic Bonnie and Clyde
    Festival, 16
Authentic Bonnie and
    Clyde Museum, 16
Avery Island, 105

B

Baton Rouge, 127–33
Barnwell Memorial Garden, 4
Bayou Folk Museum, 52
Bayou Segnette, 152
Beau Fort Plantation, 50
Beauregard-Keyes House, 151
Bep's Antiques, Inc., 154
Bernice Depot Museum, 19
Bienville Depot Museum, 17
Bienville House Hotel, 151
Bienville Parish Courthouse, 17
Billeaud House, 94
Bird City, 106
Bittersweet Plantation, 123
Blue Rose Museum, 82
Bluffs on Thompson Creek,
    The, 142
Bonnie and Clyde Ambush Site, 16
Bonnie and Clyde Trade Days, 17
Briarwood, 53
Brimstone Historical Society
    Museum, 70
British Antiques, 155
Brownell Memorial Park, 107
Button Museum, 136
Byerley House, 39

C

Cajun Man's Swamp Cruise, A, 113
Cameron Prairie National
    Wildlife Refuge, 67
Casa de Sue Winery & Vineyards, 140

INDEX

Catalpa, 139
Cathedral of St. John the
    Evangelist, 92
Centenary State Historic Site, 143
Chapel of the Madonna, 126
Charpentier Historic District, 75
Château des Cocodries, 76
Chicot State Park, 86
Children's Museum, 75
Chitimacha Tribal Museum, 106
Chopin, Kate, 52
Civil War Naval Museum, 18
Claiborne Parish Courthouse, 19
Coco Marina, 117
Collinswood School Museum, 145
Commander's Palace, 152
Contraband Days, 73
Corduroy Roads, 54
Cottage Shops, 73
Courtney Gallery of Art, 61
crabbing, 72, 117
crawfishing, 96
Creole Nature Trail, 67, 70
Crystal Rice Plantation, 82
Cypremort Point State Park, 80
Cypress Island Preserve, 80
Cypress Lake, 92

D

Delcambre Shrimp Boat
    Landing, 100
Delta Downs, 80
Delta Music Festival, 56
Delta Queen, 157
Delta Queen Steamboat
    Company, 156–57
Depot at Magdalen Place, 102
DeQuincy Railroad Museum, 70
Dorignac's, 155
Driskill Mountain, 18
Dr. Wagner's Honey Island
    Swamp Tours, 148

E

Earl K. Long State Commemorative
    Area, 55
East Feliciana Parish Courthouse, 144
Edward Douglass White
    Historic Site, 120
Emerald Hills Golf and
    Tennis Resort, 45
Emporium, 135
Emy-Lou Biedenharn Foundation, 29
Eunice, 84
Evangeline Downs, 88
Evangeline Oak, 99

F

Fairfield Place, 8
Fairview-Riverside State Park, 146
False River, 116
Feliciana Cellars Winery, 142
Fireside Antiques, 133
First United Methodist Church, 32
Fisher, 45
Floyd's Record Shop, 85
Fontainebleau State Park, 146
Ford Museum, 18
Fort St. Jean Baptiste, 47
Founder's Park, 80
Franklin, 106
French Quarter, x, 150, 151–56

G

Garden District, 152
German American Cultural Center, 157
Germantown Colony Museum, 15
Global Wildlife Center, 149
Golden Meadow, 118
Grace Episcopal Church, 135
Grambling State University, 22
Grand Coteau, 90
Grand Isle, 118
Grand Isle State Park, 118

Grandmother's Buttons, 136
Grant's Canal, 39
Great River Road, 121
Greater Baton Rouge Zoo, 129
Greenwood Plantation, 141
Gretna, 157
Griffin's Antiques, 61
Gusher Days Festival, 4

H

Hadrian, statue of, 104
H. J. Smith's Son General Store, 147
Hodges Gardens, 43
Honey Island Swamp, 148
Hughes Building, 48
Hurricane Audrey, 72

I

Iberia Savings Bank, 104
Idea Place, 22
Immaculate Conception
    Catholic Church, 49
Imperial Calcasieu Museum, 74
Isaiah Garrett House, 30
Island Oasis Bar, 117

J

Jean Lafitte (village), 73, 157
Jean Lafitte National Historical Park
    and Preserve/Acadian Cultural
    Center, 85, 91
Jean Lafitte National Park
    Barataria Unit, 160
Jeanerette Museum, 80
Jennings, 76
Jim Bowie Museum, 87
Jimmie Davis Tabernacle, 21
Jungle Gardens, 106

K

Kate Chopin House, 52
Keatchie, 14

Kent Follette Pottery Studio, 21
Kitchen Shop, The, 90
Kiroli Park, 27
Kliebert's Alligator & Turtle
    Farm, 144
Konriko Rice Mill and
    Company Store, 105

L

La Maison des Deux Soeurs, 90
Lafayette Museum–Alexander
    Mouton House, 92
Lafitte, Jean, 73
Lafitte's Landing, 123
Lake Arthur Park, 81
Lake Bistineau State Park, 7
Lake Providence, 38
Langestein's, 155
Laura, A Creole Plantation, 121
Laurel Valley Plantation, 119
Lawrence Park, 107
LeBlanc House, 94
Lee Lane Shops, 147
Le Pavillon Hotel, 150
Le Petit Paris Museum, 98
Liberty Center for the
    Performing Arts, 85
Lincoln Parish Museum, 20
Longfellow-Evangeline State
    Historic Site, 97
Los Adaes, 50
Louisiana Cotton Museum, 39
Louisiana Downs, 12
Louisiana Market, 73
Louisiana Naval War Memorial, 129
Louisiana Oil and Gas Park, 76
Louisiana Peach Festival, 19
Louisiana Political Museum and
    Hall of Fame, 54
Louisiana Purchase Bicentennial, 78
Louisiana Purchase Gardens
    and Zoo, 31

Louisiana Shrimp & Petroleum
    Festival, 107
Louisiana State Arboretum, 86
Louisiana State Capitol, 129
Louisiana State Fairgrounds, 7
Louisiana State Oil and
    Gas Museum, 3
Louisiana State Penitentiary
    Museum, 137
Louisiana State University, 127, 129,
Louisiana Tech Equine Center, 23
Louisiana Tech Farm Salesroom, 22
Louisiana Tech University, 22
Louisiana University Marine
    Consortium, 117
Louisiana Video Collection
    Library, 88
LSU Faculty Club, 128
LSU Museum of Art, 128

M

Madewood, 120
Magazine Street, 154
Magdalen Place, 102
Magnolia Mound, 131
Marais and Platins, 100
Mardi Gras, 78, 146
Marian Prayer Park, 79
Marksville State Historic Site, 62
Martin Homeplace, 31
Masur Museum of Art, 31
McGee's Landing, 97
McIlhenny Tabasco Factory, 105
Meadows Museum of Art, 10
Milbank Historic House, 143
Mile Branch Settlement, 142
Mississippi Queen, 156
Mitcham's Peach Orchard, 19
Moonwalk, 150
Mount Olivet Chapel, 58
Museum of Natural Science, 129
Myrtles, The, 137

N

Nana's Cupboard, 73
Natchitoches, 46
New Orleans, 150–56
New Roads, 133
Nicholls State University, 120
Northlake Nature Center, 144
Nottoway, 124
Nursery Row, 59

O

Oak and Pine Alley, 95
Oaklawn Manor, 106
Old Corner Antique Shop, 61
Old Courthouse, 49
Old Lecompte School, 59
Old Magnolia Gift Shoppe, 79
Old State Capitol, 127
Olde Town, 149
Opelousas Museum
    and Interpretive Center, 88
Original Swamp Gardens, 107
Ouachita River Art Guild
    Gallery, 29
Our Lady Help of Christians
    Catholic Church, 79

P

Panola Pepper Company, 39
Petit Caporal, 118
Piney Hills Gallery, 21
Pioneer Heritage Center, 12
Plaquemine Locks, 126
Pleasant Hall, 128
Ponchatoula Country
    Market, 145
Ponchatoula Feed and Seed, 145
Port Hudson, 136
Poverty Point State Historic Site, 34
prairie, 84
Presbytère, 99

R

Radisson Hotel Bentley, 56
Rayne, 82
Republic of West Florida
    Museum, 143
River Oaks Square Arts
    Center, 57
River Road, 123
Rockefeller Wildlife Refuge, 73
Roque House, 48
Rosedown Plantation
    and Gardens, 141
Rose Theater, 33
Rural Life Museum and Windrush
    Gardens, 132
Russo's Custom Framing and
    Gallery, 124
R. W. Norton Art Gallery, 11

S

Sabine National Wildlife Refuge, 67
Sallier Oak, 74
Sam Houston Jones State Park, 80
Sawmill Days, 46
Schepis Museum, 32
Sci-Port Discovery Center, 7
Shadetree Inn, 135
Shadows-on-the-Teche, 103
Snyder Memorial Museum and
    Creative Art Center, 33
Southdown Plantation House, 116
Southern Pickin' and Ginnin'
    Festival, 33
Spring Street Historical
    Museum, 9
Stagecoach Museum, 16
St. Charles College, 90
St. Charles Streetcar, 152
St. Louis Cathedral, 151
St. Martin de Tours Church Square, 98
Steen's Syrup Mill, 102
Strand Theatre, 9

Sunshine Bridge, 123
*Swapping Stories: Folktales
    from Louisiana,* 16

T

Tallulah, 37
Telephone Pioneer Museum
    of Louisiana, 80
Tensas River National Wildlife
    Refuge, 35
Thibodaux, 120
Three French Hens, 90
Three States Marker, 1
Toledo Bend Lake, 46
Touchstone Wildlife
    and Art Museum, 14
Transylvania General Store, 38
Trinity Parish Church, 49
Tunica-Biloxi Museum, 62
Tunica Hills, 134
Turn of the Century House and
    Mardi Gras Museum, 107

U

U.S.S. *Kidd,* 127

V

Vermilionville, 91
Vieux Carré. *See* French Quarter.

W

Walker House, Ltd., 147
Walter B. Jacobs Memorial
    Nature Park, 5
Watermark Saloon, 32
Webb and Webb Commissary, 12
West Baton Rouge Museum, 133
West Feliciana Historical Society
    Museum, 136
Wetlands Acadian Cultural
    Center, 120
White Castle, 124

INDEX

White Kitchen Preserve, 144
Whole Food Market, 155
W. H. Tupper General Merchandise
  Museum, 79
Wildlife Gardens, 114
Winter Quarters State Historic Site, 40

Z

Zemurray Gardens, 150
Zigler Museum, 77
Zwolle Tamale Festival, 46
Zydeco Festival, 88

Special Indexes

Bed-and-Breakfasts

Beau Fort Plantation, 50
Bittersweet Plantation, 123
Bluffs on Thompson Creek, The, 142
Butler Greenwood, 138
Chrétien Point Plantation, 89
Cottage Plantation, 139
Estorge-Norton House, 105
Fairfield Place, 8
Grand Coteau House, 90
Green Springs, 140
Greenwood Plantation, 141
Josephine, The, 154
Jubilee!, 134
leRosier Country Inn, 104
Loyd Hall Plantation, 60
Madewood, 120
Milbank Historic House, 143
Myrtles, The, 137
Nottoway, 124
Old Castillo Hotel, 100
Old Centenary Inn, 143
Rosedown Plantation and
    Gardens, 141
Seale Guesthouse, 85
Shadetree Inn, 135
Southern Colonial Bed and
    Breakfast, 55
Victoria Inn, 157

Plantation Homes

Bayou Folk Museum, 52
Beau Fort Plantation, 50
Butler Greenwood, 138,
Catalpa, 139
Chrétien Point Plantation, 89

Cottage Plantation, 139
Destrehan Plantation, 123
Frogmore Plantation and Gins, 58
Greenwood Plantation, 141
Houmas House, 123
Kent House, 55
Laura, A Creole Plantation, 121
Laurel Valley Plantation, 119
Loyd Hall Plantation, 60
Madewood, 120
Magnolia Mound, 131
Magnolia Plantation Home, 51
Melrose Plantation, 51
Myrtles, The, 137
Nottoway, 124
Oak Alley, 121
Oaklawn Manor, 106
Oakley House, 141
Olivier Plantation, 98
Parlange Plantation, 133
Pitot House, 160
Rosedown Plantation and
    Gardens, 141
San Francisco, 121
Shadows-on-the-Teche, 103
Southdown Plantation House, 116
Texcuco Plantation, 123
Winter Quarters State Historic
    Site, 40

Restaurants

A-Bear's Cafe, 115
Bee's Cafe, 23
Black's Oyster Bar, 102
Blind Tiger, 9
Bluffs on Thompson Creek, The, 142
Boudin King, 80
Boutte's Bayou Restaurant, 160

INDEX

Cafe des Amis, 95

Cafe du Monde, 151

Cafe Vermilionville, 92

Catahoula's Restaurant, 90

C'est Bon, 146

Chef Roy's Frog City Cafe, 84

Commander's Palace, 152

Dupuy's Oyster Shop, 102

Evangeline Seafood and Steakhouse, 91

Friends on the Tchefuncta, 146

Gautreau's, 156

Grapevine Restaurant, 124

House of Seafood Buffet, 141

Joe's Dreyfus Store Restaurant, 133

Jungle Club, 85

Lafitte's Landing Restaurant at
   Bittersweet Plantation, 123

Lagniappe Too Cafe, 104

Lakeshore Restaurant, 81

La Place d'Evangeline Restaurant, 100

Lasyone's Meat Pie Kitchen and
   Restaurant, 49

Lea's Lunchroom, 58

Le 'tit Cafe, 90

Lighthouse Restaurant, 117

Log Cabin Smokehouse, 22

LSU Faculty Club, 128

Magnolia Cafe, 136

Monsieur Patou, 11

Mulate's Cajun Restaurant, 94

Napoleon House, 151

Nottoway, 124

Ole Dutch Bakery, 38

Palace Cafe, 88

Pat's Fisherman's Wharf
   Restaurant, 96

Prejean's Restaurant, 92

Railroad Cafe, 124

Randol's Restaurant and Cajun
   Dancehall, 92

Restaurant des Familles, 160

Rossi's, 124

Savoie's, 13

Steamboat Warehouse, 86

Taste of Bavaria, 146

Tony Chachere's, 87

Trenton Street Bistro, 21

Tujague's, 153

Voleo's Seafood Restaurant, 160

Warehouse No. 1 Restaurant, 29

Recipes

Natchitoches Meat Pie,
   Natchitoches, 48

Peach-A-Doodle-Do with Wild about
   Peaches Rice, Ruston, 20

Rocky Mountain Oysters Napoleon,
   Chef Roy's Frog City Cafe, 83

Spinach Madeleine, Green Springs Inn
   & Cottages, 138

Tony's Chicken and Sausage
   Jambalaya, Tony Chachere's, 87

Tujague's Boiled Brisket of Beef,
   Tujague's, 153

White Chocolate Bread Pudding
   with White Chocolate Sauce,
   Alligator Bayou, 130

About the Author

Gay N. Martin, who has lived in several southeastern states, now makes her home in Alabama. She has published hundreds of articles in national newspapers and magazines and especially enjoys writing about food and travel in the Southeast. She has won numerous writing awards for fiction and nonfiction and often shares her experiences at seminars.

Before she made a New Year's resolution to turn her writing hobby into a career, Mrs. Martin taught high school for eleven years, served as resource coordinator of her school's gifted program, and sponsored the school newspaper. Her work has appeared in *Modern Bride, Boston Herald, Kiwanis, The Writer, Seventeen, Atlantic Journal-Constitution, The Times-Picayune, Far East Traveler, The London Free Press, Milwaukee Sentinel,* and other publications. She is the author of Globe Pequot's *Alabama: Off the Beaten Path* and *Alabama's Historic Restaurants and Their Recipes,* published by John F. Blair.

Mrs. Martin and her husband, a dentist, have five children.